Entscheidungsräume
Spaces of Decision-Making

Mario Fischer · Aleida Siller (Hg./ed.)

Entscheidungsräume
Die Architektur evangelischer Synodenbauten

Spaces of Decision-Making
The Architecture of Protestant Synod Halls

SCHNELL + STEINER

Geleitwort

»Synodalität« ist in den letzten Jahren zu einem Schlüsselbegriff der innerkirchlichen und ökumenischen Diskussion geworden. Dabei zeigt sich, dass wir abhängig von unseren konfessionellen Traditionen von unterschiedlichen Verständnissen ausgehen. Während in der römisch-katholischen Kirche und in den orthodoxen Kirchen bei Synoden zunächst Bischofsversammlungen gemeint sind, wird in den evangelischen Kirchen vorausgesetzt, dass Synoden die Gemeinden repräsentieren und daher aus ordinierten Amtsträgerinnen und Amtsträgern und Gemeindegliedern zusammengesetzt sind. Gemeinsam ist den verschiedenen ökumenischen Traditionen die Überzeugung, dass Synoden nicht nur Beratungs- und Entscheidungsgremien sind, sondern dass durch sie und in ihnen der Heilige Geist die Kirche leitet.

So ist dieser Bildband, der sich der Architektur von Synodenräumen widmet, nicht nur von architekturgeschichtlicher Bedeutung, sondern liefert einen wichtigen Beitrag zum evangelischen Verständnis von Synodalität.

Nicht alle der rund 100 Mitgliedskirchen der Gemeinschaft Evangelischer Kirchen in Europa haben eine »Synode«, die diesen Namen trägt. Die Bezeichnungen unterscheiden sich, doch synodale Strukturen sind in unterschiedlicher Weise in den evangelischen Kirchen vorhanden. In ihnen wird die Einheit der Kirche in ihrer Vielfalt sichtbar.

Auf Ebene der Kirchengemeinschaft in Europa kommen die Delegierten der Mitgliedskirchen alle sechs Jahre zu einer Vollversammlung zusammen. Die Vollversammlung der Gemeinschaft Evangelischer Kirchen in Europa ist keine Synode im eigentlichen Sinn. Ihre Beschlüsse werden den Synoden der Mitgliedskirchen zur Rezeption empfohlen. Die von der Vollversammlung beschlossenen Dokumente sollen von den Mitgliedskirchen bei ihren Überlegungen zu diesen Themen angemessen berücksichtigt werden.

Zugleich finden innerhalb der Gemeinschaft Evangelischer Kirchen in Europa regelmäßig Begegnungstagungen der Synoden der Mitgliedskirchen statt, bei denen diese sich auf europäischer Ebene über ihr Anliegen austauschen und aufeinander hören. Diese persönlichen Begegnungen sind wichtig. Gerade die Diskussionen um digitale Synodensitzungen in Folge der Covid-19-Pandemie haben gezeigt, dass Synoden nicht nur Entscheidungsgremien sind, sondern dass die Bedeutung des griechischen *syn-odos* »gemeinsam auf dem Weg sein« immer auch eine leibliche, sinnliche Dimension hat.

Als Präsidium der Gemeinschaft Evangelischer Kirchen in Europa sind wir froh, dass mit diesem Bildband zur Architektur von Synodenräumen ein Buch vorliegt, das einen guten Einblick in das synodale Leben und Selbstverständnis evangelischer Kirchen liefert.

Dr. John P. Bradbury, London
Marcin Brzóska, Cieszyn
Prof. Dr. Miriam Rose, Jena

Preface

In the last few years, »synodality« has become a key term in discussions within churches and in ecumenical contexts. This has shown that the way we first understand the term differs, depending on our denominational traditions. While in the Roman Catholic Church and Orthodox churches synods initially mean gatherings of bishops, in the Protestant churches it is assumed that synods represent the congregations and so consist of ordained clergy and lay church members. The various ecumenical traditions share the conviction that synods are not just bodies for consultation and decision-making but that, through and in them, the Holy Spirit guides the church.

Consequently, this illustrated volume on the architecture of synod halls is not only of significance for architectural history – it makes an important contribution to the Protestant understanding of synodality.

Not all the approximately 100 member churches of the Communion of Protestant Churches in Europe (CPCE) have a body bearing the name »synod«. The terms differ but synodal structures are found in varying ways in the Protestant churches. They demonstrate church unity in its diversity.

At the level of the communion of churches in Europe, the delegates of the member churches meet every six years for a general assembly. The general assembly of the Communion of Protestant Churches in Europe is not a synod in the actual sense. Its decisions are recommended to the synods of member churches for reception. The member churches are meant to take appropriate account of the documents adopted by the general assembly in their deliberations on these topics.

At the same time, there are regular gatherings for encounter within the CPCE attended by representatives of member church synods, at which they share their concerns and listen to one another at the European level. These personal encounters are important. Precisely the discussions about digital synod sessions following the Covid-19 pandemic have shown that synods are not only decision-making bodies. Rather, the meaning of the Greek *syn-odos*, »together on the way«, always has a physical, sensory dimension as well.

As the Presidium of the Communion of Protestant Churches in Europe we are pleased to present this illustrated volume on the architecture of synod halls, which gives a good insight into the synodal life and self-understanding of Protestant churches.

Dr John P. Bradbury, London
Marcin Brzóska, Cieszyn
Prof. Dr Miriam Rose, Jena

Vorwort

In Synoden ist der Herzschlag evangelischer Kirchen zu spüren. Hier kommen Menschen aus den Gemeinden zusammen und versuchen im gemeinsamen Hören auf Gottes Wort und aufeinander die Zeichen der Zeit zu deuten und ausgewogene Entscheidungen für die Kirche zu treffen.

In den meisten Kirchen werden Synoden in geeigneten Gemeinde- oder Kirchenräumen abgehalten, manche Kirchen mieten dafür Tagungsräume an. Einige evangelische Kirchen in Europa verfügen aber über speziell für die Abhaltung ihrer Synoden errichtete Gebäude.

Anlässlich des 450-jährigen Jubiläums der Emder Synode von 1571 entstand die Idee, in einem Bildband darzustellen, wie sich in diesen Synodenräumen das jeweilige Verständnis von protestantischer Synodalität in der Architektur und in der Ausgestaltung der Räume ausdrückt.

Fünf Synodengebäude werden in diesem Buch vorgestellt. Es handelt sich um die Versammlungsorte der Synoden der Evangelischen Waldenserkirche, der Kirche von Schottland, der Reformierten Kirche in Ungarn, der Presbyterianischen Kirche von Irland und der Evangelisch-Lutherischen Landeskirche Sachsens. Vier der Kirchen sind reformierter Tradition, eine ist lutherisch. Die Gebäude sind im 19. und 20. Jahrhundert entstanden und folgen unterschiedlicher Symbol- und Formensprache. Sie repräsentieren verschiedene kirchliche und demokratische Kulturen in Europa und zeigen zugleich, wie in ihren Kirchen die Vorstellung von Repräsentation und Partizipation, einer angemessenen Gesprächskultur und des Umgangs mit Entscheidungskompetenzen zum Ausdruck kommt.

Für die Gemeinschaft Evangelischer Kirchen in Europa (GEKE) ist dieses Buch damit ein wichtiger Beitrag, um die Vielfalt evangelischer Kirchen in Europa zu präsentieren und zugleich gemeinsame Anliegen evangelischer Leitungskultur sichtbar zu machen.

In diesem Bildband werden die Synodengebäude mit Grundrissen, Grafiken und Fotografien von Außen- und Innenansichten und einem Steckbrief vorgestellt. Artikel, die von Autorinnen und Autoren aus der jeweiligen Kirche verfasst wurden, beschreiben die Gebäude und ordnen sie in ihrer Bedeutung für die eigene Kirche ein. Daneben behandeln Querschnittsartikel die Geschichte und gegenwärtige Herausforderungen evangelischer Synoden. Eine Einleitung zeigt Gemeinsamkeiten und Unterschiede der Gebäudekonzeptionen auf und beleuchtet, wie sich darin das evangelische Verständnis von Synoden darstellt.

Um dem Buch eine breite Rezeption in Europa zu ermöglichen, ist es durchgängig zweisprachig gehalten. Alle Beiträge werden in der jeweiligen Landessprache der Kirche sowie in englischer und/oder deutscher Übersetzung abgedruckt.

Wir danken den Autorinnen und Autoren und Fotografinnen und Fotografen, die zum Gelingen dieses Buchprojekts beigetragen haben, ebenso den Institutionen, die uns Bildmaterial zur Verfügung gestellt haben.

Für die Übersetzungen haben gesorgt: Elaine Griffiths für die Übersetzungen aus dem Deutschen ins Englische, Adél und Dániel Dávid für die Übersetzung aus dem Ungarischen ins Deutsche und Benedikt Jetter für die Übersetzung aus dem Italienischen ins Deutsche. Alle weiteren Übersetzungen wurden von den Kirchen oder der Geschäftsstelle der Gemeinschaft Evangelischer Kirchen in Europa angefertigt. Ihnen allen gilt unser Dank.

Dieses Buch wäre nicht möglich gewesen, wenn nicht zwei Menschen in der Geschäftsstelle der GEKE viel Zeit und Energie investiert hätten. Kathleen Müller und Magdalena Bruckmüller haben die Kontakte zu den Kirchen und Autorinnen und Autoren gehalten, Texte bearbeitet und Fotos recherchiert und immer wieder den Fortgang des Projektes vorangetrieben. Dafür danken wir ihnen ausdrücklich.

Ein Bildband ist für die GEKE eine neue Gattung im Spektrum ihrer Veröffentlichungen. Wir danken daher Dr. Albrecht Weiland und Felix Weiland, die das Buch in das Programm des Verlags Schnell und Steiner aufgenommen haben und mit den Erfahrungen eines alteingesessenen Kunstverlags begleitet haben. Für diese kompetente Begleitung danken wir Isabell Schlott.

Wir hoffen, mit diesem Band einen Beitrag zum Verständnis von Synodalität leisten zu können, da die Räume, in denen Synoden tagen, etwas über das Selbstverständnis und das Funktionieren von evangelischen Synoden aussagen.

Wien/Hannover, an Ostern 2024

Mario Fischer
Generalsekretär der Gemeinschaft
Evangelischer Kirchen in Europa

Aleida Siller
Bis 2021 Beauftragte der Evangelisch-
reformierten Kirche für das 450. Jubiläumsjahr
der Emder Synode von 1571

Foreword

The heartbeat of Protestant churches can be felt in synods. They are places where individuals come together from the congregations and, listening to God's Word and to one another, endeavour to interpret the signs of the times and take balanced decisions for the church.

In most churches, synods are held in suitable parish or church halls, while some churches hire conference facilities. However, a number of Protestant churches in Europe have buildings that were purpose-built for holding their synods.

It was during the 450th anniversary of the 1571 Emden Synod that the idea came up – to compile an illustrated account of how these synod halls reflect the understanding of Protestant synodality in the architecture and furnishings of their respective premises.

This book showcases five such synod buildings. They belong to the Evangelical Waldensian Church, the Church of Scotland, the Reformed Church in Hungary, the Presbyterian Church of Ireland and the Evangelical Lutheran Church of Saxony. Four of the churches are in the Reformed tradition and one is Lutheran. The buildings were constructed in the 19th and 20th centuries and follow differing styles and forms of symbolism. They represent diverse church and democratic cultures in Europe and, at the same time, demonstrate the manner in which their church expresses representation and participation, practises an appropriate culture of discussion and handles decision-making competences.

Accordingly, for the Communion of Protestant Churches in Europe (CPCE) this book makes an important contribution to presenting the variety of Protestant churches in Europe and likewise to spotlighting their common concerns with respect to the Protestant culture of governance.

The synod halls are presented with their ground plans, graphics and photos of the exterior and interior, as well as a short profile. Articles written by authors from the each church describe the building and explain how the particular church understands its significance. In addition, cross-cutting articles cover the history of Protestant synods and the challenges they face today. An introduction points to the common features and the differences in the way the buildings were designed, shedding light on how that reflects the Protestant understanding of synods.

The whole book is in two languages, so that it can be widely read in Europe. All the articles have been printed in the respective national language of the church and also in English and/or German translation.

We are very grateful to the authors and photographers who have contributed to the realisation of this book project, and also to the institutions that provided illustrations.

Responsible for the translations were: Elaine Griffiths from German into English, Adél and Dániel Dávid from Hungarian into German, and Benedikt Jetter from Italian into German. All other translations were made by the churches or the head office of the Communion of Protestant Churches in Europe. Many thanks to all of them.

The book would not have been possible without the investment of much time and energy by two staff members in the CPCE head office. Kathleen Müller and Magdalena Bruckmüller kept in contact with the churches and authors, edited manuscripts, performed photo searches and constantly kept the project moving along. That was greatly appreciated.

An illustrated volume is a new genre for CPCE's range of publications. We therefore owe a debt of gratitude to Dr Albrecht Weiland and Felix Weiland for including it in the catalogue of the Schnell und Steiner publishing house and giving us the benefit of their experience as seasoned art publishers. We would like to express our gratitude to Isabell Schlott for her invaluable assistance.

It is our hope that this volume can contribute to the understanding of synodality, seeing that synod meeting-places say something about the self-understanding and functioning of Protestant synods.

Vienna/Hanover, at Easter 2024

Mario Fischer
General Secretary of the Communion of Protestant Churches in Europe

Aleida Siller
Until 2021 responsible for the 450th anniversary of the 1571 Emden Synod on behalf of the Evangelical Reformed Church

Inhalt | Contents

4 Geleitwort / Preface

6 Vorwort / Foreword

Mario Fischer · Aleida Siller

13 Einleitung

19 Introduction

Essays

Martin Friedrich

27 Synoden im Protestantismus

33 Synods in Protestantism

Peter Opitz

39 Anfänge der evangelischen Synodalkultur in der »reformierten« Reformation

48 The Beginnings of Protestant Synodal Culture in the »Reformed« Reformation

Sabine Blütchen

57 Gegenwärtige Herausforderungen evangelischer Synoden

65 Challenges to Protestant Synods

Italien / Italy / Italia

Gabriella Ballesio · Simone Baral

75 Der Synodensaal der Evangelischen Waldenserkirche

82 The Synod Hall of the Waldensian Evangelical Church

89 L'aula sinodale della Chiesa evangelica valdese

Schottland / Scotland

Rosalind Taylor

99 Das Assembly Building der Kirche von Schottland

109 The Assembly Building of the Church of Scotland

Ungarn / Hungary / Magyarország

Máté Millisits · András Czanik

119 Das Synodengebäude der Reformierten Kirche in Ungarn

125 The Synod Building of the Reformed Church in Hungary

132 A Magyarországi Református Egyház Zsinati Székháza

Irland / Ireland

Raymond Robinson · Mark Smith

141 Die Assembly Buildings der Presbyterianischen Kirche in Irland

148 The Assembly Buildings of the Presbyterian Church in Ireland

Sachsen / Saxony

Bettina Westfeld

159 Von der Ständekammer in die Dreikönigskirche

166 From the Chamber of Estates to Three Kings Church

173 Autorenverzeichnis / Index of Authors

175 Fotonachweise / Credits

Mario Fischer · Aleida Siller

Einleitung

Evangelische Kirchen werden im öffentlichen Raum oft über ihre Kirchengebäude wahrgenommen. Die Kirchen haben aber auch andere Versammlungsräume, die für ihr Leben bedeutsam sind. So haben einige für ihre Synodenversammlungen eigene Gebäude errichtet. Diese Räume sagen viel über ihr Selbstverständnis aus. Die Sitzordnung im Synodensaal, die Verwendung von Materialien, die Ausstattung mit symbolhaften Kunstwerken – all das ist wohlüberlegt und ist Teil der Identität einer Kirche. Dass Kirchen eigene Gebäude für ihre Synoden besitzen, ist allerdings nicht die Regel, sondern die Ausnahme. Denn häufig wird bewusst auf einen festen Ort verzichtet, um die Synoden in verschiedenen Regionen und Gemeinden einer Kirche abhalten zu können oder um kein zusätzliches Gebäude unterhalten zu müssen. Dann werden Synoden in kirchlichen Häusern oder in eigens dafür angemieteten Tagungsräumen abgehalten.

In diesem Bildband werden fünf Gebäude vorgestellt, die für die Durchführung von Synoden gebaut wurden: Es handelt sich um die Versammlungsorte der Synoden der Evangelischen Waldenserkirche, der Kirche von Schottland, der Reformierten Kirche in Ungarn, der Presbyterianischen Kirche von Irland und der Evangelisch-Lutherischen Landeskirche Sachsens. Im Folgenden sollen Gemeinsamkeiten und Besonderheiten der jeweiligen Gebäudekonzeptionen aufgewiesen werden, um zu erhellen, welches Verständnis von Synodalität sich darin ausdrückt und wie die Synoden in Beziehung zum Staat und zur Gesellschaft stehen.

Die Wahl des Ortes

Die vorgestellten Synodengebäude gehören jeweils zu landesweiten Kirchen oder Landeskirchen. Es ist auffällig, dass alle Synodengebäude in einer Hauptstadt erbaut wurden, wobei es sich bei der Waldenserkirche nicht um die Hauptstadt des italienischen Staates handelt, die zum Zeitpunkt der Errichtung des Synodengebäudes bereits Rom war, sondern um die faktische Hauptstadt der Kirche in den Waldensertälern, also Torre Pellice in der Nähe von Turin. Dort liegt der Synodenbau *Casa Valdese* im sogenannten »Waldenserviertel« entlang einer langgezogenen Straße. Auf beiden Seiten der Via Beckwith und der Via Arnaud befinden sich heute neben der *Casa Valdese* das Kirchengebäude, das Pfarrhaus, das Lyzeum, das Museum und das Gästehaus der Waldenser. Wenn die Synode im Sommer tagt, verwandelt sich diese Straße zu einem Volksfest und es wird deutlich, dass Torre Pellice die inoffizielle Hauptstadt der Waldenser ist.

Die Synodengebäude der Kirche von Schottland und der Presbyterianischen Kirche von Irland liegen jeweils in der Hauptstadt von Schottland und Nordirland, also in Edinburgh und in Belfast. In beiden Fällen wurden die Synodengebäude nahe bei den politischen Schaltzentralen errichtet. Die *Assembly Buildings* der Presbyterianischen Kirche von Irland sind keine 200 Meter von dem prächtigen Rathaus, der *Belfast City Hall*, entfernt, während die *Assembly Hall* der Kirche von Schottland in unmittelbarer Nähe zur Burg von Edinburgh liegt. In der sächsischen Landeshauptstadt Dresden liegt die Dreikönigskirche, in der sich der Synodensaal der Evangelisch-Lutherischen Landeskirche Sachsens befindet, in der Fußgängerzone der Dresdner Neustadt an der Hauptstraße.

Nur in Ungarn ist die Lage des Synodengebäudes nicht im Zentrum der Hauptstadt. Zwar hatte man ursprünglich geplant, das Gebäude in Budapest in zentraler Lage neben der reformierten Kirche am Kálvin-Platz zu errichten, doch entschied man schließlich, das Synodengebäude etwas weiter vom Stadtzentrum entfernt in einem Villenviertel in der Nähe des Stadtparks zu realisieren.

Die Verortung in der Hauptstadt geht für die Synoden mit einer Sichtbarkeit in der Gesellschaft, einer leichteren Verkehrsanbindung und einem schnelleren Zugang zu politischen Institutionen einher. Im Falle der Waldenserkirche fallen diese Aspekte weg.

Architektur und Finanzierung

Die Entscheidung, ein eigenes Gebäude zur Abhaltung der Synoden zu bauen, zog verschiedene weitere Fragen nach sich: Wer sollte das Gebäude entwerfen und in welchem Stil? Und wie sollte das Bauvorhaben finanziert werden?

Die Kirchen vergaben die Aufträge an Architekturbüros aus dem eigenen Land, zum Teil im Anschluss an einen Wettbewerb. Im Falle des ungarischen Synodengebäudes erhielten Alfréd Hajós und János Villányi den ersten Preis im Wettbewerb und wurden mit der Realisierung des Projekts beauftragt, das allerdings auch Elemente von vier weiteren Entwürfen aufnehmen sollte. Alfréd Hajós war zwar als Sportler berühmt, doch eröffnete er sein Architekturbüro mit János Villányi erst kurz vor Baubeginn des Synodengebäudes. Das Architekturbüro verwirklichte in der Folge namhafte Bauprojekte in Ungarn. Das repräsentative Synodengebäude nahm Stilelemente des Historismus und des Jugendstils auf. In dieser Linie arbeiteten Hajós und Villányi weiter. Ende der 1920er Jahre gestaltete Hajós Sportstätten, wie die Millenáris- (Milleniums) Turnierbahn in Budapest XIV (1928) oder das Nationale Schwimmstadion in Budapest (1930), die vom Bauhaus beeinflusst sind.

Auch bei dem Synodengebäude in Edinburgh erfolgte die Beauftragung des bekannten Architekten William Henry Playfair in Folge einer öffentlichen Ausschreibung. Die eigentliche *Assembly Hall* wurde durch David Bryce entworfen, der als bekanntester Vertreter des schottischen Baronialstils gilt. Ebenso im schottischen Baronialstil entwarf Robert Young die *Assembly Buildings* der Presbyterianischen Kirche von Irland in Belfast. Damit entschieden die Kirchen sich im Baustil für die schottische Variante der Neugotik, die sich nicht so sehr am Kirchenbau, sondern am Festungsbau orientiert.

Für die *Casa Valdese* in Torre Pellice lag zunächst ein Entwurf des Londoner Architekten und Ingenieurs William Allen Boulnois im neugotischen Stil vor. Die Kirchenleitung entschied sich jedoch für den jungen Architekten Epaminonda Ayassot, der bereits im Pellice-Tal verschiedene Bauvorhaben verwirklicht hatte. Damit wählte man einen finanziell und architektonisch weniger ehrgeizigen Bau, der stärker dem lokalen Baustil entsprach. Die Finanzierung des Projekts erfolgte durch Spenden von Waldensern im In- und Ausland sowie von befreundeten Kirchen, Komitees und einzelnen Wohltäterinnen und Wohltätern.

Zwar waren Spenden eine wichtige Säule für den Bau der Synodengebäude, doch nutzten einige Kirchen auch andere Wege der Finanzierung. Die Presbyterianische Kirche von Irland erhielt für den Bau Geld aus dem *Presbyterian Church Twentieth Century Fund* sowie ein Darlehen der *Scottish Provident Institution*. Auch die Reformierte Kirche in Ungarn war zur Finanzierung auf einen Baukredit angewiesen, an dessen Abbezahlung sich alle Kirchendistrikte der Reformierten Kirche Ungarns beteiligten. Allein die *Assembly Hall* in Edinburgh konnte vollständig durch Spenden aus der eigenen Kirche finanziert werden. Dabei ist bemerkenswert, dass die enorme Summe zur Gänze von den Frauen der *Free Church of Scotland* aufgebracht wurde.

Der Synodensaal der Evangelisch-Lutherischen Landeskirche Sachsens befindet sich in der ehemaligen Dreikönigskirche, die der Dresdner Architekt Manfred Arlt vollständig umgebaut hat. Er war beeinflusst vom Neuen Bauen und Le Corbusier und war für verschiedene große Bauprojekte in Dresden in der DDR-Zeit verantwortlich. Der Umbau der Dreikönigkirche wurde im Rahmen des Sonderbauprogramms für Kirchen in der DDR durch Spenden aus westdeutschen und westeuropäischen Kirchen finanziert.

Bei allen in diesem Buch vorgestellten Synodengebäuden entschieden die Kirchen, Entwurf und Ausführung an bekannte Architekten des eigenen Landes zu vergeben. Im Stil entschieden diese sich für repräsentative Gebäude, die dem aktuellen Zeitgeschmack und lokalen und regionalen Besonderheiten folgten. Die Finanzierung der

Gebäude ist jeweils Ausdruck dafür, dass sich Kirchenmitglieder mit dem Anliegen, für ihre Synode ein Haus zu bauen, identifizierten und aus befreundeten Kirchen Solidaritätsleistungen erfolgten.

Sitzordnung im Synodensaal

Das Wort »Synode« kommt von dem griechischen Wort *syn-odos*, was »gemeinsam auf dem Weg sein« bedeutet. Darin kommt zum Ausdruck, dass Kirche sich als Gemeinschaft versteht, die gemeinsam auf dem Weg ist. Dies wird gerade in den Synoden, in denen Delegierte aus den verschiedenen Teilen einer Kirche zusammenkommen und gemeinsam entscheiden, sehr deutlich. Der Alltag synodaler Arbeit besteht jedoch vorwiegend im Sitzen. Die Arbeit wird von »Sitzungen« geprägt, die durch einen »Vorsitz« (lateinisch: *praesidens*) geleitet werden.

In der Regel sitzt im Synodensaal vorne, für alle sichtbar, die Leitung der Synode. In einigen Fällen sitzt die Kirchenleitung neben oder hinter der Synodenleitung mit Blick in die Synode, in anderen Fällen sitzt sie der Synodenleitung gegenüber. Bei der Waldensersynode wird explizit ausgesagt, dass die Kirchenleitung der Synode gegenübersitzt, um dieser Rede und Antwort zu stehen.

Bezüglich der Anordnung der Plätze für die Synodalen gibt es unterschiedliche Modelle, die sowohl praktischen Überlegungen als auch Gewohnheiten verschiedener parlamentarischer Kulturen folgen. Wichtig ist dabei, dass sich alle gut hören und sehen können und dass durch die Anordnung der Plätze keine Hierarchie ausgedrückt wird.

In der Synodenaula der Waldenserkirche sitzen sich die Synodalen auf Bänken an drei Seiten gegenüber. Die Gestaltung erinnert an das britische Westminster-Parlament, zumal bis 1974 die Bänke auch wie im britischen Unterhaus grün gepolstert waren. Gelegentlich begegnet die Meinung, dies sei dem britischen Offizier John Charles Beckwith (1789–1862) geschuldet, der sich in den Waldensertälern niederließ und die Kirche unterstützte. Im Synodengebäude in Torre Pellice hängt ein lebensgroßes Gemälde von ihm. Doch ist eine solche Anordnung der Bankreihen auch von evangelischen Synoden wie der französisch-reformierten Synode von Montpellier von 1598 oder der Dordrechter Synode von 1618/19 bekannt.

Die reformierten Synodensäle im Vereinigten Königreich knüpfen in der Raumgestaltung jedenfalls nicht an die parlamentarische Sitzordnung des britischen Unterhauses an, was schon der Größe der Versammlungen geschuldet sein kann. Bei der Kirche von Schottland und der Presbyterianischen Kirche von Irland hat man sich für eine hufeisenförmige Sitzordnung entschieden, die eine möglichst gute Teilhabe an der Diskussion von allen Plätzen aus ermöglichen soll. Auch die Reformierte Kirche in Ungarn hat für die Sitzanordnung ihrer Synodalen eine halbrunde Bestuhlung gewählt. Nur die Synode der Evangelisch-Lutherischen Landeskirche Sachsens sitzt in geraden Tischreihen hintereinander dem Synodenpräsidium gegenüber.

Für Gäste und die Öffentlichkeit ist in der Regel ein eigener Bereich vorgesehen, häufig auf den Emporen oder Rängen, so dass sie die Synode gut verfolgen können. Ob Gäste und Öffentlichkeit berechtigt sind, ihre Zustimmung oder ihren Unmut kundzutun, folgt unterschiedlichen kulturellen Gepflogenheiten.

Synoden und Parlamente

Häufig werden evangelische Synoden vereinfachend als »Kirchenparlamente« bezeichnet, weil dort gewählte und berufene Delegierte aus den Gemeinden zusammenkommen und gemeinsam Beschlüsse fassen. Seit dem 19. Jahrhundert werden Synoden vielfach als Repräsentanz der Gemeinden angesehen. Das Verhältnis der Anzahl der Delegierten im Verhältnis zu der Gesamtzahl der Kirchenmitglieder ist sehr unterschiedlich, wie ein Blick in die hier dargestellten evangelischen Kirchen in Europa zeigt: Die Synode der Evangelischen Waldenserkirche, einer Kirche mit 20.000 Mitgliedern in Italien, zählt 180 Mitglieder. Die Evangelisch-Lutherische Landeskirche Sachsens hat 80 Synodale bei 610.000 Kirchenmitgliedern und die Kirche von Schottland 500 Synodale bei 260.000 Kirchenmitgliedern. Die *General Assembly* der Presbyterianischen Kirche von Irland umfasst 1.100 Synodale bei 190.000 Kirchenmitgliedern und die Reformierte Kirche in Ungarn hat 100 Synodale bei einer Kirchenmitgliederzahl von 944.000. Damit schwankt bei den ausgewählten Kirchen die Größe der Synode zwischen 80 (Sachsen) und 1.100 (Irland) Mitgliedern. Bezieht man die Anzahl der

Synodenmitglieder auf die Anzahl der Kirchenmitglieder, so steht ein Synodenmitglied in der Waldenserkirche für 111 Kirchenmitglieder und in der Reformierten Kirche in Ungarn für 9.440. Doch ist der Gedanke von Repräsentanz dem Gedanken der Synode erst nachträglich hinzugekommen. Die Synodalen sind nicht als Interessenvertreter ihrer Gemeinden zu verstehen, sondern sie haben im Sinne der ganzen Kirche zu entscheiden; sie sind ihrem Gewissen gegenüber verantwortlich und nicht denjenigen, die sie gewählt haben.

Auch wenn sich die Arbeitsweisen von Synoden und Parlamenten oft ähneln, bestehen doch klare Unterschiede: Synoden müssen geeignete Verfahren entwickeln, um möglichst einmütig zu entscheiden. Es gibt keine regierenden und oppositionellen Parteien, die einander gegenüberstehen. Die Synodalen tragen gemeinsam im Hören auf das Wort Gottes die Verantwortung für ihre Kirche. Daher können Synodalversammlungen nicht losgelöst von der gottesdienstlichen Feier stattfinden

Beziehung der Synode zum politischen Parlament

Oft bestanden Synoden schon vor Parlamenten, und Kirchenbauten beherbergten im 19. Jahrhundert erste Nationalparlamente, wie in Deutschland die Paulskirche in Frankfurt oder in Ungarn die große Kirche in Debrecen. Auch bei zwei der hier vorgestellten Gebäude gab es eine räumliche Beziehung zwischen Synodengebäude und Parlament.

Die Plenarsitzungen der sächsischen Landessynode fanden im 19. Jahrhundert im sächsischen Landtag statt, der sich zunächst im Landhaus in Dresden, und ab 1907 im Ständehaus befand. Auch nach dem Ende des Königreiches Sachsen und dem damit einhergehenden landesherrlichen Kirchenregiment durfte die Synode noch bis Ende der 1920er Jahre im Landtag tagen und verlegte sich von da an in kirchliche Räumlichkeiten. Zum Ende der Deutschen Demokratischen Republik konnte die sächsische Landessynode ihre neue Heimat im Saal der Dreikönigskirche – Haus der Kirche beziehen. Der erste frei gewählte sächsische Landtag – also das politische Parlament – hielt seine Sitzungen ab 1990 drei Jahre lang im Synodensaal der evangelischen Kirche ab, bis er in ein neues Parlamentsgebäude einziehen konnte. In Erinnerung daran wurde eine großformatige Fotoreproduktion des Wandgemäldes aus dem Synodensaal für das neuerrichtete sächsische Parlament angefertigt. Im dortigen Bürgerfoyer erinnert das Bild an den politischen Neuanfang im Synodensaal der Kirche.

Auch die *Assembly Hall* der Kirche von Schottland beherbergte ein Parlament. Nachdem das schottische Parlament 1707 im *Act of Union* mit dem englischen Parlament zum britischen Parlament zusammengelegt wurde, wurde erst durch zwei Referenden Ende des 20. Jahrhunderts der Weg für ein beschränkt eigenständiges schottisches Parlament frei. Dieses konstituierte sich 1999 in der *Assembly Hall* der Kirche von Schottland, die dem schottischen Parlament bis 2004 als Sitzungssaal diente. Als Reminiszenz an diese Zeit erhielt das 2004 eröffnete neue schottische Parlamentsgebäude ebenfalls einen schwarz-weißen Korridor (so benannt wegen seines schachbrettartigen Fußbodendesigns), wie die *Assembly Hall* ihn hat.

Wenngleich die sächsische Landessynode als Ausdruck des landesherrlichen Kirchenregiments zunächst im sächsischen Landtag tagte, bestehen im umgekehrten Falle für die kurzzeitige Nutzung kirchlicher Synodenräume für die staatlichen Parlamente keine inhaltlichen Gründe. Darin zeigt sich lediglich, dass die Räume nicht nur für die synodale Arbeit geeignet sind, sondern dass sie auch den Anforderungen heutiger parlamentarischer Arbeit gerecht werden.

Verweise auf staatliche Autoritäten

Die Synodenräume nehmen in ihrer Gestaltung bewusst Bezug auf staatliche Autoritäten oder nationale Symbolik.

In der *Assembly Hall* der Kirche von Schottland ist ein eigener Platz für den *Lord High Commissioner* reserviert, der die Monarchie bei der Generalversammlung vertritt. Dieser Platz, der durch eine Bekrönung zusätzlich hervorgehoben ist, befindet sich auf der Nordgalerie hinter dem Platz für den Moderator der Versammlung. Diese Galerie hat einen separaten Zugang, um zu bekräftigen, dass der *Lord High Commissioner* weder die Versammlung leitet noch an Debatten oder Entscheidungen aktiv teilnimmt. Oberhalb hinter dem Sitz des *Lord High Commissioner* stellt ein Buntglasfenster den biblischen König David dar.

Die *Assembly Hall* der Presbyterianischen Kirche von Irland hat keinen solchen hervorgehobenen Platz für die Repräsentanz der Krone. Hinter dem Präsidium der Synode befindet sich stattdessen eine Orgel, die von zwei prächtigen Buntglasfenstern umrahmt wird. An der Außenfassade des Synodengebäudes befinden sich die Wappen mehrerer irischer Städte und die irische Harfe von Leinster als Ausdruck, dass die presbyterianische Kirche für die ganze irische Insel da ist.

Auch in der *Aula sinodale* der Waldenserkirche ist der zentrale Ort für die Bezugnahme auf die staatliche Autorität hinter dem Sitz des Synodenpräsidiums in der Apsis. Dort befanden sich bis in die 1920er Jahre eine Büste und ein Porträtfoto von König Umberto I., der jedoch bereits im Jahre 1900 ermordet wurde. Er verteidigte die Religionsfreiheit der Waldenser in seiner kompromisslosen Haltung gegenüber dem Heiligen Stuhl und war der einzige italienische Monarch, der den Synodensaal, zu dessen Errichtung er auch finanziell beigetragen hatte, persönlich besuchte. An die Stelle der Respektbekundung an die Monarchie trat mit dem Apsiswandgemälde des in Torre Pellice geborenen waldensischen Künstlers Paolo Antonio Paschetto eine Bezugnahme auf die Wurzeln der Waldenserkirche. Das Gemälde zeigt eine große Eiche, deren Wurzeln im Felsen verankert sind, vor dem Hintergrund einer Berglandschaft; die Zweige des Baumes tragen eine aufgeschlagene Bibel mit einem Zitat aus Offenbarung 2,8-11: »Sei treu bis an den Tod.« Darunter befindet sich das Wappen der Waldenserkirche, der brennende Leuchter und der Treueschwur der Waldenser bei ihrer Rückkehr aus dem Exil 1689. Paschetto entwarf das Bild 1939 in der Zeit des Faschismus als Sinnbild für die verfolgte Kirche. Als 1948 der Entwurf Paschettos für ein neues Wappen der Republik Italien von der verfassungsgebenden Versammlung angenommen wurde, sahen Menschen mit Kenntnis dieses Sachverhalts in dem Wandgemälde einen Bezug zur italienischen Republik.

Im Synodensaal der Reformierten Kirche in Ungarn befinden sich keine direkten Bezüge zum ungarischen Staat. Selbst eine ungarische Fahne, die zur Ausstattung der meisten reformierten Kirchengebäude in Ungarn gehört, findet sich nicht im Synodensaal.

Der Verweis auf die staatliche Gewalt ist im Synodensaal der Evangelisch-Lutherischen Landeskirche Sachsens das Gegenteil einer Huldigung. Das monumentale Wandbild »Versöhnung« des Künstlers Werner Juza nimmt Bezug auf staatliche Ungerechtigkeit und Willkürherrschaft. Die gesichtslosen Richter sind durch Stacheldraht vom Volk getrennt und die Polizeigewalt richtet sich gegen Menschen mit offenen und leeren Händen. Das Einzige, was sie den Schilden und Gummiknüppeln entgegenzusetzen haben, ist eine Gitarre. Vor dieser Anprangerung der Unrechtsherrschaft versammeln sich nicht nur die Synodalen der Kirche, sondern tagte auch für drei Jahre der erste frei gewählte sächsische Landtag und entschied über die Neuordnung des Freistaates.

Identitätsstiftende Symbolik

Doch die Synodengebäude nehmen nicht nur Bezug auf staatliche Autoritäten. Sie enthalten auch Symbole, die in der Tradition ihrer Kirche identitätsstiftend sind. Oft verweisen sie auf die harten Kapitel in der Geschichte ihrer Kirche.

Dies ist der Fall bei der *Aula sinodale* der Waldenserkirche, wo das Wandgemälde mit Eiche, Leuchter, Treueschwur und Bibelvers an den Überlebenskampf der Kirche erinnert, die sich seit dem Mittelalter immer wieder Verfolgung ausgesetzt sah. In einem Nebenraum des Synodengebäudes, dem roten Salon, hängt andererseits aber auch ein Ölgemälde, das John Charles Beckwith zeigt, der im 19. Jahrhundert unter anderem dabei half, über einhundert Schulen in den Waldensertälern zu bauen. So gedenkt die Kirche auch ihrer Wohltäter.

Auch die Reformierte Kirche in Ungarn bringt in ihrem Synodengebäude beides zum Ausdruck. Hinter den Plätzen für das Präsidium hängt an der Wand das Wappen der Kirche. Im Wappenschild ist das Christuslamm dargestellt, das mit drei Beinen auf zwei aufgeschlagenen Büchern, dem Alten und Neuen Testament, steht und die Siegesfahne der Auferstehung mit dem Vorderbein umklammert. Die Fahne zeigt ein weißes Kreuz auf rotem Grund und verweist damit auf die Konfession der Kirche: Das helvetische Bekenntnis. Der Kopf des Lammes ist von einem Nimbus umstrahlt und hinter ihm steht ein Palmbaum. In der Interpretation der ungarischen Kirche steht die Palme für den festen Willen zum Widerstand und erinnert daran, dass die Kirche durch die Jahrhunderte für die Menschen eine Oase in der Wüste sein wollte. Über dem Wappenschild ist ein Phönix zu sehen, der aus der eigenen Asche auferstehend den Feuerflammen entsteigt und sich der Sonne zuwendet. Unter dem Wappen prangt ein Banner mit einem Satz aus Römer 8,31, der zu einem Erkennungszeichen für die Hoffnung der Reformation wurde: »Ist Gott für uns, wer kann wider uns sein?« So ist das Wappen der Reformierten Kirche in Ungarn Ausdruck ihrer Glaubenshoffnung und Zuversicht. Zugleich wird in einem anderen Raum des Gebäudes mit einer Gedenktafel der ungarischen evangelischen Prediger gedacht, die im Zuge der Gegenreformation um ihres Glaubens willen als Galeerensklaven verkauft wurden.

Sowohl die Presbyterianische Kirche von Irland als auch die Kirche von Schottland greifen in der Ausgestaltung ihrer Synodengebäude auf das Motiv des brennenden Dornbuschs zurück. Die Darstellung findet sich in der Außenfassade, in Buntglasfenstern und im Schnitzwerk der Bestuhlung. Seit 1691 ist der brennende Dornbusch ein Symbol der Kirche von Schottland, häufig untertitelt mit dem lateinischen Text *Nec Tamen Consumebatur* – »dennoch verbrannte er nicht«. Der Satz bezieht sich auf die Berufungsgeschichte Moses im Buch Exodus. Dort wird erzählt, dass Gott Mose im brennenden Dornbusch begegnete. Der Busch wurde nicht von den Flammen verzehrt. Johannes Calvin sah im brennenden Dornbusch ein Symbol für die leidende Kirche. In den Darstellungen der Presbyterianischen Kirche von Irland ziert den brennenden Dornbusch ein Spruchband mit den lateinischen Worten *Ardens sed virens* – »Brennend, aber blühend«. So zeigt sich auch hier, wie Leiden und Hoffnung in der kirchlichen Symbolik nebeneinanderstehen und aufeinander bezogen sind.

Das Wandbild im Synodensaal der Evangelisch-Lutherischen Landeskirche Sachsens prangert nicht nur das Unrecht und die Gewalt an. In der Darstellung der Kreuzigung Jesu wird, wie schon in mittelalterlichen Kreuzigungsdarstellungen, das Blut des Gekreuzigten in einem Kelch aufgefangen. Der Kelch und eine Oblate verweisen auf das Abendmahl. Nach christlichem Verständnis schenkt Gott darin neue Gemeinschaft, die als Vorgeschmack auf die himmlische Gemeinschaft verstanden wird, in welcher alles Leiden und alle Feindschaft aufgehoben sein wird. So wird das Wandgemälde zu einem Bild, das die Zuversicht auf ein befreites Leben in Gemeinschaft offenhält inmitten von Gewalt und Leid.

Alle Synodenräume nehmen in ihrer Symbolik Hoffnungsbilder auf, die die Kirche auf ihrem Weg durch die Zeiten geleitet haben und die die Synodalen an schwere Zeiten in der eigenen Geschichte erinnern.

In den Synodengebäuden, die in diesem Band vorgestellt werden, kommt das Selbstverständnis evangelischer Kirchen exemplarisch zum Ausdruck. Im Folgenden wird zunächst in die Geschichte evangelischer Synoden und ihre gegenwärtigen Herausforderungen eingeführt. Im Anschluss werden die fünf ausgewählten Synodengebäude von Vertreterinnen und Vertretern ihrer Kirchen vorgestellt.

Mario Fischer · Aleida Siller

Introduction

In the public space, Protestant churches are often recognised from their church building. But the churches have other meeting rooms of importance to their lives. For example, some churches have erected separate buildings for their synod assemblies. These premises say a lot about how they understand themselves. The seating arrangements in the synod hall, the use of materials, the furnishing with symbolic artworks – all that is well thought-out and is part of a church's identity. However, churches as proprietors of their own synod buildings is the exception rather than the rule. Frequently they go without a fixed location in order to be able to hold synods in different regions and parishes of a church, or not to have to maintain an additional building. Then synods are held in parish centres or in especially hired conference facilities.

Five buildings constructed to hold synods are presented in this illustrated volume: those of the Evangelical Waldensian Church, the Church of Scotland, the Reformed Church in Hungary, the Presbyterian Church of Ireland and the Evangelical Lutheran Church of Saxony. The following articles highlight points in common and distinguishing features of the respective building designs in order to shed light on the understanding of synodality they express and the way the synods relate to the state and society.

The choice of place

The synod buildings belong to nationwide or regional churches. It is striking that all of them were built in a capital city, although in the case of the Waldensian Church it was not the capital of the Italian state, which at the time of the erection of the building was already Rome, but the de facto church capital in the Waldensian valleys, that is, Torre Pellice, near Turin. There the synod building *Casa Valdese* stretches along a long street, the »Waldensian quarter«. Today, standing near the *Casa Valdese* on both sides of Via Beckwith and Via Arnaud, are the church building, the parsonage, the grammar school, the museum and the guesthouse of the Waldensian Church. When synod convenes in summer this area resembles a street festival and it becomes clear that Torre Pellice is the unofficial capital of the Waldensian Church.

The synod buildings of the Church of Scotland and the Presbyterian Church of Ireland lie in Edinburgh and Belfast, the respective capitals of Scotland and Northern Ireland. In both cases the synod building was erected near a centre of political power. The Assembly Buildings of the Presbyterian Church of Ireland are less than 200 metres from the splendid Belfast City Hall, while the Assembly Hall of the Church of Scotland is in close proximity to Edinburgh Castle. In Dresden, the capital of the Free State of Saxony, the *Dreikönigskirche* (Three Kings Church) building, home to the synod hall of the Evangelical Lutheran Church of Saxony, stands in the main street of the *Dresdner Neustadt* pedestrian precinct.

Only in Hungary is the synod building not located in the heart of the capital. Admittedly, the original plan was to erect the building in Budapest in a central location next to the Reformed Church in Kálvin Square, but it was ultimately decided to construct it a bit further away from the urban centre in a villa district near the city park.

The location in the capital goes hand in hand with visibility in society, easier transport connections and quicker access to political institutions. These aspects do not apply in the case of the Waldensian Church.

Architecture and financing

The decision to build a separate building for holding synods entailed various other questions: who was to design the building and in what style? And how was the project to be financed?

The churches awarded the contracts to architecture firms from their own country, sometimes after a call for tenders. In the case of the Hungarian synod building, Alfréd Hajós and János Villányi came first in the competition and were commissioned to realise the project subject to including elements from four other designs. Alfréd Hajós was famous as an athlete, but had only just opened his architecture office with János Villányi when construction of the synod building started. The architecture office subsequently carried out notable building projects in Hungary. The impressive-looking synod building included stylistic elements from historicism and art nouveau. Hajós and Villányi continued to work along these lines. At the end of the 1920s Hajós was designing sports stadia like the Millenáris (millennium) sports complex in Budapest XIV (1928) or the National Swimming Stadium in Budapest (1930), which are influenced by the Bauhaus style.

A call for tenders also took place in the case of the synod building in Edinburgh, with the commission going to a well-known architect, William Henry Playfair. The actual Assembly Hall was designed by David Bryce, who is regarded as the most eminent representative of Scottish baronial style. This style was also chosen by Robert Young when designing the Assembly Buildings of the Presbyterian Church of Ireland in Belfast. Accordingly, the churches opted for the Scottish version of neo-Gothic, which takes its inspiration more from fortresses than from church buildings.

For the *Casa Valdese* in Torre Pellice, the first draft by the London architect and engineer William Allen Boulnois was in neo-Gothic style. However, the church leadership decided in favour of the young architect Epaminonda Ayassot, who had already carried out several construction projects in the Pellice Valley. In so doing, they chose a financially and architecturally less ambitious building, corresponding more to the local architecture. The project was financed by donations from Waldensians at home and abroad, as well as friendly churches, committees and individual benefactors.

While donations were an important basis for constructing the synod buildings, some churches also resorted to other modes of financing. The Presbyterian Church of Ireland received finance for the building from the Presbyterian Church Twentieth Century Fund and a loan from the Scottish Provident Institution. The Reformed Church in Hungary, too, was dependent on a building loan for its finance, with all the church districts of the Reformed Church in Hungary contributing to its repayment. The Assembly Hall in Edinburgh was the only one to be fully financed by donations from the church concerned. It is truly remarkable that the enormous sum was entirely raised by women from the Free Church of Scotland.

The synod hall of the Evangelical Lutheran Church of Saxony is in the former *Dreikönigskirche*, which was completely rebuilt by the Dresden architect Manfred Arlt. He was influenced by the *Neues Bauen* style and Le Corbusier, and was responsible for various major building projects in Dresden during the German Democratic Republic (GDR). The *Dreikönigskirche* was financed in the context of the special building programme for churches in the GDR through donations from West German and Western European churches.

In all the cases of synod buildings presented here, the churches decided to grant the design and execution to well-known architects from their own country. In terms of style, the latter favoured imposing buildings in the contemporary taste and with local and regional features. The financing of the building is, every time, an expression of how church members identified with the concern to construct a building for their synod, with friendly churches contributing out of solidarity.

Seating arrangements in the synod hall

The word »synod« comes from the Greek word *syn-odos*, which means »together on the way«. It expresses the idea that the church understands itself as a community travelling together. This becomes very clear precisely in the synods in which delegates converge from the different parts of a church and take decisions together. Normal synodal life, however, consists mainly of sittting. The work is characterised by »sittings« chaired by a »president« (Latin: *praesidens* – sitting in front).

As a rule, the presiding officer sits up the front of the synod hall, visible to all. In some cases, the church's executive board sits beside or behind the presiding officer with a view of the synod, in other cases it sits opposite him or her. The Waldensian synod explicitly states that the church executive sits opposite the synod in order to account for itself.

There are various models of seating for the members of synod, following both practical considerations and the customs of different parliamentary cultures. The important thing is that everyone can hear and see well and that no hierarchy is reflected in the way the members sit.

In the synod hall of the Waldensian Church the members sit on benches on three opposite sides. The design recalls the Parliament of the United Kingdom, at least it did until 1974 when the benches were still upholstered in green as in the House of Commons. Occasionally the opinion is heard that this was due to the British officer John Charles Beckwith (1789–1862), who settled in the Waldensian valleys and supported the church. A life-size painting of him hangs in the synod building in Torre Pellice. Yet such an arrangement of benches is also familiar from Protestant synods like the French Reformed Synod of Montpellier in 1598 or the Synod of Dordrecht in 1618/19.

In any case, the Reformed synod halls in the United Kingdom do not follow the parliamentary seating of the House of Commons, which may be due to the size of the assemblies. The Church of Scotland and the Presbyterian Church of Ireland opted for a horseshoe pattern to allow for optimum participation in the discussion from all the places. The Reformed Church in Hungary also chose a semi-circular layout. Only the Synod of the Evangelical Lutheran Church of Saxony sits at tables one after another in parallel lines, facing the synod presidency.

A separate section is usually provided for guests and the public, frequently on the galleries or balconies, so that they can follow the synod well. Whether guests and the public are entitled to express their approval or disagreement depends on differing cultural practices.

Synods and parliaments

Protestant synods are often simply called »church parliaments« because they are locations where elected and appointed delegates from the congregations meet and take decisions together. Since the 19th century, synods have often been regarded as representing the congregations. The ratio of delegates to the total number of church members varies greatly, as shown by the Protestant churches in Europe presented here. The synod of the Evangelical Waldensian Church, with 20,000 members in Italy, has 180 delegates. The Evangelical Lutheran Church of Saxony, with 610,000 members, has 80 delegates, while the Church of Scotland, with 260,000 church members, has 500 delegates. The General Assembly of the Presbyterian Church of Ireland comprises 1,100 delegates for 190,000 church members and the Reformed Church in Hungary has 100 delegates for a church membership of 944,000. The synod size of the selected churches ranges between 80 (Saxony) and 1,100 (Ireland) members. Relating the number of synod members to church members, the ratio in the Waldensian Church is 1:111 and in the Reformed Church in Hungary 1:9,440. Yet the idea of representation was only a late addition to the concept of synod. Members of synod should not be understood as stakeholders of their congregations – they have to take decisions in the interest of the whole church; they are accountable to their conscience and not to those who have elected them.

Even if the procedures of synods and parliaments are often similar there are still clear differences; synods have to develop appropriate procedures in order to take decisions that are as consensual as possible. There are no governing and opposition parties confronting one another. The members of synod share responsibility for their church while listening to God's word. Hence synod assemblies cannot be disconnected from services of worship.

Relation of the synod to the political parliament

Often synods existed before parliaments, and church buildings in the 19th century accommodated the first national parliaments, like Germany's *Paulskirche* in Frankfurt or, in Hungary, the Great Reformed Church in Debrecen. In the case of the following two buildings there was also a spatial relationship between the synod building and the parliament.

In the 19th century, the plenary meetings of the Saxon synod took place in the Saxon state parliament, which was located first in the patrician *Landhaus* building in Dresden, and from 1907 in the *Ständehaus* (House of Estates). Even after the end of the Kingdom of Saxony (in 1918) and, with it, the ecclesiastical authority of the territorial ruler, the synod was still permitted to meet in the parliament until the late 1920s, moving then to church premises. At the end of the German Democratic Republic the Saxon synod was able to move into the hall of *Dreikönigskirche – Haus der Kirche*. The first freely elected Saxon parliament conducted its sessions for three years from 1990 in the synod hall of the Protestant church until a purpose-built house of parliament was ready. In memory of that interim period, a large-scale photographic reproduction of the mural in the synod hall was made for the newly erected Saxon parliament. Displayed in the lobby, the picture recalls the fresh political start in the synod hall of the church.

The Assembly Hall of the Church of Scotland was also home to a parliament. After the Scottish parliament was merged with the English parliament through the 1707 Act of Union, it took until the end of the 20th century to clear the way for a Scottish parliament with limited autonomy, through two referendums. It convened for the first time in 1999 in the Assembly Hall of the Church of Scotland, which served as a debating chamber for the Scottish Parliament until 2004. In memory of this period, the new Scottish Parliament building, opened in 2004, was given a Black and White Corridor (so named after its chequerboard tiled floor) like the one at the Assembly Hall.

Although the Saxon synod initially held its sessions in the Saxon Parliament as an expression of the territorial ruler's authority over the church, in the converse case there have been no substantive reasons for the short-term usage of church synod premises by state parliaments. All it shows is that the facilities are not only suited to the work of synod but can also do justice to the demands of present-day parliamentary work.

References to state authorities

In their designs, the synod halls deliberately refer to state authorities or national symbols.

In the Assembly Hall of the Church of Scotland, a special place is reserved for the Lord High Commissioner, who represents the monarchy at the general assembly. Marked by a crown, this place is on the northern gallery behind the seat of the moderator (presiding officer). This gallery has a separate access to underline that the Lord High Commissioner neither chairs the assembly nor participates actively in decision-making. High up behind the seat of the Lord High Commissioner, a stained-glass window portrays the biblical King David.

The Assembly Hall of the Presbyterian Church of Ireland reserves no such prominent place for the representative of the crown. Instead, behind the presidency there is an organ framed by two magnificent stained-glass windows. On the external facade of the synod building are found the coats-of-arms of several Irish cities and the Irish harp, expressing the fact that the Presbyterian Church is there for the whole island of Ireland.

In the Waldensian Church's *Aula sinodale* the central place referring to state authority is the apse behind the seat of the synod presidency. A bust and portrait photo of King Umberto I were on display there into the 1920s, well after his murder in 1900. He defended the Waldensians' freedom of religion in his uncompromising stance towards the Holy See and was the only Italian monarch to personally visit the synod hall, which he had supported financially. This gesture of respect towards the monarchy was replaced by the painting on the apse wall by Torre Pellice-born Waldensian artist Paolo Antonio Paschetto, evoking the origins of the Waldensian Church. The painting shows a mighty oak, enrooted in the rock, in a mountain landscape; the branches of the tree bear an open Bible with a verse from Revelations 2:8-11: »Be faithful unto death.« Under it is the emblem of the Waldensian Church, the candlestick and the oath of the Waldensians on their return from exile in 1689. Paschetto created the picture in 1939 during the Fascist period as a symbol of the persecuted church. When in 1948 the constituent assembly accepted Paschetto's design of a new coat-of-arms for the Italian Republic, people with this knowledge saw a reference to the Italian Republic in the mural.

The synod hall of the Reformed Church in Hungary contains no direct references to the Hungarian state. Not even a Hungarian flag, which is part of the furnishings in most Reformed Church buildings in Hungary, is to be found in the synod hall.

The reference to state power in the synod hall of the Evangelical Lutheran Church of Saxony is the opposite of paying homage. The monumental mural »Reconciliation« by the artist Werner Juza relates to state injustice and arbitrariness. The faceless judges are separated from the people by barbed wire and police use violence against people with open, empty hands. The only thing they have to counter the shields and rubber batons is a guitar. This denunciation of tyranny is the backdrop not only for the members of synod – for three years the first freely elected Saxon parliament met here and determined the new order of the Free State of Saxony.

Identity-creating symbolism

Yet the synod building does not just refer to state authorities. They contain symbols creating a sense of identity in the tradition of their church. Often they point to the hard times in their church history.

This is the case with the *Aula sinodale* of the Waldensian Church, where the mural with its oak, candlestick, oath of loyalty and Bible verse recall the church's struggle to survive, having repeatedly been exposed to persecution since the Middle Ages. On the other hand, in an adjacent room in the synod building, the Red Salon, hangs an oil painting of John Charles Beckwith, who inter alia helped to build over one hundred schools in the Waldensian valleys. This is also a way of remembering the church's benefactors.

The Reformed Church in Hungary likewise expresses both in its synod building. The church's emblem hangs behind the places for the presidency. It depicts Christ as a lamb, standing with three legs on two open books, the Old and New Testaments, and gripping the victorious flag of the resurrection with its front leg. The flag shows a white cross on a red background, thereby indicating the church's confession: the Helvetic Confession. The lamb's head is surrounded by a nimbus and behind it is a palm tree. In the interpretation of the Hungarian church, the palm stands for the firm will to resist and recalls that the church throughout the centuries wanted to be like an oasis in the desert for their people. Above the emblem, a phoenix rises from the flames and its own ashes, turning towards the sun. Below it is a banner with a phrase from Romans 8:31, which became a trademark of Reformation hope: »If God is for us, who can be against us?« Hence the emblem of the Reformed Church in Hungary expresses its faithful hope and confidence. At the same time, in another room of the building a plaque recalls the Hungarian Protestant preachers who were sold as galley slaves for their faith during the Counter-Reformation.

Both the Presbyterian Church of Ireland and the Church of Scotland had recourse to the motif of the burning bush when decorating their synod building. The image is found on the external facade, in stained-glass windows and seat carvings. Since 1691 the burning bush has been a symbol of the Church of Scotland, frequently subtitled with the Latin text *Nec tamen consumebatur* – »yet it was not burnt up«. The phrase relates to the calling of Moses, as narrated in the Book of Exodus. It says that God encountered Moses in the burning bush. The bush was not consumed by the flames. John Calvin saw in the burning bush a symbol of the suffering church. In the symbolic depictions of the Presbyterian Church of Ireland, the burning bush is adorned by a ribbon with the Latin words *Ardens sed virens* – »Burning, but flourishing«. We see here, too, how suffering and hope are closely related in church symbolism.

The mural in the synod hall of the Evangelical Lutheran Church of Saxony not only denounces wrong-doing and violence. In the depiction of Jesus' crucifixion, the blood of the crucified Christ is collected in a cup as in medieval pictures of the crucifixion. The cup and a wafer evoke the Lord's Supper. According to Christian understanding, God graciously gifts us with renewed communion in the elements, understood as a foretaste of the heavenly communion in which all suffering and hostility will pass away. This way the mural becomes a picture that keeps open the confidence in a liberated life in community, in the midst of violence and suffering.

In their symbolism, all synod buildings include images of hope that have guided the church on its way through the ages and remind the members of synod of difficult times in their own history.

The synod buildings described are examples of the self-understanding and history of Protestant churches. The following chapters will first introduce the history of Protestant synods and their present challenges. Then the five selected synod buildings will be described by representatives of their churches.

Essays

Martin Friedrich

Synoden im Protestantismus

Synoden gehören zum Protestantismus; sie sind gewissermaßen sogar eins seiner Markenzeichen. Das war mehr oder weniger bereits im 16. Jahrhundert so. Allerdings sind nur die Synoden, die sich in den reformierten Minderheitskirchen herausbildeten, die direkten Vorläufer der Synoden, wie sie heutzutage in unseren Kirchen bestehen. Die Synoden, die es in den lutherischen Kirchen der Reformationszeit gab, sind durch zwei Merkmale von den heutigen Synoden zu unterscheiden. Erstens waren sie nicht die Inhaber der höchsten Autorität in den Kirchen. Und zweitens bestanden sie im Allgemeinen nur aus Geistlichen.

Die Vorgeschichte

Mit dem letzteren knüpfte die Reformation an die Tradition von Alter Kirche und Mittelalter an. Synoden waren in den ersten Jahrhunderten das wichtigste Instrument, um Differenzen in Lehre und Leben zu behandeln und so die einzelnen Gemeinden zu einer Kirche zusammenzubringen. Spätestens seit Ende des zweiten Jahrhunderts kamen Vertreter der Gemeinden einer bestimmten Region zusammen, um Streitfragen zu schlichten, Häretiker auszuschließen und grundlegende Fragen zu besprechen. Stimmberechtigt waren die Bischöfe der städtischen Gemeinden; anfangs konnten Priester und Diakone zumindest als Berater teilnehmen. »Synodos« hieß die Veranstaltung auf Griechisch, »concilium« auf Lateinisch. Erst mit der Zeit wurde die Bezeichnung Synode vorrangig für die regionalen Beratungen verwendet, Konzil für die erst seit der Konstantinischen Wende möglichen universalen Versammlungen der gesamten Kirche, die für die Lehrentwicklung der Kirche so bedeutsam waren.

Im Mittelalter setzte sich die Entwicklung fort. Es gab im Westen weiterhin von Bischöfen beschickte Diözesan- und Metropolitansynoden (nur im Frankenreich gehörten zeitweise auch Adlige, also Laien, zu den Teilnehmern) und auf gesamtkirchlicher Ebene die sogenannten ökumenischen Konzilien, auch wenn ihre Ökumenizität von der Ostkirche nicht anerkannt wurde. Im 14. Jahrhundert setzte sich sogar zeitweise die Theorie des Konziliarismus durch, wonach das Konzil in seiner Autorität noch über dem Papsttum stehe (Abb. 1).

Die Reformation in Deutschland und Ostmitteleuropa

Die Wittenberger Reformation war in ihrer Stellung zu Konzil/Synode in einer Zwickmühle. Auf der einen Seite hatte Martin Luther (1483–1546) schon im November 1518 gefordert, dass ein Konzil die Lehrstreitigkeiten in der Kirche lösen solle. Nachdem er aber bei der Leipziger Disputation im Sommer 1519 festgestellt hatte, dass auch Konzilien irren könnten, war klar, dass dieses Instrument allein nicht der Universalschlüssel sein konnte. Luther hat stets (am ausführlichsten in der Schrift *Von Conciliis und Kirchen* 1539) argumentiert, dass ein Konzil nur anerkannt werden könne, wenn es sich der Autorität der Heiligen Schrift unterstelle. Das galt für alle Ebenen, so dass eine Beteiligung der Protestanten an dem vom Papst einberufenen und geleiteten Konzil von Trient (1545–1563) nicht in Frage kam (Abb. 2). Aber auch im Aufbau der evangelischen Kirchen spielten synodale Elemente zunächst keine entscheidende Rolle. Philipp Melanchthon (1497–1560) setzte größere Hoffnungen in die

| Aus den Bischofssynoden der alten Kirche entwickelten sich die ökumenischen Konzilien, die von den Kaisern einberufen wurden. Im späten Mittelalter wurde im sogenannten »Konziliarismus« die Position vertreten, dass Konzilien Autorität über Päpste haben. (Wandmalerei im Kloster Megistis Lavras auf dem Berg Athos, Griechenland). | *The ecumenical councils convened by the emperors evolved from the bishops' synods of the early church. »Conciliarism« in the late Middle Ages represented the position that supreme authority resided in ecumenical councils, even against popes (mural in Megistis Lavras Monastery on Mount Athos, Greece).*

Konfliktlösung durch synodale Beratungen, sah die Voraussetzungen dafür aber nicht gegeben.[1]

Das wichtigste Instrument in der schweizerischen und reichsstädtischen Reformation waren die Disputationen oder Religionsgespräche, die Elemente der Synoden mit denen der akademischen Disputationen verbanden.[2] In Ulm (1532, sogar mit Laienbeteiligung)[3] und Straßburg (1533) ist dabei sogar ausdrücklich von Synoden die Rede. Dieses Vorbild wurde in der Wittenberger Reformation jedoch kaum aufgenommen. Die auffälligste Ausnahme ist die Homberger Synode, bei der 1526 auf Einladung von Landgraf Philipp (1504–1567) Adlige und Theologen zusammenkamen und den Übergang Hessens zur Reformation beschlossen (Abb. 3). Die von Franz Lambert (1487–1530) auf Grundlage der Lehre vom allgemeinen Priestertum entworfene Kirchenordnung wurde zwar nicht beschlossen, aber ab 1531 fanden regelmäßig Synoden statt. Bis zur Bildung eines Konsistoriums waren die Generalsynoden, die aber nur bis 1582 zusammenkamen, die eigentlichen Träger des Kirchenregiments in Hessen.[4] Auch in Pommern hatten die General- und Regionalsynoden im 16. Jahrhundert einen erheblichen Einfluss auf die Kirchenpolitik, wie in Hessen aber dem landesherrlichen Kirchenregiment unterstellt.

In anderen lutherischen Territorien, z. B. nach der württembergischen Synodalordnung von 1537, waren die Synoden eher Fortbildungs- und Disziplinierungsveranstaltungen für die Pfarrer. Der württembergische »Synodus« dagegen war, entgegen seinem Namen, keine Synode, sondern ein Gremium, das aus den Mitgliedern des Kirchenrats (einem Konsistorium entsprechend) und den vier Generalsuperintendenten bestand. Zusätzlich wurden 1644 Kirchenkonvente mit Laienbeteiligung eingerichtet, die aber nur für Kirchenzucht zuständig waren.[5] Nur in Jülich-Kleve-Berg gab sich die lutherische Kirche bei den Synoden in Unna und Dinslaken 1612 eine presbyterial-synodale Ordnung nach dem reformierten Modell der Emder Synode (siehe Opitz' Beitrag in diesem Band).

In den anderen lutherischen Territorien waren die Synoden reine Geistlichkeitssynoden. Das gilt auch in Ostmitteleuropa. Die Geschichte der evangelischen Kirchen in Polen, Ungarn und Siebenbürgen in der Frühen Neuzeit kann geradezu als Geschichte ihrer Synoden geschrieben werden. Bei den Synoden von Mediasch und

Erdöd 1545, Prešov/Eperies 1546, Hermannstadt 1563 und Leutschau 1597 mit ihrer Festlegung auf das lutherische Bekenntnis und von Sillein 1610 mit der Schaffung einer einheitlichen Kirchenstruktur hatten nur die Pfarrer mitzureden. Die Synoden waren hier zwar ein wesentliches Element der Kirchenleitung, aber kein Ausdruck der Lehre vom allgemeinen Priestertum. Obwohl, anders als in Deutschland, das landesherrliche Kirchenregiment nicht das bestimmende Verfassungsprinzip war, setzte der westeuropäische Typ der Kirchenleitung sich nicht durch.

Neue Entwicklungen im 18. Jahrhundert

Bei den reformierten Kirchen in diesem Gebiet sah es nicht anders aus. Die Reformierte Kirche in Ungarn war seit der konstituierenden Synode von Debrecen 1567 synodal verfasst, aber nicht presbyterial-synodal. Im 17. Jahrhundert versuchten ungarische Theologen, die auf Studienreisen in Westeuropa die Verfassung der dortigen calvinistischen Kirchen kennengelernt hatten, auch in ihrer Kirche die Beteiligung von Ältesten in der Verfassung zu verankern, aber zunächst ohne Erfolg. Erst 1791 führte die reformierte Synode von Buda (gemeinsam mit der gleichzeitigen lutherischen Synode von Pest) die presbyterial-synodale Kirchenverfassung ein.[6]

Schon zuvor waren in zwei weiteren Traditionen des Protestantismus Synoden mit einem starken Laienelement etabliert worden. Sowohl Nikolaus Graf Zinzendorf als auch John Wesley hatten in ihren Bewegungen bereits regelmäßige Konferenzen als ein wesentliches Element des kirchlichen Lebens eingeführt. Was während ihres Lebens noch ihrer charismatischen Leitung unterworfen war, wurde nach ihrem Tod zum bestimmenden Verfassungselement. Seit 1764 wird die Herrnhuter Brüdergemeine durch Generalsynoden (heute Unitätskonferenzen) geleitet, an denen neben Amtsträgern auch gewählte Vertreter der Provinzen teilnehmen.[7] Die Bischöfliche Methodistenkirche (einer der Vorgänger der heutigen *United Methodist Church*) konstituierte sich 1784 auf der *Christmas Conference* in Baltimore (damals noch ausschließlich aus Geistlichen gebildet) und hat seit 1794 als oberstes Organ die alle vier Jahre stattfindende *general conference*, an der zwischen 600 und 1000 Abgeordnete teilnehmen.

2 Mit dem Konzil von Trient (1545–1563) antwortete die katholische Kirche auf die Reformation und wurde zur Konfessionskirche. Protestanten waren zu dem vom Papst einberufenen und geleiteten Konzil nicht eingeladen. Für Martin Luther konnte ein Konzil ohnehin nur anerkannt werden, wenn die Heilige Schrift oberste Autorität sei. | *The Council of Trent (1545–1563) was the Catholic Church's response to the Reformation, making it a confessional church. Protestants were not invited to the council, which the pope called and presided over. In any case, according to Martin Luther, a council could only be recognised if Scripture was the supreme authority.*

Der Durchbruch im 19. Jahrhundert

Im 19. Jahrhundert kam dann auch in den evangelischen Kirchen im deutschen Sprachraum das presbyterial-synodale Element zum Durchbruch. Zu den Ursachen gehört zum einen natürlich das Vorbild der westeuropäischen Kirchen, insbesondere der aus den preußischen Westprovinzen. Zum anderen spielte aber auch die politische Verfassungsdiskussion eine Rolle. So wie unter dem Schlagwort des Konstitualismus allenthalben eine Beteiligung des Volkes an der Legislative durch Parlamente gefordert wurde, sprach man auch vom »kirchlichen Konstitualismus«. Ohne den Summepiskopat der Landesfürsten insgesamt in Frage stellen zu wollen, wurde eine repräsentative Vertretung des Kirchenvolkes als Element der Kirchenverfassung gefordert. Damit veränderte sich das Verständnis von presbyterial-synodal, denn nach der alten reformierten Tradition waren die Presbyter und Synodalen keine Repräsentanten der Gemeinden, sondern wie die Pastoren Amtsträger und Sachwalter des göttlichen Willens.

Die Haltung derer, die nach 1800 für die Etablierung von Synoden eintraten, ist nicht immer klar einem der beiden Grundmotive zuzuordnen; oft vermischten sich auch beide. Bei den Diskussionen in Preußen nach den Befreiungskriegen war für die kirchlichen Vertreter sowohl in den Westprovinzen als auch in Berlin, wo Friedrich Schleiermacher bei der Synode von 1819 einen Verfassungsplan vorlegte, die Anlehnung an die calvinistische Ordnung entscheidend. Populär wurde die Forderung aber auch durch die politischen Implikationen, und sie waren es auch, die die anfangs erfolgversprechenden Ansätze zum Scheitern brachten: 1821 brach König Friedrich Wilhelm III. (1770–1840) den Prozess der Beratung einer neuen Kirchenverfassung ab, weil er auf keinen Fall der Forderung nach einer Repräsentativverfassung für sein Königreich Vorschub leisten wollte (Abb. 4).[8]

So waren es andere Landeskirchen, in denen erstmals Synoden mit Beteiligung der Laien tagten: 1818 ließ der bayerische König für den pfälzischen Landesteil eine Generalsynode zusammentreten, die nicht nur die Union der reformierten und lutherischen Kirche beschloss, sondern auch weitere wesentliche Entscheidungen über Lehre, Ordnung und Gottesdienst der Kirche fällte. Ein Drittel der Synodalen waren gewählte Gemeindeglieder. 1823 kamen auch in Bayern diesseits des Rheins zwei Generalsynoden zusammen, bei denen Geistliche und Laien im Verhältnis 6 zu 1 vertreten waren; erst ab 1849 waren sie paritätisch besetzt.[9] Bei der ebenfalls vom Landesherrn, dem Großherzog von Baden, zusammengerufenen badischen Unionssynode von 1821 waren die Nichtgeistlichen sogar in einer knappen Mehrheit.

Von großer Bedeutung für die weitere Entwicklung war die Rheinisch-Westfälische Kirchenordnung (Abb. 5) von 1835. Um die Akzeptanz seiner Agende zu sichern, sah sich der preußische König zu einer Konzession an die Gemeinden in den Westprovinzen gezwungen, die eine Rückkehr zu den bei ihnen seit Jahrhunderten geltenden Verfassungsprinzipien wünschten. So wurden auf der Ebene der Kirchenkreise und der Provinzialkirchen paritätisch zusammengesetzte Synoden geschaffen, die in ihren Kompetenzen allerdings den vom König besetzten Konsistorien untergeordnet blieben. Das Mischsystem von konsistorialer und presbyterial-synodaler Verfassung war zwar nur ein Kompromiss, wurde aber an vielen Stellen als vorbildlich angesehen.

Im Vormärz kam es wieder verstärkt zu Forderungen, die evangelische Kirchenverfassung zu reformieren, und zwar sowohl aus politischen als auch aus kirchlichen Motiven. König Friedrich Wilhelm IV. ließ 1843/44 Kreis- und Provinzialsynoden (in den Ostprovinzen rein aus Pfarrern bestehend) und 1846 eine Preußische Generalsynode (mit einer größeren Anzahl von Laien, die allerdings von den Provinzialsynoden gewählt wurden) tagen. Ihren Vorschlag, im gesamten Königreich Presbyterien und Synoden einzurichten und so (in noch einmal abgeschwächter Form) Elemente der Rheinisch-Westfälischen Kirchenordnung zu übernehmen, wies er jedoch zurück, weil er die presbyterial-synodale Ordnung aufgrund ihrer politischen Implikationen ablehnte. Während der Märzrevolution 1848 betrieb Kultusminister Maximilian Graf von Schwerin-Putzar (1804–1872) die Einführung einer presbyterial-synodalen Verfassung für die gesamte Landeskirche, konnte sie aber in seiner kurzen Amtszeit nicht erreichen.[10] So wurde erst unter Kultusminister Adalbert Falk (1827–1900) 1873 durch die Kirchengemeinde- und Synodalordnung und 1876 durch die Generalsynodalordnung die Konsistorialverfassung nach dem Vorbild der Rheinisch-Westfälischen Kirchenordnung durch konsultative Synoden ergänzt. Zuvor waren schon in einigen anderen Territorien (z. B. Oldenburg 1853, Baden 1861, Hannover 1864) ähnliche Mischverfassungen eingeführt worden; fast alle anderen folgten bis zum Beginn des 20. Jahrhunderts. Das Vorhandensein von Synoden war eine entscheidende Voraussetzung dafür, dass die Selbstorganisation der deutschen evangelischen Kirchen nach dem Ende der Monarchien 1918, mit dem auch das landesherrliche Kirchenregiment endete, relativ reibungslos gelang.

In allen deutschen Landeskirchen waren nun die Synoden die obersten Entscheidungsgremien. Auch dort wo, vor allem in lutherischen Kirchen, parallel dazu das personale Bischofsamt geschaffen und mit eigenen Kompetenzen auch gegenüber den Synoden ausgestattet wurde, waren es die Synoden, die die Bischöfe (oder auch andere leitende Geistliche) wählten, über den Haushalt und die Schwerpunkte der kirchlichen Arbeit bestimmten und in letzter Instanz auch die Kirchenordnung festlegten. In ihrer Arbeitsweise mit Ausschüssen und Plenarsitzungen ähnelten die Synoden den Parlamenten im politischen Bereich, und so kam der Begriff der »Kirchenparlamente« auf. Dieser wurde aber auch immer wieder zurückgewiesen, weil für die Synodalen nicht der Wille ihrer Wähler, sondern das Mandat durch Jesus Christus, den obersten Herrn seiner Kirche, bestimmend sein soll.

Das große Arbeitspensum, das die Synoden und Konferenzen der neueren Zeit haben, ließ es kaum noch zu, dass größere Debatten über Lehre und Bekenntnis geführt wurden. Umso wichtiger ist es, abschließend die Synode zu erwähnen, die im Mai 1934 die Barmer Theologische Erklärung verabschiedete (Abb. 6). Sie knüpfte auch darin wieder an die reformierten Synoden des 16. und 17. Jahrhunderts an, dass sie als Versammlung der Bekennenden Kirche in Deutschland ohne jegliche Unterstützung, ja sogar gegen die Behinderung durch staatliche Stellen durchgeführt werden musste. Dennoch waren die bis 1936 auf Reichsebene und bis 1943 in der preußischen Landeskirche durchgeführten Bekenntnissynoden (darunter die von Halle 1937 mit ihrer wegweisenden Erklärung zur Abendmahlsgemeinschaft) theologische Höhepunkte des Kirchenkampfes und auch Meilensteine auf dem Weg zur Leuenberger Konkordie.

Abschließend noch ein Blick auf die Orte, an denen die Synoden stattfanden. Hierzu gibt es bislang anscheinend weder explizite Überlegungen der Zeitgenossen noch Überblicksdarstellungen. Synoden wurden dort

3 Auf Einladung von Philipp dem Großmütigen diskutierten Vertreter der geistlichen und weltlichen Landstände der Landgrafschaft Hessen bei der Homberger Synode über die Einführung der Reformation in der Landgrafschaft. (Kirchenfenster in Homberg, Efze). | *At the invitation of Landgrave Philipp the Magnanimous, representatives of spiritual and secular estates in the landgraviate of Hesse discussed the introduction of the Reformation in their territory at the Homburg Synod (church window in Homberg, Efze).*

abgehalten, wo ein geeigneter Ort zur Verfügung stand. Bei der waldensischen Synode in Chanforan 1532 war das nur ein freies Feld, bei der Pariser Nationalsynode 1559 ein Keller in einem Privathaus in der Vorstadt Saint-Germain-des-Prés, bei der Emder Synode 1571 das Erdgeschoss des städtischen Zeughauses, in dem sich sonst die französischsprachige Flüchtlingsgemeinde versammelte. Meist waren große Stadtkirchen der Schauplatz der Synoden, von der Homberger Stadtkirche 1526 über die Große Kirche von Debrecen 1567 und die Westminster Abbey 1649 bis zur Karlsruher Stadtkirche 1821. Bisweilen waren es auch fürstliche oder kommunale Räume, wie das Stadthaus von Kaiserslautern bei der Unionssynode von 1818 (nur der Abschlussgottesdienst fand in der Stiftskirche statt) oder das Berliner Stadtschloss, das der König 1846 zum Schauplatz der Generalsynode bestimmt hatte. Erst zum Ende des 19. Jahrhunderts kam das Bedürfnis auf, eigene Versammlungsräume für die Synoden zu schaffen.

---

1 Christoph Markschies: *Theologie der Synode*. In: René Dausner, Florian Bruckmann (Hg.): *Im Angesicht der Anderen. Gespräche zwischen christlicher Theologie und jüdischem Denken*. Paderborn 2013, 35–58, 45–47.
2 Volker Leppin: *Disputation und Religionsgespräch. Diskursive Formen reformatorischer Wahrheitsfindung*. In: Ecclesia disputans. Die Konfliktpraxis vormoderner Synoden zwischen Religion und Politik. Hg. v. Christoph Dartmann u. a. Berlin 2015, 231–251.
3 Marc Mudrak: *Reformation und alter Glaube. Zugehörigkeiten der Altgläubigen im Alten Reich und in Frankreich (1517–1540)*. Berlin 2015, 48 f.
4 Karl Dienst: *Darmstadt und die evangelische Kirchengeschichte in Hessen*. Darmstadt 2007, 378–381.
5 Anneliese Sprengler-Ruppenthal: *Kirchenordnungen II / 1. Reformationszeit*. In: TRE 18 (1989), 670–703.
6 Jan-Andrea Bernhard: *Konsolidierung des reformierten Bekenntnisses im Reich der Stephanskrone: Ein Beitrag zur Kommunikationsgeschichte zwischen Ungarn und der Schweiz in der frühen Neuzeit (1500–1700)*. Göttingen 2017.
7 Dietrich Meyer: *Zinzendorf und die Herrnhuter Brüdergemeine: 1700–2000*. Göttingen 2009, 63–66.
8 Markschies: *Theologie der Synode*, 53–56.
9 Hans-Peter Hübner: *Gemeindeleitung in der Evangelisch-Lutherischen Kirche in Bayern*. In: Zeitschrift der Savigny-Stiftung für Rechtsgeschichte: Kanonistische Abteilung 100, 2014, 495–533.
10 Martin Friedrich: *Die preußische Landeskirche im Vormärz*. Waltrop 1994.

Martin Friedrich

Synods in Protestantism

Synods belong to Protestantism; they are even one of its trademarks, so to speak. That was more or less the case back in the 16th century. However, only the synods that emerged in the minority Reformed churches are the direct precursors of those existing in our churches nowadays. The Lutheran synods at the time of the Reformation differ from today's synods for two reasons. First, they were not the highest authority in the churches. And, second, they generally only consisted of clergy.

Prehistory

On the role of clergy, the Reformation picked up the tradition of the early church and the Middle Ages. In the first centuries, synods were the most important instrument for dealing with differences in teaching and life, and hence for forging the individual congregations into one church. By the end of the second century, representatives of the congregations of certain regions were coming together to resolve contentious issues, expel heretics and discuss fundamental questions. The bishops of urban communities had the right to vote; in the beginning, priests and deacons could attend at least as advisors. The meeting was called a »synodos« in Greek and »concilium« in Latin. Only with time was the term »synod« primarily used for regional deliberations. And only after Constantine made Christianity the official religion was »council« used for the universal gatherings of the whole church that were so important for developing its doctrine.

The development continued in the Middle Ages. In the West there continued to be diocesan and metropolitan synods consisting of bishops (sometimes with the attendance of lay people in the form of nobles, but only in Francia). At the level of the whole church, »ecumenical councils« were still held, even though the Orthodox Church did not recognise their ecumenical character. The 14th century saw the theory of conciliarism prevailing from time to time, according to which the council's authority was even higher than that of the papacy (Fig. 1).

The Reformation in Germany and eastern central Europe

The Wittenberg Reformation was in a dilemma regarding its stance on the council/synod issue. On the one hand, Martin Luther (1483–1546) had, as early as in November 1518, called for a council to resolve the doctrinal disagreements in the church. However, after the Leipzig Disputation in summer 1519 convinced him that councils, too, could err, it was clear that this instrument alone could not be the solution. Luther always argued (in most detail in the 1539 treatise *Of Councils and Churches*) that a council could only be recognised if it submitted to the authority of Scripture. That applied to all levels, so that there was no question of Protestants participating in the Council of Trent (1545–1563), which the Pope convened and presided over (Fig. 2). But synodal elements did not initially play a key role in building up the Protestant churches, either. Philipp Melanchthon (1497–1560) pinned greater hopes on synodal deliberations for resolving conflicts but did not see the preconditions existing for this.[1]

In the Reformation taking place in Switzerland and the imperial cities, the most important instruments were disputations, or religious discussions linking elements

4 König Friedrich Wilhelm III. von Preußen befürchtete mit der Einführung repräsentativer Synoden dem Parlamentarismus Tür und Tor zu öffnen. | *King Friedrich Wilhelm III of Prussia feared that introducing representative synods would open the floodgates to parliamentarianism.*

of synods with those of academic disputations.[2] Documents from Ulm (1532, even with lay participation)[3] and Strasbourg (1533) actually mention the term »synod«. However, the Wittenberg Reformation rarely followed this example. The most striking exception is the Synod of Homberg, at which, in 1526, nobles and theologians met on the invitation of Landgrave Philipp (1504–1567) and decided to forward the progress of the Reformation in Hesse (Fig. 3). A church order was drafted by Franz Lambert (1487–1530) on the basis of the doctrine of the priesthood of all believers and, although it was not adopted, synods took place regularly from 1531. Up until the forming of a consistory, the general synods, albeit only held until 1582, were actually in charge of church governance in Hesse.[4] In Pomerania, too, the general and regional synods had a considerable influence on church policies in the 16th century, which, however, as in Hesse were subject to the ecclesiastical authority of the respective territorial ruler.

In other Lutheran territories the synods were more like training and disciplinary events for the pastors, to judge by the Württemberg synodal order of 1537. Despite its name, the »synodus« in Württemberg was not a synod, but a body consisting of members of the church council (corresponding to a consistory) and the four general superintendents. In addition, church conventions (*Kirchenkonvente*) were established in 1644 but they were only responsible for church discipline.[5] Only in Jülich-Kleve-Berg did the Lutheran church – at the synods in Unna and Dinslaken in 1612 – adopt a presbyterial-synodal order on the Reformed model of the Emden Synod (see the article by Peter Opitz).

In the other Lutheran territories, the synods were purely made up of clergy. That also applied to eastern central Europe. The history of the Protestant churches in Poland, Hungary and Transylvania in the early modern age can, indeed, be written as the story of their synods. Only the pastors had a say at the synods of Mediaş and Ardud (both in Transylvania) in 1545, Prešov (Slovakia) in 1546, Sibiu (Transylvania) in 1563 and Levoča in 1597, which adopted the Lutheran confession, and of Žilina (both in Slovakia) in 1610, which created a unified church structure. In these cases, the synods were an essential element of church governance but did not reflect the doctrine of the priesthood of all believers. Although, unlike in Germany, the defining constitutional principle was not the ecclesiastical preference of the territorial ruler, this region did not follow the western European type of church governance.

New developments in the 18th century

The situation with the Reformed churches in central Europe was no different. The Reformed Church in Hungary had had a synodal constitution since the first Synod of Debrecen in 1567, but it did not give a role to presbyteries. The 17th century saw attempts by Hungarian theologians to enshrine the participation of elders in the constitution, having got to know the constitution of Calvinist churches on their visits to western Europe. Initially they were unsuccessful. It was not until the Reformed Synod of Buda (held at the same time as the Lutheran Synod of Pest) that the presbyterial-synodal church constitution was introduced in 1791.[6]

Two other Protestant traditions had already established synods giving a strong role to the laity. Both Nikolaus Count Zinzendorf (1700–1760) and John Wesley (1703–1791) had already introduced regular conferences in their movements, as an essential element of church life. What was still subject to their charismatic leadership during their lifetime became a defining constitutional element after their death. From 1764 the Moravian Church was governed by general synods (today called Unity Synods) attended by elected representatives of the provinces, besides the clergy.[7] The Episcopal Methodist Church (a predecessor of the present United Methodist Church) constituted itself in 1784 at the Christmas Conference in Baltimore (at the time composed exclusively of clergy) and has since 1794 a general conference taking place every four years as its highest governing body, attended by between 600 and 1000 delegates.

The breakthrough in the 19th century

The 19th century saw the breakthrough of the presbyterial-synodal element in the German-speaking Protestant churches, as well. The reasons naturally included, first, the model of the western European churches, particularly from the western provinces of Prussia. Second, discussions about the political constitution also played a role. Just as everywhere people were demanding participation in law-making through parliaments, under the heading of constitutionalism, there was also talk of »church constitutionalism«. Without wanting to challenge the ecclesiastical authority of the territorial rulers as a whole, people called for a fair representation of the church population as an element of the church constitution. That brought about a change in the understanding of ›presbyterial-synodal‹, since according to the old Reformed tradition the presbyters and members of synods were not representatives of the congregations but ministers and stewards of the divine will, like the pastors.

The attitude of those who, after 1800, pressed for the establishment of synods, is not always clearly attributable to one of the two basic motives; often it was a mixture of both. At the discussions in Prussia after the wars of liberation (1813–15, ending Napoleonic rule), similarity with the Calvinist order tipped the balance for the church representatives both in the western provinces and in Berlin, where Friedrich Schleiermacher (1768–1834) presented a constitutional plan to the synod of 1819. The demand was also popular due to its political implications but, despite its initially promising beginnings, they were nipped in the bud. In 1821 King Friedrich Wilhelm III (1770–1840) interrupted the process of discussing a new church constitution because, above all, he did not want to promote the call for a representative constitution for his kingdom (Fig. 4).[8]

Hence synods with the participation of lay people were first introduced in other regional churches. In 1818 the King of Bavaria called a general synod for the part of his realm that lay in the Palatinate, which not only decided to unite the Reformed and Lutheran churches but also took other essential decisions on the church's doctrine, order and worship. A third of the members of synod were elected members of congregations. In 1823 two general synods met in in the part of Bavaria which lay on the right side of the Rhine at which clergy and lay people were represented with a ratio of 6 to 1; only from 1849 was

5 Die Rheinisch-Westfälische Kirchenordnung von 1835 wurde durch ihre Verbindung der presbyterial-synodalen Ordnung mit der traditionellen Konsistorialverfassung zum Vorbild für weitere evangelische Kirchenordnungen des 19. und 20. Jahrhunderts. | *The Rhenish-Westphalian church order of 1835 became the model for further Protestant constitutions in the 19th and 20th centuries, because it combined the presbyterial-synodal order with the traditional consistorial constitution.*

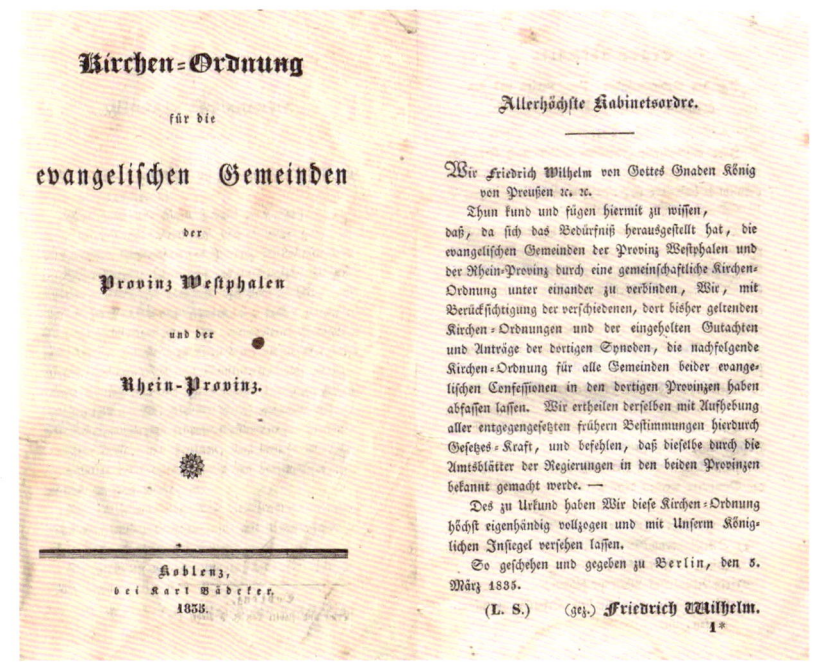

there parity of membership.⁹ At the Union Synod of 1821, likewise called by the ruler, the Grand Duke of Baden, there was even a slight majority of lay people.

The Rhenish-Westphalian church order of 1835 was of great significance for further development (Fig. 5). In order to ensure the acceptance of his liturgical orders, the King of Prussia saw himself forced to make a concession to the congregations in the western provinces who wished to return to the constitutional principles prevailing in their regions for centuries. For example, synods with parity representation were created at the level of the church districts and provincial churches, the powers of which still remained subordinate to the consistories appointed by the king. The mixed system of consistorial and presbyterial-synodal constitutions was only a compromise but regarded as exemplary at many points.

The decade beginning with 1840 (pre-March period) again saw increasing demands to reform the Protestant church constitution, for both political and ecclesiastical reasons. King Friedrich Wilhelm IV (1795–1861) promoted two types of synod – district and provincial synods (consisting solely of pastors in the eastern provinces) in 1843/44 and a Prussian general synod (with a larger number of lay people, albeit elected by the provincial synods) in 1846. However, he dismissed their proposal to establish presbyteries and synods in the whole kingdom and thereby adopt elements of the Rhenish-Westphalian church constitution (in even more watered-down form), because he rejected the presbyterial-synodal order due to its political implications. During the March revolution in 1848 the cabinet minister responsible for churches, Maximilian Count von Schwerin-Putzar (1804–1872), attempted to introduce a presbyterial-synodal constitution for the whole regional church, but was unable to accomplish this in his short term of office.¹⁰ It was only under the minister Adalbert Falk (1827–1900) that the consistorial constitution, following the model of the Rhenish-Westphalian church, was supplemented by consultative synods through the parish and synodal order of 1873 and the general synod order of 1876. Before that, similar mixed constitutions were introduced in some other territories (Oldenburg in 1853, Baden in 1861, Hanover in 1864); almost all the others had followed by the beginning of the 20th century. The availability of synods was a key precondition for the relatively smooth transition to self-organisation by the German Protestant churches after the end of the monarchies in 1918, which also spelled the end of the ecclesiastical authority of territorial rulers.

6 In der Zeit des Nationalsozialismus führte die Bekennende Kirche (BK) eigene Synoden durch mit dem Ziel, das christliche Bekenntnis zu bezeugen. Das Foto entstand auf der freien reformierten Synode am 3./4. Januar 1934 in Barmen. | *In the National Socialist period the Confessing Church held its own synods with the goal of witnessing to the Christian confession. The photo was taken at the free Reformed synod on 3/4 January 1934 in Barmen.*

In all German regional churches, the synods were now the highest decision-making body. This was also the case in places where, particularly in Lutheran churches, the personal ministry of bishop was created in parallel and equipped with its own powers, including vis-a-vis the synods. It was the synods that elected the bishops (or other leading clergy), established the budget and the priorities of church work, and ultimately also laid down the church order. In its way of working with committees and plenary meetings, the synods resembled parliaments in the political sphere and so the term »church parliament« began to be used. But this was regularly rejected because what was supposed to matter for the members of synods was not the will of those who elected them but their mandate through Jesus Christ, the supreme Lord of his church.

The large workload that synods and conferences have had in recent times has hardly allowed for major debates on doctrine and confession. It is all the more important, in conclusion, to mention the synod that adopted the Barmen Theological Declaration in May 1934 (Fig. 6). It recalled the Reformed synods of the 16th and 17th centuries in that, as a gathering of the Confessing Church in Germany, it had to be carried out without any support, indeed even in face of the efforts of state authorities to hinder it. Nevertheless, the confessional synods held until 1936 under the Third Reich and until 1943 in the Prussian church (including that of Halle in 1937 with its pioneering statement on table fellowship) were theological highpoints of the church struggle (*Kirchenkampf*) and also milestones on the way to the Leuenberg Agreement.

In conclusion, let us take a look at the places where the synods were held. It appears that no explicit thinking by the people at the time is known to date, nor are there any overviews. Synods were held wherever a suitable location was available. At the 1532 Waldensian Synod of Chanforan it was only an open field; at the Paris national synod of 1559 it was a cellar in a private house in the area of Saint-Germain-des-Prés; at the Emden Synod in 1571 it was the ground floor of the city arsenal, where the French-speaking refugee congregation normally met. Mostly big city churches were the setting for synods, from the Homberg City Church in 1526 to the Large Church of Debrecen in 1567, from Westminster Abbey in 1649 to the Karlsruhe City Church in 1821. Sometimes it was also courtly or municipal rooms, such as the town hall of Kaiserslautern at the Union Synod of 1818 (only the final service took place in the Collegiate Church) or the Berlin Palace, which the king chose as the venue for the general synod in 1846. It was not until near the end of the 19th century that the need arose to create separate meeting facilities for synods.

---

1 Christoph Markschies: *Theologie der Synode*. In: René Dausner, Florian Bruckmann (ed.): *Im Angesicht der Anderen. Gespräche zwischen christlicher Theologie und jüdischem Denken*. Paderborn, 2013, 35–58, 45–47.
2 Volker Leppin: *Disputation und Religionsgespräch. Diskursive Formen reformatorischer Wahrheitsfindung*. In Ecclesia disputans. Die Konfliktpraxis vormoderner Synoden zwischen Religion und Politik. Ed. Christoph Dartmann et al., Berlin, 2015, 231–251.
3 Marc Mudrak: *Reformation und alter Glaube. Zugehörigkeiten der Altgläubigen im Alten Reich und in Frankreich (1517–1540)*, Berlin, 2015, 48 f.
4 Karl Dienst: *Darmstadt und die evangelische Kirchengeschichte in Hessen*, Darmstadt, 2007, 378–381.
5 Anneliese Sprengler-Ruppenthal: *Kirchenordnungen II / 1. Reformationszeit*. In TRE 18 (1989), 670–703.
6 Jan-Andrea Bernhard: *Konsolidierung des reformierten Bekenntnisses im Reich der Stephanskrone: Ein Beitrag zur Kommunikationsgeschichte zwischen Ungarn und der Schweiz in der frühen Neuzeit (1500–1700)*, Göttingen, 2017.
7 Dietrich Meyer: *Zinzendorf und die Herrnhuter Brüdergemeine: 1700–2000*, Göttingen, 2009, 63–66.
8 Markschies: *Theologie der Synode*, 53–56.
9 Hans-Peter Hübner: *Gemeindeleitung in der Evangelisch-Lutherischen Kirche in Bayern*. In Zeitschrift der Savigny-Stiftung für Rechtsgeschichte: Kanonistische Abteilung 100, 2014, 495–533.
10 Martin Friedrich: *Die preußische Landeskirche im Vormärz*. Waltrop 1994.

Peter Opitz

Anfänge der evangelischen Synodalkultur in der »reformierten« Reformation

Evangelisch und »synodal«

Die Reformation war das Unternehmen, neu auf die biblische Christusbotschaft, »das Evangelium«, zu hören, möglichst gereinigt von Verdunkelungen und Verzerrungen, die sie im Lauf der Kirchengeschichte erfahren hatte. Daraus ergab sich nicht nur eine Änderung der individuellen Glaubens- und Frömmigkeitspraxis, sondern auch die Notwendigkeit, die »christliche Kirche« als organisierte Gemeinschaft von Christen in direkter Orientierung an den neutestamentlichen Zeugnissen umzugestalten. Grundlegende, dem Neuen Testament entnommene Einsichten über das Wesen einer christlichen Gemeinde führten dabei mit innerer Logik zu »synodal« organisierten Kirchen.

Als Erstes ist die Einsicht zu nennen, die unter dem missverständlichen Schlagwort des »allgemeinen Priestertums« (im Anschluss an 1. Petr 2,9) bekannt ist. Gemeint ist damit nicht eine Ausbreitung, sondern das Ende allen menschlichen Priestertums. Christen brauchen keine Priester, die sie mit Gott in Beziehung bringen, und überhaupt keine kirchliche Institution mit Ämtern und Riten als Vermittlungsinstanz zwischen Gott und den Menschen. Denn Christen leben in einer direkten, persönlichen Gottesbeziehung, ermöglicht durch Christus, den einzigen »Priester«, und vermittelt durch Gottes Geist, der in den Menschen Glauben und damit Gemeinschaft mit Gott wirkt. Das bedeutet auch: Vor diesem Gott gibt es keine geistlichen Hierarchien unter Menschen; alle Christen stehen vor Gott auf derselben Ebene.

Die zweite Einsicht: Wenn das Neue Testament von »Kirche« spricht, spricht es einerseits von der geistlichen Gemeinschaft aller Christen mit Christus, einer Gemeinschaft, welche alle Glaubenden aller Zeiten umfasst: Die »eine«, »allgemeine« Kirche, wie das Nizänische Glaubensbekenntnis formuliert. Sie ist der geistliche »Leib Christi« (z. B. 1. Kor 12,12–27). Wenn im Neuen Testament andererseits von der christlichen Kirche als irdischer, menschlicher Gemeinschaft die Rede ist, geht es um bestimmte Ortsgemeinden und konkrete christliche Versammlungen. Eine »evangelische« Kirche muss organisatorisch hier ansetzen.

Die dritte Einsicht: Das Neue Testament kennt eine Vielzahl von Bezeichnungen für »Ämter«, die sich bzgl. Aufgaben und Tätigkeiten vielfältig überschneiden. Gemeinsam ist ihnen, dass sie nicht »Amtsvollmachten« bezeichnen, sondern Dienste. Die Reformatoren (im Folgenden beziehe ich mich auf Heinrich Bullinger und Johannes Calvin, die das reformierte Kirchenverständnis entscheidend geprägt haben) fassten sie in drei Bereiche zusammen: Die Verkündigung, die Leitung und Beaufsichtigung der Gemeinde und die Fürsorge für die Armen (Pastorenamt, Ältestenamt und Diakonenamt). Das bei Calvin als Viertes erwähnte Amt des »Lehrers« spielte nur dort eine Rolle, wo eine theologische Schule oder Akademie bestand. Alle drei »Ämter« sind *diakonische* Aufgaben, weshalb gerade die Pastoren konsequent als »Diener« (am göttlichen Wort) bezeichnet werden. Sie werden nicht von einer mit bestimmten Kompetenzen ausgestatteten Einzelperson ausgeübt (etwa einem einzelnen »Bischof«), sondern gemeinsam mit anderen.

So ist das Ältestenamt (griechisch: *Presbyter*, vgl. Apg 20,17) ein Leitungsamt innerhalb eines von einer Ortsgemeinde gewählten Gremiums, das von dieser mit einer bestimmten Aufgabe betraut ist. Auch hier geht es um einen Dienst an der Gemeinde und nicht um

Die Darstellung der Zürcher Disputation in einer um 1600 angefertigten Handschrift. | *The depiction of the Zurich Disputation in a manuscript produced around 1600.*

(die von den Reformatoren dazu angeführten klassischen Texte sind neben anderen v. a. 1. Petr 5,1–3; 1. Tim 3,1–3 und Tit 1,5–9).

Und schließlich war den Reformatoren als humanistisch gebildete Bibelexegeten bewusst: Dem Neuen Testament sind zwar konstitutive Eckpunkte, Kriterien und Modelle für eine christliche Gemeinde zu entnehmen, die ihren Namen verdient, nicht aber eine festgelegte, zeitlos gültige Kirchenordnung oder Ämterstruktur. Flexibilität und Beweglichkeit in Fragen der Ordnung und Gestaltung der christlichen Gemeinschaft und Kirche in Berücksichtigung der jeweiligen kulturellen und politischen Situation gehörten von Anfang an zum »evangelischen« Verständnis von Kirche.[1]

Allerdings sollten kirchliche Strukturen der Verkündigung des wiederentdeckten »Evangeliums« ebenso Raum geben wie dessen Konsequenzen für das Miteinander in einer christlichen Kirche. Die Koordinaten hingegen waren durch die jeweils eigene politische und kulturelle Situation gegeben. Vertraut waren die Reformatoren zudem mit antiken Theorien des guten »politischen« Zusammenlebens. Dabei leuchtete ihnen die Abwägung der Vor- und Nachteile der verschiedenen politischen Modelle durch Aristoteles grundsätzlich ein: Während die Monarchie fast zwangsläufig in Tyrannenherrschaft führt und auf der anderen Seite eine extreme Demokratie als Herrschaft der Masse leicht in gesetzlose Pöbelherrschaft abgleitet und Raum für Volksverführer (Demagogen) öffnet, bietet die Aristokratie, die Leitung des Gemeinwesens durch einen kleinen Kreis »der Besten«, die größte Gewähr für eine Politik im Dienst des Gemeinwohls.[2] Dies trug zweifellos dazu bei, dass die Reformatoren einerseits unermüdlich das Recht der Ortsgemeinde betonten, Menschen in ein kirchliches Amt zu berufen. Dass die römische Papstkirche der Gemeinde dieses Recht genommen und begonnen hat, kirchliche Amtsträger gleichsam von oben her ohne Einbezug der Gemeinde zu ernennen, gehört zu den zentralen Verunstaltungen des Christentums durch sie. Zugleich waren die Reformatoren gegenüber einem demokratischen Mehrheitsentscheid skeptisch. Die Gemeinde muss ernsthaft konsultiert werden und Einspruchsmöglichkeiten besitzen, letztlich aber sollen die Entscheidungen – nach Anhörung der Stimmen aus der »Volk« – von einem kleinen, von der Gemeinde gewählten Gremium aus fähigen Leuten gefällt werden. Das Ideal christlicher

Herrschaftsausübung (in 1. Kor 12,28 ist griechisch von »Kybernetik« die Rede, der Kunst der Steuerung lebendiger Prozesse). Entsprechend muss ein Ältester sowohl die dazu nötigen Fähigkeiten besitzen, als auch im Blick auf seine Lebensführung eine Vorbildfunktion einnehmen

»Einmütigkeit« (vgl. 1. Kor 1,10; Röm 15,5; Apg 15, 23–26) und die erforderliche »Weisheit« in den Entscheidungen waren mehr als das, was mit einer bloßen Mehrheitsentscheidung erreicht werden kann. Calvin zitiert dazu Vergil: »Die Menge ist unbestimmt und spaltet sich in einander widersprechende Bestrebungen auf«.[3] Entsprechend suchten die Reformatoren die Mitwirkung der Gemeinde auf ein Vorschlags- und Einspruchsrecht zu beschränken, standen für dieses Recht aber auch entschieden ein.

Modern und leicht anachronistisch formuliert könnte man die Richtung, in welche die Reformatoren im Blick auf die Ordnung und Leitung einer »evangelischen« Kirche zeigten, als repräsentative Demokratie mit direktdemokratischen Elementen bezeichnen. Damit sind wir nahe beim heutigen presbyterial-synodalen Gedanken angelangt. Und so wurde die alte christliche Tradition von »Synoden« für die evangelischen Kirchen wieder wichtig, nicht nur für außerordentliche Zusammenkünfte wie etwa die Synode von Dordrecht 1618 oder die »Westminster Synode« 1643–49, sondern auch als Begriff zur Bezeichnung regelmäßiger, institutionalisierter Treffen mit »kybernetischer« Funktion, zunächst innerhalb einer Ortsgemeinde und dann auch darüber hinaus.

Die Geschichte der Synodalkultur der evangelischen Kirchen spiegelt dabei die Ausbreitung und Entwicklung des evangelischen Christentums in unterschiedlichen politischen und kulturellen Kontexten.

Synodalkultur im Dienst der Gemeindereformation

Schon früh findet man bei den Reformatoren als Gegenentwurf zu der das gesamte »christliche Abendland« umspannenden, hierarchisch organisierten römischen Bischofskirche das Bestreben, die konkrete Ortsgemeinde in ihren Kompetenzen zu stärken, unter Berufung auf biblische Texte wie 1. Kor 14,30 f., wo Paulus grundsätzlich jedem Christen die Erlaubnis und Kompetenz erteilt, zu lehren, und zugleich der gesamten Gemeinde, alle Lehre zu prüfen. Luther folgerte daraus, *Dass eine christliche Versammlung oder Gemeinde Recht und Macht habe, alle Lehre zu beurteilen und Lehrer zu berufen, ein- und abzusetzen,* so der Titel einer Schrift von 1523.[4] In der lutherischen Reformation, wie sie sich aus politischen und geografischen Gründen vornehmlich als »Fürstenreformationen« entwickelt und etabliert hat, blieb für eine unmittelbare Umsetzung derartiger Gedanken vorerst wenig Raum, zumal Luthers Verständnis der Predigt und der »Sakramentsverwaltung« dem kirchlichen Amt als einem Gegenüber zur Gemeinde eine starke Stellung zumaß.

In der Schweizer-oberdeutschen Reformation, aus der sich die evangelisch-»reformierte« Tradition entwickelt hat, war die Ausgangslage etwas anders. Im Unterschied zu den allermeisten anderen Territorien in Europa bestand die Eidgenossenschaft nicht aus Fürstentümern. Hier herrschte eine starke Tradition der Selbstverwaltung mit vergleichsweise flachen Hierarchien. Städte wurden durch gewählte Räte und Bürgermeister regiert, aber auch in Talschaften und Dörfern wurden politische Behörden und Richter gewählt. Politische Entscheidungen wurden nicht von einzelnen Landesfürsten, sondern in Gremien und Kommissionen getroffen, und Entscheidungen von großer Tragweite wurden nicht ohne Konsultation der Bevölkerung gefällt.

Die erste Zürcher Disputation vom Januar 1523, an der Zwingli seine 67 Thesen präsentieren und öffentlich verteidigen musste, passt in dieses politische Klima (Abb. 1). Um die Religionsstreitigkeiten in der Stadt zu beenden, lud der Zürcher Rat alle Prediger und Priester in Stadt und Land ein, sich am Gespräch zu beteiligen und setzte fest, dass es in deutscher Sprache durchgeführt werden soll. Er knüpfte damit nicht nur an die akademische Tradition der akademischen »Disputation« über theologische Fragen an, sondern auch an die kirchliche Tradition der »Synode«, und nahm für sich als weltliche Behörde zugleich in Anspruch, im Dienst des Religionsfriedens auf dem eigenen Staatsgebiet eine solche einberufen zu können (wie einst Konstantin I. in Nicäa 325). Dem Einwand der bischöflichen Delegation, dass derartige theologische Fragen auf eine Konferenz von Bischöfen und Gelehrten gehören, antwortete Zwingli unter Berufung auf biblische Texte wie Mt 18,20 mit dem Hinweis auf die Priorität der versammelten Ortsgemeinde vor einer kirchlichen Großorganisation: »In diesem Raum ist eine wahrhaft christliche Kirche versammelt!«[5]

In den Städten und Gebieten der Eidgenossenschaft, aber auch in Städten des Reiches, die sich durch Ratsbeschluss der Reformation zuwandten, setzte sich das Modell einer Gemeindereformation durch. Sie bestand in einer engen Zusammenarbeit von kirchlichen und bürgerlich-politischen Instanzen, die sich ja durchaus ernsthaft als evangelisch-christliche Obrigkeit und als Teil der Kirche verstanden. Hier wurde der Synodalgedanke im Blick auf die *innere Organisation* der neuen evangelischen Kirchen wichtig.

In Zürich kam die erste »Synode«, von Zwingli angeregt, am 21. April 1528 zusammen. Institutionalisiert wurde sie in der am 22. Oktober 1532 verabschiedeten Synodalordnung, welche bis zum Ende des *Ancien Régimes* die Grundlage der Zürcher Kirche bildete. Von nun an wurde die Synode zweimal jährlich, jeweils im Frühjahr und im Herbst durchgeführt. In diesen für alle Pfarrer auf dem Zürcher Staatsgebiet obligatorischen Synoden unter Beisitz von acht Ratsmitgliedern als Vertreter der Gemeinde ging es um Koordination und Informationsaustausch. Im Zentrum aber stand die »Zensur«: Die Synodalordnung sah vor, dass die Amtsführung, die Lehre und der Lebenswandel jedes Pastors behandelt und Ermahnungen ausgesprochen wurden. Dabei sollten nicht nur der Fleiß und die Liebe im Studium der Heiligen Schrift und das familiäre Leben zur Sprache kommen, sondern auch charakterliche Mängel wie Neid, Anmaßung oder allfällige Tendenzen zu Herrschsucht (vgl. 1. Tim 3, 2–13; 1. Petr 5, 1–4). Ausdrücklich sollten auch die Dekane dieser kollegialen Zensur unterworfen sein, damit sie ihre Stellung nicht missbrauchen.[6]

Die bisherige Ämterhierarchie, in welcher geweihte Einzelpersonen höheren geistlichen Ranges als »Bischöfe« die Aufsicht über ein ganzes Gebiet und die dort tätige Pastorenschaft hatten, wurde damit in eine Form kollektiver, wechselseitiger Selbstkontrolle von gleichgestellten Pastoren im Blick auf das ihnen anvertraute Pfarramt umgestaltet. Das Gewicht lag auf der Vermeidung von geistlichen Hierarchien: Alle, die Dorfpfarrer wie die gelehrten Lehrer an der »Hohen Schule« sollen sich »als Brüder und Mitarbeiter im Evangelium Christi« achten und entsprechend miteinander umgehen.[7]

Die Kompetenz der Anstellung neuer Pfarrer behielt sich der Rat vor, wobei eine Examenskommission, bestehend aus zwei Pfarrern, zwei Räten und zwei Lehrern aus der Zürcher »Hohen Schule« die Kandidaten prüfte und ihr Gutachten abgab. Die feierliche Ablegung des Amtseids erfolgte dann wiederum vor der Synode, und erst damit war der Kandidat offiziell in den Kirchendienst aufgenommen. In anderen reformierten Orten der Eidgenossenschaft wurden ähnliche synodale Formen der inneren Kirchenleitung eingerichtet.

Leicht anders gestaltete sich die Kirchenorganisation im kleinen Stadtstaat Genf zur Zeit Calvins. Unter Aufnahme von Anregungen aus Straßburg und Basel sah Calvin in der Kirchenordnung von 1541 zwei Gremien zur (inneren) Leitung der Kirche vor: Hier sollte ein Ältestenrat (*Konsistorium*), zusammengesetzt aus Pfarrern und geeigneten Räten, über die Kirchendisziplin der Gemeindeglieder wachen. Gleichzeitig schuf Calvin mit der *Compagnie des pasteurs* ein Treffen der gesamten Genfer Pfarrerschaft, das wöchentlich stattfinden sollte, was aufgrund des kleinen Territoriums Genfs möglich war. Es wurde von einem gewählten Moderator geleitet. Neben dem gemeinsamen Bibelstudium hatte die *Compagnie des pasteurs* eine den Synoden der größeren Kirchen entsprechende Funktion: Die Selbstzensur der Pfarrerschaft im Blick auf Amtsführung, Lehre und Leben. Auch Fragen der inneren Kirchenorganisation wurden hier besprochen, und neue Kandidaten für das Pfarramt geprüft und dem Rat zur Wahl vorgeschlagen, der sich auch hier das entscheidende Wort vorbehielt.

Synodalkultur in Diasporakirchen und im Dienst übergemeindlicher Koordination und Kooperation

Anders war die Lage dort, wo der evangelische Glaube keine Unterstützung von der Obrigkeit erhielt, sondern im Gegenteil durch sie unterdrückt wurde. Dies war etwa in Frankreich, in Oberitalien und den habsburgisch-spanisch verwalteten niederländischen Provinzen (das Gebiet der heutigen Benelux-Länder) der Fall. Trotz oft blutiger Verfolgung entstanden auch in diesen Gebieten evangelische Kirchen in großer Zahl. Ohne Schutz, aber auch ohne Gängelung durch eine politische Obrigkeit, mussten sie sich selber organisieren.

Die Synode von Chanforan

Einen besonderen Fall stellte die Waldenserbewegung dar. Bereits vor der Reformation existierte in der Einrichtung eines »Consilium Generale«, einer jährlichen Versammlung der waldensischen Prediger, eine Form von

»synodaler« Tradition avant la lettre. Das *Consilium Generale* von 1530 in Merindol (Provence) beschäftigte sich mit der Frage eines möglichen Anschlusses an die Reformation. Nach Erkundigungen bei Schweizer-oberdeutschen Reformatoren und beraten durch den Westschweizer Reformator Wilhelm Farel besiegelte zwei Jahre später die »Erklärung der Synode von Chanforan« die Hinwendung der Waldenser zur Reformation (Abb. 2). Dies bedeutete unter Anderem die Abkehr von der bislang konstitutiven Wanderpredigertradition. Die Einführung von Synoden war hingegen eine veränderte Fortsetzung des *Consilium Generale*.

Die Synode der protestantischen französischen Kirchen von 1559 und die Discipline ecclésiastique

Die evangelischen Kirchen in Frankreich[8] führten in der Regel die drei Ämter Pfarrer, Ältester (Presbyter) und Diakon ein. Dabei wurde der Ältestenrat (das Presbyterium, dem auch Pfarrer und Diakonen angehören konnten) bald zu einem echten kirchlichen Leitungsgremium, weit über Kirchenzuchtfragen hinaus. Er bestand aus gewählten Vertretern der Gemeinde, und besaß, frei von Ansprüchen einer bürgerlichen Obrigkeit, die Kompetenz, Pfarrer anzustellen oder zu entlassen, ihre Amtsführung zu beaufsichtigen, aber auch renitente Gemeindeglieder aus der Gemeinde auszuschließen. Seine Aufgaben waren diejenigen eines »Senats« im kirchlichen Bereich, wie Johannes a Lasco in seiner Kirchenordnung für die Flüchtlingsgemeinde in London formulierte. Nach Calvin war dies schon in der Zeit der ersten Kirche so.[9]

Aus dem Bedürfnis nach zwischen- und übergemeindlicher Kooperation, Koordination und Unterstützung in der Situation der Unterdrückung entwickelte sich hier seit der Mitte des 16. Jahrhunderts eine übergemeindliche presbyterial-synodale Kultur. Delegierte verschiedener Gemeinden trafen sich in regionalen Synoden zur Besprechung gemeinsamer Anliegen unter Wahrung der Autonomie der Einzelgemeinden. Wie das Vorgehen bei der Besetzung lokaler Presbyterien und deren Kompetenzen auf Gemeindeebene sich entwickeln und ausgehandelt werden mussten, so auch die Regeln für regionale Synoden: Wer soll die einzelnen Gemeinden dort vertreten? Wer soll sie leiten und mit welchen Kompetenzen ausgestattet? Wie verbindlich sollen die Beschlüsse dieser Synoden für die Lokalgemeinden sein? Die eingangs

2 Mit der Synode von Chanforan, die auf einem freien Feld stattfand, nahmen die Waldenser 1532 die Reformation schweizerischer Prägung an. | *With the Synod of Chanforan, which took place in an open field, the Waldensians adopted the Swiss-style Reformation in 1532.*

aufgezählten Elemente »reformierter« Ekklesiologie, Einflüsse aus dem französischsprachigen, westlichen Teil der Berner Kirche (dem heutigen Kanton Waadt) und lokale Traditionen – abgesehen von den vorgegebenen geographischen Bedingungen formten sich zu einer eigenen Synodentradition, deren Ziel nicht ein Zusammenschluss der Einzelgemeinden zu einer nationalen Großkirche war, sondern eine Art Kirchenverband ohne übergreifende hierarchische Struktur, was ein sorgfältiges Austarieren der Zuständigkeiten und Kompetenzen der verschiedenen Ebenen nötig machte. Dass dies nicht ohne Diskussionen und Konflikte möglich war, können die Diskussionen um ein stärker »basisdemokratisch« orientiertes Leitungsmodell illustrieren, wie es Jean Morely (1524–ca. 1594) propagiert hatte und wie es auf mehreren regionalen Synoden schließlich abgelehnt wurde.

Die Kombination verschiedener »synodaler« Ebenen mit dem Ziel einer »brüderlichen« Koordination und Kooperation bei gleichzeitiger Verhinderung von kirchlicher Herrschaftsausübung prägt dann auch die *Discipline ecclésiastique*, die auf der ersten nationalen Synode der verstreuten evangelischen Kirchen im Mai 1559 in Paris beschlossen wurde.[10] Sie wurde zu einem grundlegenden Dokument einer übergreifenden Synodalordnung, die presbyterial geleitete evangelische Ortsgemeinden Frankreichs miteinander verband, sowohl in regionalen Synoden oder »Kolloquien« als auch auf nationaler Ebene (Abb. 3). Als gemeinsame Bekenntnisgrundlage diente die auf der gleichen Pariser Synode verabschiedete *Confessio Gallicana*. Während gemäß Artikel 4 nationale Synoden je nach Bedarf stattfinden sollten, legte Artikel 5 fest, dass sich in jeder Kirche oder Provinz die Pfarrer und mindestens ein Ältester oder Diakon zweimal jährlich treffen sollten. Darüber hinaus legte sie eine gewisse Harmonisierung der inneren Organisation der einzelnen Kirchen fest, etwa bezüglich der Wahl der Pfarrer (durch den Ältestenrat, aber nicht ohne Berücksichtigung der Gemeinde), und wies den Regionalsynoden koordinierende und die Gemeinden unterstützende Aufgaben zu. Gleichzeitig war sie darauf bedacht, keine »Herrschaft« oder Hierarchie aufkommen zu lassen, weder auf der personalen Ebene, noch auf der Ebene der Kirchen. So wurde der Vorsitzende der Synode jeweils gewählt, begrenzt auf die Dauer der Synode, und er war der »freundschaftlichen und brüderlichen« Zensur ebenso unterworfen wie alle anderen Synodenmitglieder (Art. 2 und 4). Dass auf kirchlicher Ebene keine Kirche gegenüber anderen einen Vorrang beanspruchen darf, wurde gleich im ersten Artikel festgehalten, noch vor jeder inhaltlichen gemeinsamen Entscheidung.

Die Emder Synode von 1571

In Emden, einer Stadt mit einem großen Seehafen, kamen im Jahr 1571 Abgesandte der reformierten niederländischen Exilgemeinden zusammen, um ihr kirchliches Leben zu organisieren (Abb. 4). Die Synode der niederländischen Gemeinden »unter dem Kreuz« von 1571 steht auf der Grundlage des skizzierten reformierten Kirchenverständnisses und knüpfte zugleich an die französische Synodaltradition an.[11] Das Einladungsschreiben zur Synode stützt sich auf die gleichen Bibelstellen, die bereits zu Beginn der Zürcher Reformation ein knappes halbes Jahrhundert zuvor wichtig waren, und begründet die Form der Synode ausführlich als dem evangelischen Glauben und der daraus fließenden »brüderlichen« Gemeinschaft gemäß. Wie die *Discipline ecclésiastique* lehnt sie gleich im ersten Artikel jede Art von Hierarchie oder Überordnung ab, sowohl auf der Ebene der Gemeinden wie unter Amtsträgern (Abb. 5). Die *Emder Synode* stand darüber hinaus vor der Herausforderung, Pastoren und Älteste aus einer Vielzahl unterschiedlicher, französischsprachiger und deutsch- bzw. niederländischsprachiger Exilgemeinden zu versammeln, aus einem Gebiet, das sich von Friesland bis in die Pfalz erstreckte. So suchte auch sie einen synodalen Weg der Harmonisierung und Verständigung bei gleichzeitiger Wahrung der Freiheit der einzelnen Gemeinden. Der in den französischsprachigen Gemeinden in Gebrauch stehende *Genfer Katechismus* wurde ebenso anerkannt wie der in den deutschsprachigen Gemeinden gebräuchliche *Heidelberger Katechismus*. Aber auch Gemeinden, die andere Katechismen verwenden, sofern diese »mit Gottes Wort übereinstimmen«, sind nicht ausgeschlossen. Angesichts der bereits bestehenden Unterschiede innerhalb des reformierten Lagers, die einerseits sprachlich-kultureller Art waren, aber auch mit unterschiedlich großer Nähe zu Luthers Abendmahlslehre zu tun hatten, praktizierte die *Emder Synode* damit eine binnenreformierte Form von »versöhnter Verschiedenheit« in der Lehre. Konkreter als die *Discipline ecclésiastique* gehen die Synodenbeschlüsse aber auf Fragen der Abendmahls- und Kirchenzuchtspraxis ein, wobei den Gemeinden gerade in der Praxis der Abendmahlsfeier großer Spielraum gelassen wird. Gemeinsames Anliegen ist die klare Abgrenzung gegenüber einer sakramentalen Heilsvermittlung. So soll »gewönliches« Brot verwendet, und der Eindruck einer »Weihe« der Abendmahlselemente unbedingt vermieden werden. Die Spannung zwischen den Abendmahlsverständnissen des *Genfer Katechismus* und des *Heidelberger Katechismus* wird nicht thematisiert.

Beschlossen wurde überdies die Abhaltung von regelmäßigen Provinzsynoden an wechselnden Orten. Vor allem im niederländischen und norddeutschen Raum, aber auch darüber hinaus, wirkten die Beschlüsse der *Emder Synode* gleichsam als Katalysator zur Verbreitung presbyterial-synodaler Leitungs- und Ordnungsstrukturen im evangelischen Raum (Abb. 6).

3 Die Nationalsynode der reformierten Kirchen in Frankreich bei einer Sitzung 1598 in Montpellier. Auf dem Tisch der Synodenleitung liegen die Bibel, das Glaubensbekenntnis, die Kirchenordnung (Discipline) und die Synodalakten als verbindliche Schriften. | *The National Synod of the Reformed churches in France at a session in Montpellier in 1598. The Bible, the Confession of Faith, the Church Order (Discipline) and the Synodal Acts lie on the table of the synod leadership as documents of reference.*

Die vom November 1618 bis Mai 1619 im niederländischen Dordrecht abgehaltene *Dordrechter Synode* war im Kern eine niederländische Zusammenkunft, die das Ziel hatte, die reformierten Kirchen geschlossen auf ein »strenges« Verständnis der göttlichen Gnadenwahl zu verpflichten; dies auf dem Hintergrund von (»neuen«) Lehren, die dem menschlichen Willen im Gegenüber zum göttlichen Wirken einen größeren Freiraum zu geben versuchten. Auch politische Faktoren spielten dabei keine geringe Rolle. Die Einladung zu einer solchen »Generalsynode« erging allerdings nicht nur an niederländische Provinzsynoden, sondern an zahlreiche Kirchen des reformierten Protestantismus von England bis in die Schweiz, die in der Folge auch ihre Delegierten nach Dordrecht entsandten. Damit war das Dordrechter Treffen zu einer gesamteuropäischen Synode des reformierten Protestantismus geworden. Die dort schließlich verabschiedeten Lehrregeln (*Canones*) verpflichteten die reformierten Kirchen auf ein konsequent prädestinatianisches Gnadenverständnis.

Während die Zusammenkunft von Dordrecht um eine spezifische theologische Frage kreiste, besaß die dreißig Jahre später stattfindende und sich über sechs Jahre erstreckende *Westminster Synode* (1643–1649) ein umfassenderes Ziel. Hintergrund war der Bürgerkrieg zwischen der (»puritanischen«) Armee des Parlaments – mit schottischer Unterstützung – und den Truppen Königs Karl I. aus dem Hause Stuart, dessen Regierung absolutistische Züge besaß, und der durch seine Heirat mit der katholischen Tochter des französischen Königs Heinrich IV. des Katholizismus verdächtigt wurde. Politische und religiös-konfessionelle Motive waren dabei, wie oft im 17. Jahrhundert, eng miteinander verschränkt. Die *Westminster Synode* wurde auf Weisung des Parlaments einberufen mit dem Ziel, den englischen Protestantismus in Lehre und Kirchenorganisation klarer zu regeln und gleichzeitig eine größere Abstimmung mit der Schottischen (reformierten) Kirche, aber auch mit reformierten Kirchen auf dem Kontinent zu erreichen. Die zu diesem Zweck zusammengerufenen 121 Geistlichen und 30 »Laien« – nicht alle waren stets anwesend – vertraten sehr unterschiedliche Konzepte bezüglich der Organisation einer Gottes Wort entsprechenden Kirche. Aus zahllosen Sitzungen und Debatten gingen schließlich eine Gottesdienstordnung, eine Kirchenordnung, das »Westminster Bekenntnis« und zwei Katechismen von unterschiedlicher Ausführlichkeit

4 Im Erdgeschoss dieses Lagerhauses fand 1571 die Emder Synode statt. Sie war eine Synode niederländischer reformierter Flüchtlingsgemeinden und prägte durch ihre Beschlüsse das Selbstverständnis und die presbyterial-synodale Kirchenordnung vieler reformierter Kirchen. | *The Synod of Emden was a synod of Dutch Reformed refugee congregations and has had a decisive influence on the self-understanding and the presbyterial-synodal church order of the Reformed Churches.*

Außerordentliche »reformierte« Synoden von historischer Tragweite

Es waren die ekklesiologischen Grundentscheidungen der durch sie repräsentierten Tradition, welche auch die bekannten außerordentlichen Synoden im 17. Jahrhundert prägten. Zu nennen sind hier vor allem die *Dordrechter Synode* (Abb. 7) von 1618 und die in einem ganz anderen politischen und kulturellen Klima stattfindende *Westminster Synode* von 1643–1649 (Abb. 8).

hervor. Die Beschlüsse wurden vom englischen Parlament verabschiedet, allerdings im Rahmen der »Wiederherstellung« der Stuart-Monarchie 1660 wieder aufgehoben. Die Schottische Kirche hingegen übernahm die Synodenbeschlüsse dauerhaft. Die Wirkungsgeschichte der *Westminster Synode* geht allerdings weit über das 17. Jahrhundert und über die Britischen Inseln hinaus. Für zahlreiche reformierte Kirchen im englischen Sprachraum gilt sie bis heute – von ihren theologischen Entscheidungen ganz abgesehen – als ekklesiologischer Orientierungspunkt für eine presbyterial-synodale Kirchenleitung.

Fazit

Das »allgemeine Priestertum« aller Gläubigen, die Ortsgemeinde als Ausgangspunkt des Kirchenverständnisses und das nicht-hierarchische Verständnis der kirchlichen Ämter als Dienstämter führten in den reformierten Kirchen zur Herausbildung dauerhafter synodaler Strukturen und Formen der kirchlichen Entscheidungsfassung.

---

1 Die GEKE-Studie »Die Kirche Jesu Christi« (1994) brachte dies in ihrer Unterscheidung von Grund, Gestaltung und Bestimmung der Kirche als Kern evangelischen Kirchenverständnisses zum Ausdruck.
2 Vgl. beispielsweise Calvins Überlegungen zur Wahl kirchlicher Amtsträger in: Weber, Otto (Hg.), Johannes Calvin, Unterricht in der christlichen Religion, 4. Aufl., Neukirchen-Vluyn 1986, Buch IV,4,10–13.
3 Weber, Otto (Hg.), Johannes Calvin, Unterricht in der christlichen Religion, 4. Aufl., Neukirchen-Vluyn 1986, Buch IV,4,12.
4 Siehe: Bornkamm, Karin; Ebeling, Gerhard (Hgg.), Martin Luther ausgewählte Schriften, Bd. 5: Kirche, Gottesdienst, Schule, Frankfurt am Main 1990, 10.
5 Siehe Egli, Emil u. a. (Hg.), Huldreich Zwingli sämtliche Werke, Berlin, Leipzig, Zürich 1905–2013, Band I, 491–495.
6 Siehe Campi Emidio; Roth Detlef; Stotz Peter (Hgg.), Heinrich Bullinger Schriften, Zürich 2004–2007, Bd. 5, 27.66–73.
7 Egli, Emil (Hg.), Aktensammlung zur Geschichte der Zürcher Reformation in den Jahren 1519–1533, Zürich 1879, Neudruck Aalen 1973, 834 (Nr. 1899).
8 Vgl. zum folgenden Thema: Sunshine, Glenn S., Reforming French Protestantism. The Development of Huguenot Ecclesiastical Institutions, 1557–1572, Kirksville/Missouri 2003.
9 Vgl. Weber, Otto (Hg.), Johannes Calvin, Unterricht in der christlichen Religion, 4. Aufl., Neukirchen-Vluyn 1986, Buch IV,3,8.
10 Fornerod, Nicolas und Opitz, Peter (eds), Die Discipline ecclésiastique von 1559, in: Reformierte Bekenntnisschriften, vol. 2/1 (1559–1563), ed. Andreas Mühling and Peter Opitz, Neukirchen-Vluyn 2009, 57–83.
11 Freudenberg, Matthias und Siller, Aleida. Emder Synode 1571. Wesen und Wirkungen eines Grundtextes der Moderne, Göttingen, 2020.

Peter Opitz

The Beginnings of Protestant Synodal Culture in the »Reformed« Reformation

Protestant and ›synodal‹

The Reformation undertook to find new ways of hearing the Gospel – the biblical message of Christ – in its purest possible form, clearing away the accretions and distortions it had suffered in the course of church history. That led not only to a change in the practice of individual faith and piety but also to the need to reshape the Christian church as an organised community of Christians with direct orientation to New Testament testimony. Fundamental insights derived from the New Testament led, logically, to organising churches in a ›synodal‹ fashion.

The first insight to mention is known from the misleading catchword of ›priesthood of all believers‹ (following from 1 Pet 2:9). This does not mean a proliferation of priests but the end of all human priesthood. Christians do not need priests to bring them into relationship with God, nor do they need any church institution with offices and rites as a mediator between God and human beings. That is because Christians live in a direct, personal relationship with God, enabled through Christ, the only ›priest‹, and mediated through the workings of God's Spirit, giving rise to faith and thereby to communion with God. That also means that before this God there are no spiritual hierarchies among people; all Christians stand before God on the same level.

The second insight: when the New Testament speaks of the »church« it means, on the one hand, the spiritual community of all Christians with Christ, a community embracing all believers of all ages: the »one«, catholic church, as stated in the Nicene Creed. It is the spiritual »Body of Christ« (e.g. 1 Cor 12:12–27). On the other hand, when the New Testament refers to the Christian church as an earthly, human community it means certain local congregations and real-life Christian assemblies. This is where an ›evangelical‹ (Gospel-based) church must start, in terms of organisation.

The third insight: the New Testament has a host of names for ›offices‹, which in many ways overlap in terms of tasks and activities. Common to them is that they designate ministries, not authorities. The Reformers (in the following I refer to Heinrich Bullinger and John Calvin, who decisively shaped Reformed understanding of the church) summed them up in three areas: proclamation, leadership and supervision of the congregation, and caring for the poor (pastoral ministry, offices as elders, and diaconal ministry). The fourth ministry of teaching, mentioned by Calvin, is particularly relevant where there was a theological school or academy. All three ›offices‹ are *diaconal* tasks, which is why precisely the pastors are consistently called ›ministers‹ (of God's Word). These ministries are not exercised by a single individual with certain competences (for example, a single ›bishop‹) but together with others.

Hence there is the office of elder (Greek: presbyter, see Acts 20:17), a leading office within a body elected by a local congregation, and one entrusted with a certain task. Here too it is a matter of serving the congregation and not of exercising domination (1 Cor 12:28 uses a Greek term derived from ›cybernetics‹, the art of controlling living processes). Consequently, an elder has to possess both the necessary abilities and lead an exemplary life (the classical texts cited by the Reformers include 1 Pet 5:1–3; 1 Tim 3:1–3; Titus 1:5–9).

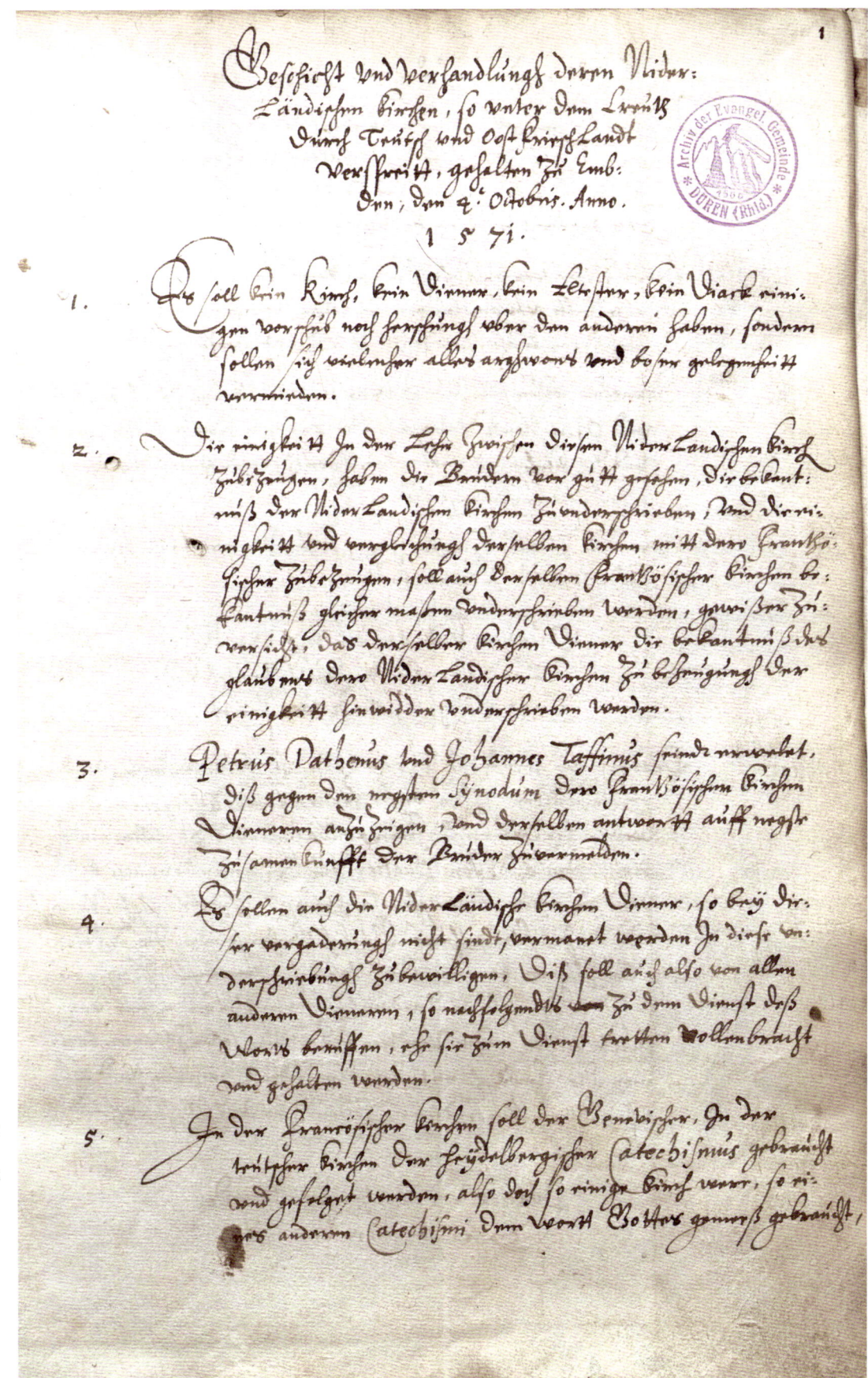

5 Erste Seite einer deutschsprachigen Abschrift der Beschlüsse der Emder Synode von 1571. Der erste Artikel hält fest: »Keine Gemeinde soll über andere Gemeinden, kein Pastor über andere Pastoren, kein Ältester über andere Älteste, kein Diakon über andere Diakone Vorrang haben oder Herrschaft beanspruchen.« | First page of a germanspeaking copy of the minutes of the Emden Synod of 1571. The first paragraph states: »No church shall take precedence or lord it over other churches, no pastor over other pastors, no elder over other elders, no deacon over other deacons.«

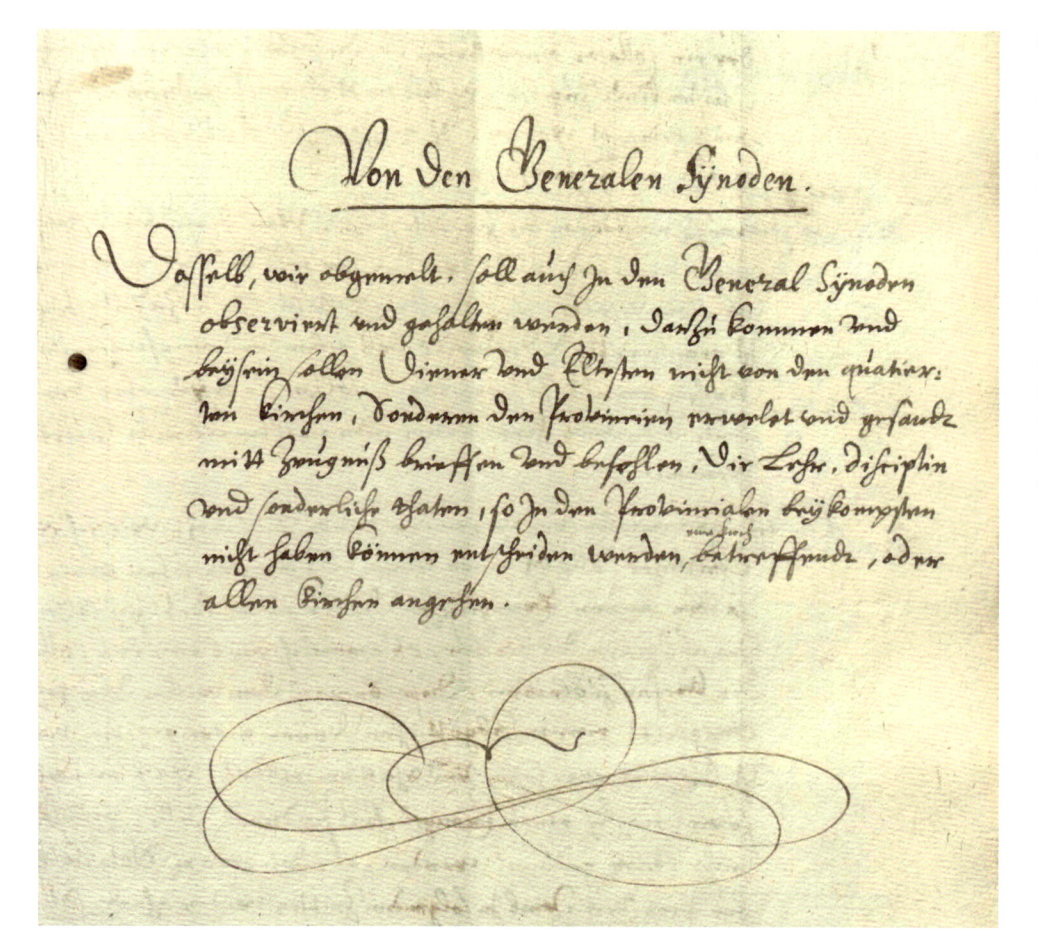

6 Die Emder Synode legte fest, dass wichtige Themen zu Lehre und Kirchendisziplin sowie Fragen, die auf den Provinzsynoden nicht entschieden werden konnten, von der Generalsynode behandelt werden sollten. Pastoren, Älteste und Diakone entschieden auf allen Ebenen mit gleichem Stimmrecht. | *The Emden Synod determined that matters pertaining to doctrine and church discipline, as well as queries that could not be resolved at the provincial synods, should be addressed by the general synod. At all levels, pastors, elders and deacons were accorded equal voting rights.*

And, finally, the Reformers – being humanist-trained biblical exegetists – were aware that while basic elements, criteria and models for a Christian congregation deserving of its name must be taken from the New Testament, this does not extend to an established, timelessly valid church order or ministry structure. Flexibility and mobility in questions of order and the shaping of Christian community and church considering the respective cultural and political situation were part of the ›evangelical‹ understanding of church.[1]

However, church structures were also to make room for proclaiming the rediscovered ›Gospel‹ and for its impact on mutual relations in a Christian church. By contrast, the coordinates were given by the respective specific political and cultural situation. The Reformers were also familiar with ancient theories of good ›political‹ living together. Basically they were in agreement with the way Aristotle weighed up of the advantages and disadvantages of different political models: while monarchy almost automatically leads to tyranny and, on the other hand, an extreme democracy as the rule of the masses easily slides into lawless rule of the rabble and gives space to demagogues, the aristocracy offers leadership of the community by a small group of ›the best‹, the greatest guarantee of a policy at the service of the common good.[2] This doubtless contributed to the way the Reformers untiringly emphasised the right of the local congregation to call individuals to an ecclesiastical ministry. The fact that the Roman pontifical church deprived the parish of this right and began to appoint church office-bearers top-down, so to speak, without any involvement of the congregation, is one of its central distortions of Christianity. At the same time, the Reformers were sceptical about a democratic majority decision. The parish must be seriously consulted and have opportunities for objections, but ultimately the decisions – having heard the voices from the ›people‹ – are taken by a small body of capable individuals elected by the congregation. The ideal of Christians »united in the same mind« (see 1 Cor 1:10; Rom 15:5; Acts 15:23–26) and the required »wisdom« in the decisions were more than what can be achieved with a mere majority decision. Calvin quotes Virgil in this context: »The crowd is uncertain and divides into contradictory aspirations.«[3] Accordingly, the Reformers attempted to restrict the congregation's participating in the right to propose and object, but also decisively stood up for this right.

In modern and slightly anachronistic terms, the direction in which the reformers pointed with regard to the organization and leadership of a »Protestant« church could be described as representative democracy with direct democratic elements. That brings us close to present-day presbyterial-synodal thinking. And so the old Christian tradition of synods again became important for the Protestant churches, not just for special gatherings such as the Synod of Dordrecht in 1618 or the Westminster Synod of 1643–49, but also as a term to designate regular, institutionalised meetings with a cybernetic – i.e. church leadership – function, first within a local congregation and then beyond.

The history of the synodal culture of the Protestant churches mirrors the spread and development of Protestant Christianity in different political and cultural contexts.

Synodal culture at the service of congregational Reformation

At an early stage, the Reformers strove to strengthen the competences of the local congregation as a counter-model to the hierarchical Roman episcopal church spanning the entire ›Christian West‹. Appealing to biblical passages like 1 Corinthians 14:30f., where Paul basically grants each Christian the permission and competence to teach and, at the same time, the whole congregation to examine all teachings, Luther concluded *That a Christian Assembly or Congregation has the Right and Power to Judge all Teaching, and to Appoint, Employ and Dismiss Teachers*, to quote the title of a treatise (1523).[4] In the Lutheran Reformation – for political and geographical reasons developed and established chiefly as a ›Reformation of the princes‹ – there was little room at first for the immediate implementation of such thinking, particularly as Luther's understanding of preaching and the administration of the sacraments attributed a strong position to the ordained ministry over against the congregation.

In the Swiss and Upper-German Reformation from which the Evangelical ›Reformed‹ tradition developed, the starting situation was somewhat different. By distinction with the vast majority of other territories in Europe, the Swiss confederation did not consist of princedoms. Here there was a strong tradition of self-government with comparably flat hierarchies. Cities were governed by elected councils and mayors, but political authorities and judges were also elected in the valleys and villages. Political decisions were not made by individual princes but in committees and commissions, and decisions of great consequence were not taken without consulting the population.

The first Zurich Disputation of January 1523, at which Zwingli had to present and publicly defend his 67 theses, fits into this political climate (Fig. 1). In order to end the religious arguments, the Zurich Council invited all preachers and priests in the town and region to take part in the conversation, declaring that it was to take place in German. He here was linking up not only with the tradition of the academic disputation about theological questions but also with the church tradition of the synod, and claiming as a secular authority to be able to convene a disputation in the service of religious peace on his own state territory (as Constantine I had once done in Nicaea in 325). Answering the objection of the episcopal delegation that such theological questions belonged at a conference of bishops and scholars, referring to biblical texts like Matthew 20:28 giving priority to the assembled local congregation over a big church organisation, Zwingli asserted: »A truly Christian church is assembled in this room.«[5]

In the cities and territories of the confederation, but also in the imperial cities that espoused the Reformation by decision of the city council, the model of a congregational Reformation won the day. It consisted of close cooperation between ecclesiastical and political authorities, which seriously understood each other to be the Evangelical Christian authorities and part of the church. Here the synodal idea became important with respect to the *internal organisation* of the new Protestant churches.

The first synod, proposed by Zwingli, met in Zurich on 21 April 1528. It was institutionalised in the synod order adopted on 22 October 1532, which formed the basis of the Zurich church until the end of the *ancien régime*. From now on, the synod met twice a year, in spring and in autumn. These synods were compulsory for all pastors in the Zurich state territory with eight council members as representatives of the community. The topics were questions of coordination and the exchange of information. The main focus, however, was on »censure«: the synod rules provided for examining the conduct of office, teaching and way of life of each pastor, and issuing admonishments. Reference was made not only to the diligence and love in studying scripture, and family life, but also character faults like envy, arrogance or any tendency towards dominance (see 1 Tim 3:2–13; 1 Pet 5:1–4). Deans, too, were to be subjected to this appraisal by colleagues so that they did not misuse their position.[6]

The previous hierarchy of offices, in which consecrated individuals of higher spiritual rank had, as bishops, oversight over a whole area and the pastors working there, was revamped into a form of collective, reciprocal checking by pastors of equal rank with respect to the pastoral office they had been entrusted with. The emphasis lay on avoiding spiritual hierarchies. Everyone, the village pastor and the learned teacher at the »Theological School« (Schola Tigurina) were to respect one another »as brothers and workers in the Gospel of Christ« and act towards one another accordingly.[7]

The council retained the right to employ new pastors, with an examination commission, consisting of two pastors, two councillors and two teachers from the Zurich »Theological School« (Schola Tigurina) examining the candidates and submitting their opinions. The solemn pronouncing of the official oath then took place before the synod, and only then was the candidate officially admitted to the ministry of the church. Other Reformed towns in the confederation set up similar forms of internal church governance.

In Calvin's time, the church in the small city state of Geneva was organised slightly differently. Taking up suggestions from Strasbourg and Basel, Calvin provided for two bodies for (internal) church management in the church order of 1541. A council of elders (*consistory*), composed of pastors and suitable councillors, was to watch over the church discipline of the members of the congregation. At the same time, with the *compagnie des pasteurs* Calvin created a body of all the Genevan pastors that was to meet weekly, which was possible in view of the small size of Geneva. It was led by an elected moderator. Besides common Bible study, the *compagnie des pasteurs* had a function corresponding to the synods of larger churches: the mutual appraisal of the pastors in terms of their conduct of office, doctrine and their personal lives. Questions of internal church organisation were also discussed here and new candidates for the ministry examined and proposed for election by the council, which had the last word on these matters as well.

Synodal culture in diaspora churches and at the service of cross-community coordination and cooperation

The situation was different where Protestant faith received no support from the authorities, but, on the contrary, was oppressed by them. This was, for example, the case in France, Upper Italy and the Habsburg-Spanish administered Dutch provinces (the area of today's Benelux countries). Despite often bloody persecution, Protestant church sprang up in large numbers even in these regions. They had to organise themselves without protection, but also without a political authority telling them what to do.

The Synod of Chanforan

The Waldensian movement was a special case. Even before the Reformation the *consilium generale*, an annual assembly of Waldensian preachers, established a form of early ›synodal‹ tradition. The general council of 1530 in Merindol (Provence) dealt with the question of possibly joining the Reformation. After inquiries among Swiss and Upper-German Reformers, and advised by the West Swiss Reformer William Farel (1489–1565), the Declaration of the Synod of Chanforan two years later sealed the Waldensians' accession to the Reformation (Fig. 2). Amongst other things, this meant turning away from their previously core tradition of wandering preachers. By contrast, the introduction of synods was tantamount to continuing the *consilium generale* in adapted form.

The synod of the French Protestant churches of 1559 and the Discipline ecclésiastique

The Protestant churches in France[8] generally introduced three ministries – pastor, elder (presbyter) and deacon. The council of elders (presbytery, to which the pastor and deacons could also belong) soon became a genuinely ecclesiastical governing body, going far beyond questions of church discipline. It consisted of elected representatives of the congregation and – free from the claims of a civic authority – had the competence to employ or dismiss pastors, supervise their conduct of office, and also to exclude incorrigible members of the congregation. Its tasks were those of a »senate« in the church field, to quote John a Lasco (1499–1560) in his church order for the refugee congregation in London. According to Calvin, this was already the case at the time of the early church.[9]

From the mid-16th century, a cross-community presbyterial-synodal culture developed from the need for cooperation between and across communities. They needed to coordinate their actions and support one another in situations of oppression. Delegates from various congregations met in regional synods to discuss common concerns while preserving the autonomy of the individual communities. Just as procedures for staffing local presbyteries and defining their competences needed to be developed and negotiated at the congregational level, so did the rules for regional synods. Who was to represent the individual congregations there? Who was to lead them, equipped with what powers? How binding were the decisions of these synods for the local congregations? The elements of »Reformed« ecclesiology, influences on the French-speaking, western part of the Bern church (today's Canton Waadt) and local traditions – apart from the given geographical conditions – formed into a synodal tradition of their own, the goal being not a merging of individual congregations into a large national church, but a kind of church association without an over-arching hierarchical structure, which called for a careful balancing of the responsibilities and powers at the different levels. This was not possible without discussions and conflicts, as illustrated by the discussions about a strongly ›grassroots‹ democratic model, such as that propagated by Jean Morely (1524–ca. 1594), which was finally rejected at several regional synods.

The combination of different ›synodal‹ levels with the goal of ›fraternal‹ coordination and cooperation with the simultaneous prevention of the exercise of domination in the church also featured in the *Discipline ecclésiastique*, which was passed at the first national synod of the scattered Protestant churches in May 1559 in Paris.[10] It became

7 Die Dordrechter Synode fand vom 13. November 1618 bis zum 9. Mai 1619 statt. Sie war eine nationale Versammlung der niederländischen reformierten Kirche unter Beteiligung von ausländischen reformierten Delegationen und fasste Beschlüsse zur Prädestinationslehre. | *The Dordrecht Synod took place from 13 November 1618 to 9 May 1619. It was a national assembly of the Dutch Reformed Church with the participation of foreign Reformed delegations and made decisions on the doctrine of predestination.*

a fundamental document of an overarching synodal order connecting the presbyterial Protestant local congregations in France, both in regional synods or »colloquies« and at the national level (Fig. 3). The *Confessio Gallicana*, which had been adopted at the same Paris synod, served as the common confessional basis. While, pursuant to Article 4, national synods were to take place when needed, Article 5 stated that in every church or province the pastors and at least one elder or deacon should meet twice a year. Furthermore, they laid down a certain harmonisation of the internal organisation of individual churches, e.g. regarding the election of pastors (by the council of elders, but with some congregational involvement), and assigned to regional synods the work of coordinating and supporting the congregations. At the same time, this document was careful not to allow any ›dominance‹ or hierarchy to arise, neither at the personal level nor at the level of churches.

8 Die Westminstersynode (engl.: Westminster Assembly) wurde vom britischen Parlament zur Neuordnung der Kirche von England einberufen. Die Synode dauerte insgesamt sechs Jahre (1643–1649). Hier in einer historischen Darstellung von John Rogers Herbert um 1840. | *The Westminster Assembly was convened by the British Parliament to reorganise the Church of England. The synod lasted a total of six years (1643-1649). Here in a historicist depiction by John Rogers Herbert around 1840.*

The president of synod was elected, for the duration of the synod, and was subjected to »friendly and brotherly« appraisal along with all other members of synod (Articles 2 and 4). The fact that, at the church level, no church was allowed to claim priority over another was stated in the very first article, even before any substantive common decision.

The Emden Synod of 1571

In Emden, a city with a large marine trade port, envoys from the Reformed Dutch exile congregations met together in 1571 in order to organise their church life (Fig. 4). The synod of the Dutch congregations »under the cross« of 1571 is based on the Reformed church understanding (outlined above) and, at the same time, linked up with French synodal tradition.[11] The letter of invitation to the synod is based on the same Bible passages that were important at the start of the Zurich Reformation nearly half a century before, and justifies the form of synod in detail as being in accordance with Protestant faith and the consequent »fraternal« community. Like the *Discipline ecclésiastique*, it rejects any kind of hierarchy in the very first article, both at the level of the congregations and among the clergy (Abb. 5). Furthermore, the *Emden Synod* confronted the challenge of gathering pastors and elders together from a host of different, French-speaking and German or Dutch-speaking exile congregations in an area stretching from Frisia to the Palatinate. They, too, sought a synodal path of harmonisation and understanding while simultaneously preserving the freedom of the individual congregations. The *Geneva Catechism* was recognised and used in the French-speaking congregations, as was the *Heidelberg Catechism* in the German-speaking congregations. But communities using other catechisms were not excluded as long as they »agree[d] with God's Word«. In view of the differences existing within the Reformed camp, which were of a linguistic and cultural nature but also linked to the differing affinity with Luther's teaching on the Lord's Supper, the *Emden Synod* ratified an internally reformed style of »reconciled diversity« in doctrine. However, the synod decisions dealt with questions of eucharistic practice and church discipline more in detail than the *Discipline ecclésiastique* while leaving the congregations a lot of freedom in their practice of celebrating the Lord's Supper. They shared the concern to draw the line at a sacramental mediation of salvation. For example, ordinary bread was to be used and the impression that the communion elements were consecrated was to be avoided at all cost. The tension between the way the *Geneva Catechism* and the *Heidelberg Catechism* understand the Lord's Supper was not mentioned.

In addition, the synod decided to hold regular provincial synods at changing venues. Above all in the Dutch and North German region but also beyond, the decisions of the *Emden Synod* served as a catalyst for spreading presbyterial-synodal governance and administrative structures in the Protestant sphere (Fig. 6).

Extraordinary Reformed synods of historical importance

The prominent extraordinary synods in the 17th century were also marked by fundamental ecclesiological decisions stemming from the traditions they represented. The most significant were the *Dordrecht Synod* (Fig. 7) of 1618 and the *Westminster* Synod (Fig. 8) of 1643–1649, which took place in a completely different political and cultural climate.

The Dordrecht Synod, held from November 1618 until May 1619 in Dordrecht, the Netherlands, was basically a Dutch meeting with the aim of aligning the Reformed churches along a ›strict‹ understanding of divine election by grace; this against the background of (›new‹) doctrines attempting to give greater freedom to the human will by contrast with divine action. Political factors played a considerable role here, as well. The invitation to such a ›general synod‹ did not go only to Dutch provincial synods, however, but also to numerous churches representing Reformed Protestantism from England to Switzerland, who consequently also sent their delegates to Dordrecht. That made the Dordrecht gathering a pan-European synod of Reformed Protestantism. The doctrines finally adopted there (*canones*) committed the Reformed churches to an understanding of grace consistently oriented to predestination.

While the Dordrecht gathering focused on a specific theological question, the *Westminster Synod* (1643–1649), convening thirty years later and extending over six years, had a more comprehensive goal. The background was the civil war between the (»Puritan«) army of parliament – with Scottish support – and the troops of King Charles 1 (1600–1649) from the House of Stuart, whose government had absolutist features and who was suspected of Catholicism through his marriage to the Catholic daughter of the King of France, Henri IV (1553–1610). Political and religious-confessional motifs were closely interwoven, as often happened in the 17th century. The *Westminster Synod* was convened on the instruction of parliament with the aim of achieving more clarity in the doctrine and church organisation of English Protestantism and, at the same time, greater agreement with the Scottish (Reformed) church, but also with Reformed churches on the Continent. The 121 clergy and 30 lay people convening for this purpose – not all of them were present all the time – held very differing opinions regarding the organisation of a church corresponding to God's Word. Countless meetings and debates finally produced a worship order, a church order, the Westminster Confession and two catechisms of different length. The decisions were adopted by the English but cancelled during the Restoration of the Stuart monarchy in 1660. The Church of Scotland, by contrast, adopted the synodal decisions on a permanent basis. The history of the impact of the *Westminster Synod* goes far beyond the 17th century and beyond the British Isles. To this day, a large number of Reformed churches in the English-speaking world – quite apart from their theological positions – regard it as a point of ecclesiological orientation for presbyterial-synodal church governance.

Conclusion

The »priesthood of all believers«, the local congregation as the starting point for defining the church, and the non-hierarchical understanding of church offices as ministries led to the forming of lasting synodal structures and ways of church decision-making in the Reformed churches.

---

1 The CPCE study »The Church of Jesus Christ« of 1994 expressed this in its distinction between the ground, form and purpose of the church as the core of Protestant understanding of it.
2 See e.g. Calvin's thinking on the election of clergy in: Weber, Otto (ed.), Johannes Calvin, Unterricht in der christlichen Religion, 4th ed., Neukirchen-Vluyn, 1986, Buch IV, 4,10–13.
3 Weber, Otto (ed.), op. cit., vol. IV, 4,12.
4 Bornkamm, Karin; Ebeling, Gerhard (eds), Martin Luther ausgewählte Schriften, vol. 5: Kirche, Gottesdienst, Schule, Frankfurt am Main, 1990, 10.
5 Egli, Emil et al. (ed.), Huldreich Zwingli sämtliche Werke, Berlin, Leipzig, Zürich, 1905–2013, vol. I, 491–495.
6 Campi, Emidio; Roth Detlef; Stotz Peter (eds), Heinrich Bullinger Schriften, Zürich, 2004–2007, Bd. 5, 27.66–73.
7 Egli, Emil (ed.), Aktensammlung zur Geschichte der Zürcher Reformation in den Jahren 1519–1533, Zürich, 1879, reprint Aalen 1973, 834 (No 1899).
8 See on the following topic Sunshine, Glenn S. Reforming French Protestantism. The Development of Huguenot Ecclesiastical Institutions, 1557–1572, Kirksville/Missouri 2003.
9 Weber, Otto (ed.), op. cit. vol IV, 3,8.
10 Fornerod, Nicolas and Opitz, Peter (eds), Die Discipline ecclésiastique von 1559, in: Reformierte Bekenntnisschriften, vol. 2/1 (1559–1563), ed. Andreas Mühling and Peter Opitz, Neukirchen-Vluyn 2009, 57–83.
11 Freudenberg, Matthias and Siller, Aleida. Emder Synode 1571. Wesen und Wirkungen eines Grundtextes der Moderne, Göttingen, 2020.

Sabine Blütchen

Gegenwärtige Herausforderungen evangelischer Synoden

Am Beginn des 21. Jahrhunderts, gut 500 Jahre nach der Reformation, steht die Legitimation einer Synode als Leitungsorgan evangelischer Kirchen außer Frage. Theologische und dogmatische Diskussionen über ihre Daseinsberechtigung sind längst geführt. Heute sehen sich die Synoden anderen Herausforderungen gegenüber.

»Synode« bedeutet wörtlich Weggemeinschaft. In den meisten Kirchen setzt sie sich schon lange aus Pfarrpersonen und Laien zusammen. Synoden treffen sich in vielen Kirchen ein- oder zweimal jährlich, um ihrem Auftrag nachzukommen. Wolfgang Huber, der frühere Bischof der Evangelischen Kirche Berlin-Brandenburg-schlesische Oberlausitz und Ratsvorsitzende der Evangelischen Kirche in Deutschland, beschreibt ihre Aufgabe mit »Teilnahme an der Kirchenleitung, Verantwortung für den Vollzug des Bekennens, Auftrag gegenüber der Öffentlichkeit«.[1]

In den wenigen vorstehenden Absätzen klingen wesentliche Herausforderungen der Gegenwart für unsere Synoden schon an. Die Zusammensetzung dieser Weggemeinschaft, das Wahl- und/oder Berufungsverfahren und dessen Auswirkungen auf die Entscheidungsfindung haben Bedeutung für die Arbeit der jeweiligen Synode. Außerdem trägt jede der von Huber genannten Aufgaben ihre eigenen Herausforderungen in sich: das Miteinander von Synoden, den weiteren Organen der Kirchenleitung und der kirchlichen Verwaltung hat für die synodale Arbeit durchaus Relevanz. Die Aufgabenfelder einer Synode, die Huber als »Verantwortung für den Vollzug des Bekennens« und »Auftrag gegenüber der Öffentlichkeit« bezeichnet, haben auch im 21. Jahrhundert besondere Bedeutung.

Zusammensetzung von Synoden

Synoden als Leitungsorgane evangelischer Kirchen verbinden Predigtamt und Gemeinde, also Laien und ordinierte Hauptamtliche, die gemeinsam die geistliche und rechtliche Leitung innehaben.

In den verschiedenen Kirchen differieren die Größe der Synoden und die genaue Zusammensetzung ihrer Mitglieder stark. So hat z. B. die Synode der Evangelisch-Lutherischen Landeskirche Sachsens 80 Mitglieder, die Kirche von Schottland 500, die reformierte Kirche Ungarns 100, die der Evangelischen Waldenserkirche 180 Synodale, die Presbyterianische Kirche in Irland 1300 Delegierte.

In vielen Kirchen müssen die nicht-ordinierten Personen Mitglieder der lokalen Kirchengemeindeleitung sein, in anderen von diesen ausgewählte Gemeindemitglieder. Meist kommen berufene Mitglieder hinzu.

Wer im einzelnen Mitglied einer Synode werden kann, ist in jeder Ordnung ausdifferenziert geregelt. Ein besonderes Beispiel dafür ist die Synodalordnung für die 1975 gegründete Verwaltungsunion der Waldenser- und Methodistenkirche in Italien. Diese Ordnung regelt in zehn Abschnitten die Sitzverteilung. Dabei wird den besonderen Gegebenheiten dieser Kirche Rechnung getragen, um eine ausgewogene Vertretung von Gemeinden unterschiedlicher Größe zu gewährleisten. Zudem stehen weitere Sitze den Mitgliedern der Theologischen Fakultät zu. Ferner gibt es eine Reihe von beratenden Mitgliedern

Der Präsident der Synode wird jeweils für ein Jahr gewählt. Da die Waldenserkirche vom Rio de la Plata eine Einheit mit den italienischen Waldensern bildet, gibt es hier auch in Bezug auf die spezifischen Aufgaben zusätzliche Herausforderungen.

Der so genannten Generalversammlung der *Church of Scotland* gehören Kommissare an, die jährlich zu bestimmen sind, Hauptamtliche und Älteste, die nicht Mitglieder der regionalen Bezirkskirchenleitung sein müssen. Dazu kommen Jugendvertreterinnen und -vertreter, die Rede- aber kein Stimmrecht haben, gleiches gilt für Gastvertreter aus Partnerkirchen. Der Moderator der Versammlung wird ebenfalls nur jeweils für ein Jahr gewählt.

Der irischen Generalversammlung gehören alle Geistlichen einschließlich der pensionierten sowie ein Ältester aus jeder Gemeinde an. Der Moderator wird jährlich gewählt.

Der sächsischen Landessynode gehören 60 gewählte Synodale an, gewählt in 20 Wahlkreisen. Wahlberechtigt sind lokale Kirchenvorsteherinnen und Kirchenvorsteher sowie die Pfarrpersonen. Jeder Wahlkreis entsendet drei Synodale, darunter eine Pfarrperson. 20 Synodale werden von der Kirchenleitung berufen, darunter sollen Superintendenten, zwei Jugendvertreter und ein Vertreter der Theologischen Fakultät sein. Der Präsident der Landessynode wird für die gesamte Amtsdauer von sechs Jahren gewählt.

Vielfältige Belastungen der Synodenarbeit

Bedenkt man, dass nicht nur in evangelischen Kirchen, sondern ganz allgemein die Bereitschaft, sich in Gewerkschaften, Vereinen und Parteien ehrenamtlich zu engagieren, in den vergangenen Jahren deutlich gesunken ist, wird schnell erkennbar, wie schwierig es sein kann, die für unsere Kirchen so wichtigen Gremien zu besetzen, insbesondere, wenn es sich in einigen Fällen um eine sehr große Anzahl zu besetzender Plätze handelt. Dabei sind die häufig angeführten Hinderungsgründe, sich für ein synodales Amt zur Verfügung zu stellen, unterschiedlich.

Pfarrpersonen führen ihre zunehmende Belastung durch die ständig steigenden Anforderungen ihres Amtes an. Neben Seelsorge und Verkündigung – oft nicht nur für einen Pfarrbezirk – sind zahlreiche Verwaltungsaufgaben zu versehen, für die es auch bei mehrtägiger Teilnahme an einer Synode keine Entlastung gibt. Auch die Organisation von Vertretung für Amtshandlungen, etwa anfallende Beerdigungen während einer Synode, gestaltet sich oft schwierig.

In vielen Kirchen stellen die Laien oder Ehrenamtlichen die Mehrheit der Synodalen, in einigen Ordnungen heißen sie (regierende) Älteste.

Sind sie zwingend bereits Älteste in ihren Gemeinden, haben sie also bereits mindestens ein Ehrenamt inne. Das synodale Amt kommt als ein weiteres hinzu. Der damit verbundene Zeitaufwand nicht nur der Tagungen, sondern auch von Vorbereitung und ergänzenden Ausschusssitzungen wird häufig als Argument gegen eine Kandidatur genannt.

Können die Mitglieder direkt aus der Mitte der Gemeinde in die Synode gewählt werden, fehlt ihnen häufig die Kenntnis von Struktur und Aufgabenverteilung in der Kirche. Diese Synodalen haben es schwer, im Gremium Fuß zu fassen, da ihnen auch das Netzwerk fehlt, um nötige Informationen einzuholen. Sie als neue Synodale mit frischem Blick von außen wertzuschätzen und ihnen den Start zu erleichtern, etwa über ein Mentoring oder zusätzliche Informationsangebote, ist sinnvoll und sehr lohnend.

Allen »echten« Laien gemein ist die als abschreckend empfundene Überlegung, dass bei der Vielzahl an Themen einer Synode, die häufig eher rechtlicher oder betriebswirtschaftlicher Art sind und weniger theologische Fragen betreffen, die eigene Kompetenz fehlen könnte. Dass der gesunde Menschenverstand und die eigene Lebenserfahrung als Christ in der Gemeinde wichtige Argumente gerade im Gegenüber zu reinem Fachwissen sein können, wird häufig unterschätzt.

Laien im Wortsinn der Synodalordnungen sind alle außer den Pfarrpersonen oder ordinierten Hauptamtlichen. Allerdings nimmt die Zahl der hauptamtlich in der Kirche Beschäftigten auf der Bank der Laien in allen Synoden deutlich zu. Sie sind Kirchenmusikerinnen, Diakoninnen, Religionspädagogen und Verwaltungsmitarbeitende. Diese Synodalen haben selbstverständlich eine Vielzahl zusätzlicher Informationen bzw. Informationsquellen über das allen zur Verfügung stehende Material hinaus, was insbesondere auf unerfahrene Synodale einschüchternd oder beeinflussend wirken kann.

Dass »hauptamtliche Laien« versucht sein können, Berufsinteressen zu wahren, ist verständlich, kann aber dem Auftrag einer Synode, das Interesse der ganzen Kirche zu

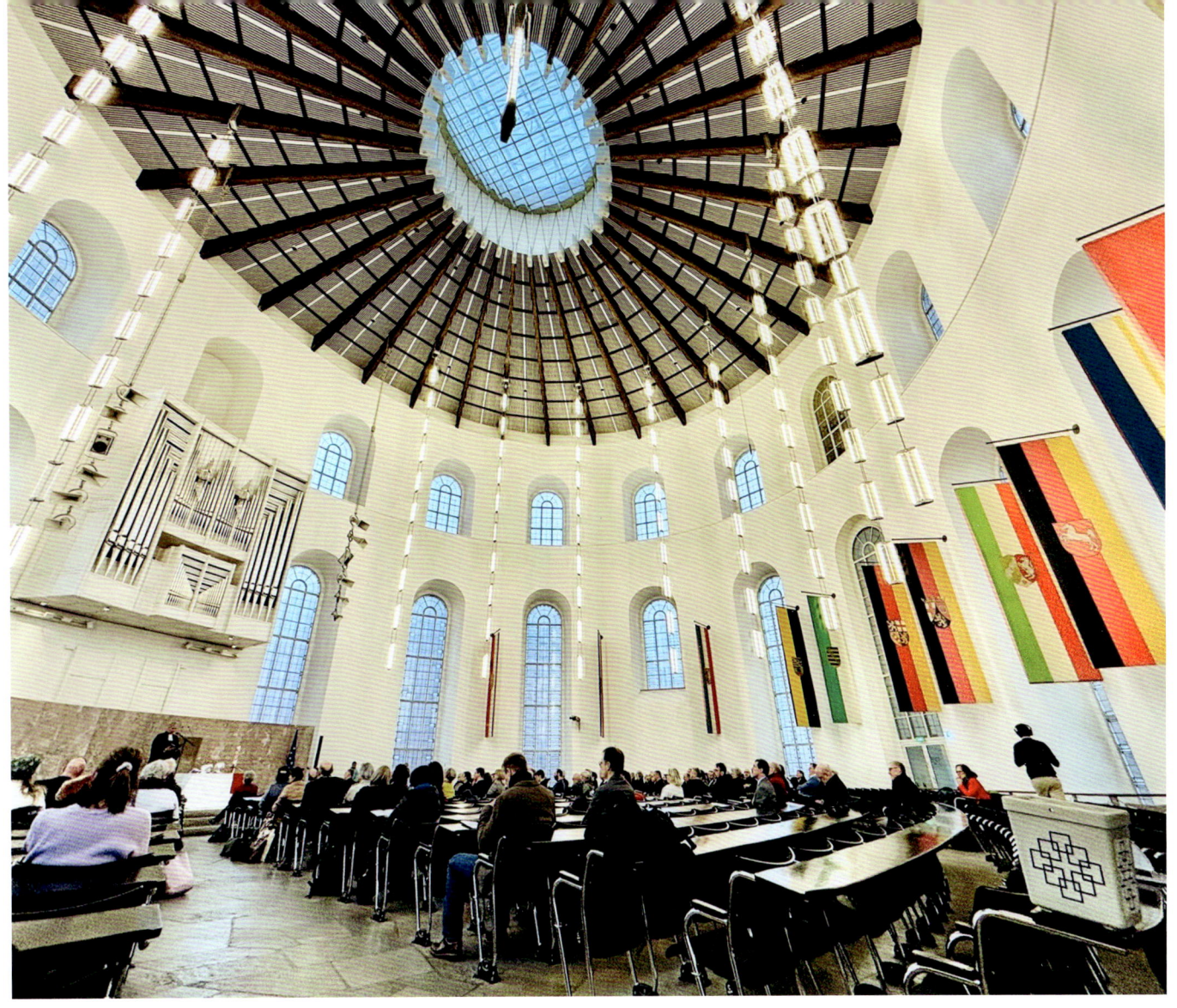

| Synodeneröffnungsgottesdienst der Evangelischen Kirche in Hessen und Nassau im November 2023 in der Frankfurter Paulskirche. | *Synod opening worship service of the Protestant Church in Hesse and Nassau in Frankfurt's St. Paul's Church in November 2023.*

vertreten, zuwiderlaufen. Gesetzliche Regelungen, nicht nur die Pfarrpersonen von Abstimmungen über ihre Besoldung auszuschließen, sondern auch Vertreter anderer Berufsgruppen, kennen viele Synodalordnungen bislang nicht.

Die Laien sollen möglichst die ganze Vielfalt der Gemeinde Christi abbilden. Das ist in der Regel nur sehr bruchstückhaft der Fall. In allen Synoden sind Männer und Frauen vertreten, auch wenn das Verhältnis noch nicht ausgeglichen ist. Bestimmte Berufsgruppen sind in allen Synoden unterrepräsentiert, so vor allem Handwerker oder auch Freiberufler. Auch Personen, die Kinder oder ältere Angehörige betreuen, lassen sich meist nicht für das synodale Amt gewinnen. Die Tagungsdauer von mehreren Tagen und die häufig lange Synodalperiode von bis zu sechs Jahren sind ernstzunehmende Hinderungsgründe.

Längst nicht jede Ordnung regelt die Beteiligung junger Menschen und wenn, häufig noch ohne Stimmrecht. Ethnische Minderheiten einer Kirche haben in Einzelfällen Anspruch auf einen Synodensitz, so z. B. die Sorben in Sachsen.[2] Dass Menschen mit Beeinträchtigung Mitglied einer Synode werden können, ist grundsätzlich völlig unbestritten. Die praktische Umsetzung stellt diese Synodalen und auch die Organisatoren in der Praxis oft vor zusätzliche Herausforderungen, denn nicht alle Tagungsorte sind barrierefrei und etwa die Sicherstellung der tagelangen Anwesenheit mehrerer Gebärdendolmetscher ist aufwendig und kostenintensiv. Aber gerade die Perspektive von Menschen, die mit besonderen Herausforderungen leben müssen und dennoch leicht aus dem Blick geraten, bereichern die Diskussionen ungemein.

Neben den gewählten Vertreterinnen und Vertreter gehören einer Synode weitere berufene oder entsendete

2 Die Vollversammlung der Gemeinschaft evangelischer Kirchen in Europa (GEKE) im September 2018 im Basler Münster. | *The General Assembly of the Communion of Protestant Churches in Europe (CPCE) in Basel Cathedral in September 2018.*

Mitglieder an. Dabei handelt es sich häufig um Angehörige theologischer Fakultäten, großer Einrichtungen, der Diakonie oder auch staatlicher Institutionen. Ihre Expertise und der Blick von außen sind es, die für eine Synode wichtig und bereichernd sein können.

Leitung der Synode und Entscheidungsfindung

Geleitet werden die synodalen Diskussionen von einem Präsidenten bzw. einer Präsidentin oder einem Moderator bzw. einer Moderatorin. Berichte und Vorlagen für die anstehenden Entscheidungen sowie Gesetzesentwürfe werden von Ausschüssen oder Räten vorbereitet. Jede Synodalordnung kennt genaue Vorschriften für mögliche Änderungsanträge und das nachfolgende Abstimmungsverfahren. Gerade das Antragsverfahren stellt sicher, dass abweichende Meinungen nicht nur in die Diskussion eingebracht werden können, sondern sich das Gremium deutlich positionieren muss. Ob ein Antrag letztlich mehrheitlich unterstützt wird, hängt sicher immer auch von der Güte der Argumente ab, gelegentlich aber auch davon, welche Mechanismen zur Meinungsbildung noch gebräuchlich sind. Hier können die Synodalen, die hauptberuflich in der Kirche beschäftigt sind, oft bereits auf ein eigenes Netzwerk zurückgreifen.

In einigen Kirchen sind auch synodale Gruppen üblich, die fest in den Ablauf der Tagung integriert sein können. So gibt es Synoden, die die Plenumsdiskussion regelmäßig unterbrechen, wenn sich die Gruppen zu einem Thema zunächst austauschen oder abstimmen wollen. Üblich sind auch bilaterale Gespräche außerhalb des Plenums, um die jeweiligen Interessen an einzelnen Tagesordnungspunkten oder Wahlvorschlägen auszuloten und gegebenenfalls wechselseitige Unterstützung abzusprechen.

Die Zuordnung der Synodalen zu den Gruppen ist freiwillig. Gerade für unerfahrene Mitglieder einer Synode kann der Austausch in der Gruppe eine gute Möglichkeit sein, ergänzende Informationen zu bekommen. Wenn sich die Mitglieder an die Entscheidungen der Gruppe gebunden fühlen, können Gruppensitzungen die Erörterung im Plenum deutlich verkürzen. Andererseits bleiben Aspekte, die zwar in einer Gruppe geäußert werden, dort aber nicht mehrheitsfähig sind, im Plenum oft ungehört.

In vielen Synoden sind Gruppen völlig unüblich. Dort hat das Prinzip der Unabhängigkeit des einzelnen Synodalen einen hohen Stellenwert. Mehrheiten finden sich von Fall zu Fall, was wiederum zu sehr überraschenden Ergebnissen führen kann.

Insbesondere über Abänderungsanträge, die nicht bereits in Ausschüssen vorberaten, sondern nur im Plenum erörtert werden, können Beschlüsse eine völlig neue Gewichtung bekommen, wenn sie von starken Meinungsführern unterstützt werden.

Die Versammlungsleitung wird bestrebt sein, dass möglichst alle Argumente für und wider angesprochen werden und nicht nur die jeweiligen Wortführenden ihre Sichtweise darstellen. Gelegentlich müssen die Laien ausdrücklich ermuntert werden, sich zu äußern, wenn die Pfarrpersonen mehrheitlich und häufig sehr eloquent für ein Ergebnis eintreten. Das Ziel synodaler Entscheidungsfindung ist ja nicht die Durchsetzung von Partikularinteressen, sondern ein möglichst einmütiges Abstimmungsergebnis zu erreichen. Gerade, wenn wie vorstehend ausgeführt, über Abänderungsanträge ganz neue Aspekte eingeführt werden, kann sich die Dauer der Diskussion erheblich verlängern, bis ein von einer großen Mehrheit getragenes Ergebnis erzielt werden kann. Anders als in einem staatlichen Parlament geht es in einer Synode jedoch gerade nicht darum, die eigenen Interessen, gleich ob die einer Berufsgruppe oder einer Gemeinde, durchzusetzen, sondern im Dienste des Herrn die Kirche zu leiten. Bei aller Anstrengung gelingt es dennoch nicht immer, einmütige oder gar einstimmige Beschlüsse zu fassen.

Zusammenarbeit von Synoden, Kirchenleitung und kirchlicher Verwaltung

Da die Synoden jeweils nur ein- oder zweimal jährlich tagen, liegen die Umsetzung ihrer Beschlüsse sowie gegebenenfalls zwischenzeitlich erforderliche weitere Entscheidungen in den Händen der Kirchenleitungen und -verwaltungen.

Die Synode als oberstes Organ der Kirche kann alle Maßnahmen, die von ihr Beauftragte ausführen, kontrollieren und auch korrigieren – so der rechtliche, theoretische Grundsatz. In der Praxis gestaltet sich das Miteinander von Synode mit Kirchenleitung und -verwaltung oft schwierig. Insbesondere für die kirchliche Verwaltung sind gelegentlich Entscheidungen einer Synode, die zu erheblichen Veränderungen in den geübten Abläufen oder Zuständigkeiten führen, nur schwer nachvollziehbar. Andererseits erfordern staatliche Vorgaben, z. B. im Bereich des Bau- und Denkmalschutzrechts oder auch des Steuerrechts, die Anpassung kirchlichen Rechts. Die in Verwaltung und hauptamtlicher Kirchenleitung versammelte und gewachsene theologische, juristische und verwaltungstechnische Kompetenz ist für die Leitung der Kirche unverzichtbar. Ohne kompetente Zuarbeit der Profis in Verwaltung und Kirchenleitung kann eine Synode den heutigen Anforderungen, die an eine so große Institution gestellt werden, kaum entsprechen. Die Herausforderungen bestehen daher wesentlich in der Kommunikation zwischen den Organen und Gremien. Je besser diese gelingt und Vertrauen aufgebaut werden kann, desto besser können alle Akteure ihre Aufgaben im Rahmen der Leitung einer Kirche und damit ihren Dienst für die Kirche ausüben.

Entscheidungsfindungen in Zeiten geringer werdender Ressourcen

Die Aufgaben einer Synode sind vielfältig. Mit der kirchlichen Gesetzgebung einschließlich der Zuständigkeit für die Verabschiedung des Haushalts nimmt eine Synode wichtige kirchenpolitische Weichenstellungen vor. Diese erfordern aktuell angesichts deutlich geringer werdender personeller und – fast überall – auch finanzieller Ressourcen massive Einschnitte in fast allen Bereichen des kirchlichen Lebens. Um diese gut begründen zu können, ist die Synode auf eine kompetente Zuarbeit aus der Verwaltung mit exakten Daten und Analysen angewiesen. Es bedarf intensiver Beratungen, häufig ist zusätzlich ein Beteiligungsprozess weiterer Ebenen oder Gremien erforderlich, um Verständnis für die Entscheidungen zu erreichen. Sowohl die rückläufigen Studierendenzahlen in der Theologie wie auch die in einigen Kirchen sinkenden Mitgliederzahlen zwingen zum Überdenken bisheriger Gemeindemodelle. Und im Rahmen dieser scheinbar rein politisch-strukturellen Entscheidungsprozesse dürfen die theologischen Fragen, die damit unmittelbar verbunden sind, nicht vernachlässigt werden.

Synoden als Spiegel der gesellschaftlichen Wirklichkeit

Neben den Themen, die originär die jeweils eigene Kirche betreffen, beschäftigen sich Synoden mit den Fragen, die die Gesellschaft insgesamt beschäftigen und zu denen eine substantiierte, evangelische Positionierung wichtig ist. So geht es etwa beim Thema des Klimaschutzes, das häufig unter vorwiegend marktwirtschaftlichen Aspekten behandelt wird, darum, den Blick zu weiten und an den uns als Menschen gegebenen Auftrag zur Bewahrung der Schöpfung zu erinnern.

Das Thema Segnung oder Trauung gleichgeschlechtlicher Paare führt bzw. führte in fast allen Kirchen zu tiefgreifenden theologischen Auseinandersetzungen. Auch die jüngst – leider – wieder entbrannte Diskussion zur Friedensethik fordert jede Synode heraus, aber sie muss sich dem stellen. Gerade bei diesen Themen erweist es sich als besonderes Gut, wenn junge und lebenserfahrene Menschen, Theologinnen und Laien ihre jeweiligen Standpunkte in die Diskussion einbringen können und jeweils die Argumente der Konsynodalen bewusst hören. Anders als in einem Parlament geht es gerade nicht darum, andere von der eigenen Meinung zu überzeugen, sondern am Ende geschwisterlicher Beratungen zu möglichst einmütigen Entscheidungen zu kommen.

Neben den bereits angesprochenen Aufgaben können Synoden historisch gewachsene weitere Befugnisse haben. So fungiert z. B. die Generalversammlung der *Church of Scotland* auch als Gericht, in geistlichen Angelegenheiten ist sie oberste Instanz.

Große Meinungsvielfalt, Fake news und Orientierungslosigkeit angesichts existentieller Fragen charakterisieren die gesellschaftliche Wirklichkeit. Dem Öffentlichkeitsauftrag von Kirche und damit auch von Synoden kommt damit große Bedeutung zu, wenn sich das Leitungsorgan der Kirche mit aktuellen gesellschaftspolitischen oder sozialen Fragen befasst, wie z. B. der Segnung oder Trauung gleichgeschlechtlicher Paare oder dem Klimaschutz. Eine Synode behandelt ein Thema unabhängig vom Zeitgeist auf dem Hintergrund der Bekenntnisse der Kirche in ihrer Bedeutung für die Gegenwart. Wie diese jeweils von den Synoden ausgelegt werden, unterscheidet sich zum Teil erheblich, abhängig von theologischen Auslegungen in einer Kirche. Aber gleich, wie im jeweils konkreten Fall entschieden wird, jede dieser Entscheidungen soll dazu dienen, dem Auftrag der Kirche gerecht zu werden. Diese Entscheidungen in die Welt und damit in den allgemeinen Meinungsbildungsprozess zu bringen, ist angesichts der Flut von Meldungen keine kleine Herausforderung. Es überrascht daher nicht, dass die Berichterstattung über Synodentagungen in der Presse nur im zeitlichen Kontext zu den jeweiligen Tagungen, also nur ein- bzw. zweimal jährlich erfolgt.

Akzeptanz für synodale Entscheidungen

Über die kirchlichen und die sozialen Medien ist jedoch eine umfassende und vertiefte Information möglich. Grundsätzlich muss die Relevanz ihrer Entscheidungen für die »Öffentlichkeit«, zunächst die kirchliche und nachgeordnet die breite, den Synodalen bei ihren Beschlussfassungen immer bewusst sein.

Gerade die Beschlüsse, mit denen eine Synode unmittelbar in das gemeindliche Leben eingreift, sei es durch Änderung von Finanzierungsregelungen oder personelle Entscheidungen, müssen nachvollziehbar kommuniziert werden. Ein bloßer Hinweis auf die rechtliche Kompetenz und Zuständigkeit eines Gremiums reicht im 21. Jahrhundert in keinem Bereich mehr aus. Zudem können die Synodalen sich, anders als die Abgeordneten eines staatlichen Parlaments nicht auf das Mehrheitsvotum der Wähler berufen, sind sie doch fast überall nur von einem kleinen Teil der Kirchenmitglieder gewählt bzw. von wenigen berufen worden.

In der Begründung von Entscheidungen sollte daher immer deutlich werden, dass nicht die Interessen Einzelner oder auch ganzer Gruppen maßgebend sind, sondern jeder Beschluss der Kirche und ihrem Auftrag – Seelsorge, Verkündigung und den Dienst am Nächsten sicherzustellen – dienen muss. Das gilt auch oder gerade in Zeiten, in denen Kirchenmitgliedschaft nicht mehr selbstverständlich ist und auch synodale Beschlüsse kritisch hinterfragt werden. Daher sind Erläuterungen, wie die jeweils zur Verfügung stehenden Mittel eingesetzt werden, unerlässlich.

3 Tagung der Gesamtsynode der Evangelisch-reformierten Kirche im November 2023 in der Johannes a Lasco Bibliothek, der ehemaligen Großen Kirche von Emden. | *Autumn session of the synod of the Protestant Reformed Church in the Johannes a Lasco Library, the former Great Church of Emden, in November 2023.*

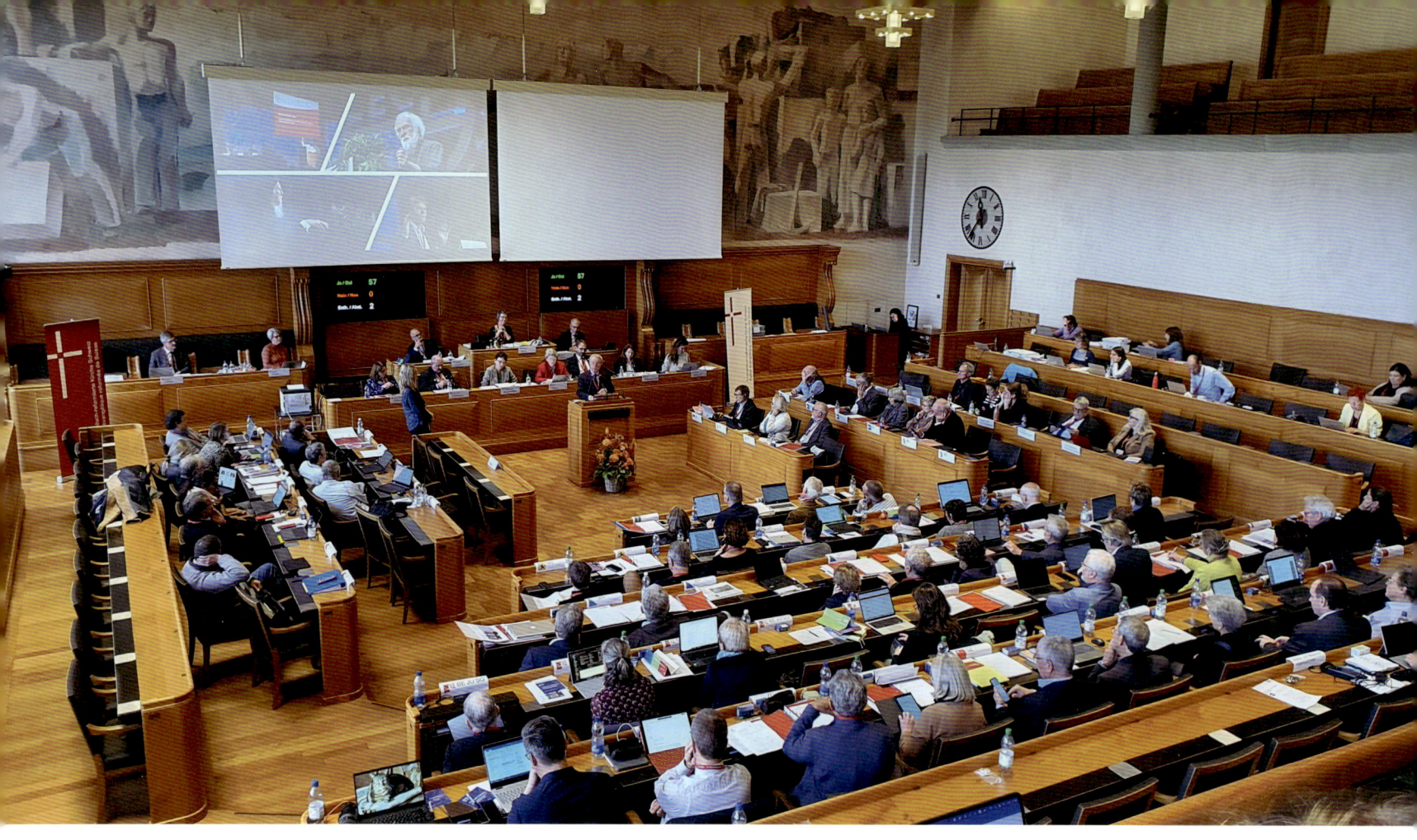

4 Die Synode der Evangelisch-reformierten Kirche Schweiz bei ihrer Sitzung im Grossratssaal im Rathaus Bern im November 2023. | *The Synod of the Protestant Church in Switzerland at its meeting in the Grossratssaal in Bern City Hall in November 2023.*

Schluss

Evangelische Synoden bringen zum Ausdruck, dass die Leitung der Kirche nach evangelischem Verständnis der ganzen Kirche zukommt. Die gemeinsame Kirchenleitung ist ein hohes Gut und diese Aufgabe kann nicht einer einzelnen Person oder einem kleinen Gremium überlassen werden. Synodenarbeit erfordert Verantwortung, ermöglicht ebenso aber auch die mündige Mitsprache aller Beteiligten in der Kirche. Die gegenwärtigen Herausforderungen, mit denen Synoden und jedes einzelne synodale Mitglied konfrontiert sind, sind vielfältig und sie sind im besten Sinne herausfordernd. Aber im Miteinander mit den übrigen Haupt- und Ehrenamtlichen in den verschiedenen Organen und der Verwaltung und im Vertrauen auf den Heiligen Geist können diese Herausforderungen bestanden werden.

---

1 Wolfgang Huber, Synode und Konziliarität. Überlegungen zur Theologie der Synode, in: Gerhard Rau/Hans-Richard Reuter/Klaus Schlaich (Hgg.), Das Recht der Kirche Bd. III: Zur Praxis des Kirchenrechts, Gütersloh 1994, 319–348, 335.

2 Verfassung der Evangelisch-Lutherischen Landeskirche Sachsens, 1950, §20 Abs. 1.

Sabine Blütchen

Challenges to Protestant Synods

Nowadays, in the early 21st century and a good 500 years after the Reformation, there is no further need to justify the role of synods as governing bodies of Protestant churches. Theological and dogmatic discussions about their raison d'être are long over. Today the synods face other challenges.

›Synod‹ literally means ›travelling together‹. In most churches the synod has consisted of both clergy and lay people for a long time now. Synods in many churches convene once or twice a year to accomplish their mission. Wolfgang Huber, the former bishop of the Evangelical Church of Berlin-Brandenburg-Silesian Upper Lusatia and Chair of the Council of the *Evangelische Kirche in Deutschland* (Protestant Church in Germany – EKD), describes its task as »sharing in church governance, responsibility for witness, mission towards the public«.[1]

The above paragraph already resonates with substantial present-day challenges for our synods. The composition of this ›travelling community‹, the election and/or appointment procedure and its impact on decision-making – all this is important for the work of the respective synod. Furthermore, each of the three tasks Huber names entails its own challenges. First, the cooperation between a synod, the other governing bodies and the church administration are very relevant to its work. And the other two areas of synodal activity, which Huber calls »responsibility for witness« and »mission towards the public«, are of particular significance in the 21st century.

Composition of synods

Synods as governing bodies of Protestant churches connect the preaching ministry and the congregation, that is to say, ordained ministers and lay people, who together exercise spiritual and legal leadership.

The size of synods and exact composition of their members differs greatly according to the respective churches. For example, the synod of the Evangelical Lutheran Church of Saxony has 80 members, in the Church of Scotland it is 500, the Reformed Church of Hungary 100, the Waldensian Evangelical Church 180 and the Presbyterian Church in Ireland 1300.

In many churches, the non-ordained persons must be members of the local parochial council, while in others they have to be members of the congregation whom the council selects. Usually there are coopted members as well.

Those eligible to become members of synod are always described in detail in the rules. A particular example of this is the Synod of the Union of the Waldensian and Methodist Churches in Italy, which has seen shared administration since 1975. Its procedural order contains ten sections on the seating arrangements. It takes account of the special circumstances of the churches in order to guarantee a balanced representation of congregations of varying size. Further seats go to members of the Faculty of Theology and there are also a number of places for advisers.

The President of Synod is elected for one year. Since the Waldensian Church of Rio de la Plata forms a union with the Italian Waldensians, this gives rise to additional challenges in relation to the specific tasks.

The General Assembly of the Church of Scotland is made up of ›commissioners‹ appointed annually, who are ministers, deacons and elders, who do not need to be members of the presbytery (district executive body). In addition, there are youth representatives who have the right to speak but not to vote. The same applies to guests from partner churches. The Moderator of the Assembly, like the Waldensian President of Synod, is elected for only one year.

The members of the General Assembly of the Presbyterian Church in Ireland comprise all the clergy, including those in retirement, as well as one elder from every congregation. The Moderator is elected annually.

The Synod of the Evangelical Lutheran Church of Saxony has 60 elected members, elected in 20 constituencies. Eligible for election are members of local parish councils and the clergy. Each constituency sends three members to synod, including one pastor. 20 members of synod are appointed by the church board and should include superintendents, two youth representatives and one representative of the Faculty of Theology. The President of Synod is elected for the entire six-year term.

Multifarious strain of synod work

Considering that the willingness to serve in an honorary capacity has clearly declined in past years – not only in Protestant churches, but also generally in trade unions, associations and political parties – it is easy to see how difficult it can be to fill the positions on such important bodies, particularly if, as sometimes happens, the number of places is very high. Yet people frequently give a number of reasons why they do not stand for a synodal office.

Clergy say they are under increasing strain through the constantly rising demands made on their ministry. Besides pastoral care and preaching – often in more than one church district – they have to perform a large number of administrative tasks that no one can do for them when they attend a synod for several days. It is also often difficult to organise substitutes for occasional offices that crop up during a synod, e.g. holding funerals.

In many churches the lay people or non-church employees make up the majority of members of synod, and some regulations call them (governing) elders. If, according to the rules, they are elders in their congregations they already have at least one honorary office. Synod membership is yet another one. As a consequence, preparing for synodal sessions, and attending them and additional committee meetings are extremely time-consuming.

If the members may be elected to synod from the midst of the parish they frequently lack knowledge of the structure and distribution of tasks in the church. These members of synod find it hard to get a foothold in the body since they also lack a network from which to obtain necessary information. It makes sense and is very rewarding to appreciate them as new members of synod with a fresh view of things, and to facilitate their start, e.g. by mentoring or additional briefings.

All ›genuine‹ lay people are deterred by the idea that they will be incompetent to deal with the plethora of topics at a synod, which are frequently legal or management-oriented rather than related to theological questions. They often underestimate the fact that sheer common sense and their own life experience as Christians in the congregation can be important arguments precisely by contrast with pure expertise.

›Lay people‹ in the literal sense of the synod orders means everyone apart from clergy or ordained staff. However, the number of church employees sitting on the benches for lay people is steadily growing in all synods. They are church musicians, deacons, teachers of religious education and administrative staff. These members of synod naturally have access to a great deal of additional information, or resources going beyond the material available to all, which may intimidate or influence inexperienced members of synod.

The fact that ›lay staff‹ may be tempted to stand up for professional interests is understandable, but can counteract the mission of a synod to represent the interest of the whole church. Many synod orders have not yet included rules to exclude not only clergy from votes about their own pay but also representatives of other professional groups.

Lay people are supposed to reflect, as far as possible, the whole of Christ's church in its diversity. That generally only happens in a fragmentary way. Men and women are represented in all synods, even if not yet on a parity basis. Certain professional groups are underrepresented everywhere, e.g. tradespersons or self-employed

5 Das Präsidium der Synode der Evangelischen Kirche der Böhmischen Brüder bei ihrer Tagung im Saal des Multikulturellen Zentrums Fabrika in Svitavy im Jahr 2022. | *The Presidium of the Synod of the Evangelical Church of Czech Brethren at its meeting in the hall of the Multicultural Centre Fabrika in Svitavy in 2022.*

individuals. People caring for children or older relatives can mostly not be won over to stand for synodal office, either. The length – several days – and the frequently long synodal term lasting up to six years are serious grounds for not doing so.

Not every order provides for the participation of young people, far from it, and if they do, it is frequently still without the right to vote. Ethnic minorities of a church have the right to a seat in synod in individual cases, e.g. the Sorbs in Saxony.[2] It is basically beyond dispute that persons with impairments can become members of synod. The practical implementation often confronts these members and also the organisers with additional challenges, because not all venues are accessible and e.g. guaranteeing days of presence of several sign interpreters is complicated and cost-intensive. But precisely the perspective of people who have to live with special challenges and who still are easily overlooked is extremely enriching for the discussions.

Apart from the elected representatives, a synod has other coopted or seconded members. They are frequently representatives of theological faculties, large institutions, diaconal ministries or public bodies. Their expertise and view from outside is important and can be enriching for a synod.

Presiding at synod and taking decisions

Synodal discussions are chaired by a president or a moderator. Reports and proposals for upcoming decisions as well as draft laws are prepared by committees or councils. Each synodal order has exact regulations for possible amendments and subsequent voting procedures. Precisely the motion procedure makes sure not only that different opinions can be raised in the discussion but also that the body takes a clear position. Whether a motion is ultimately supported by a majority will certainly depend on the quality of the arguments, but occasionally also on what mechanisms are still usual for forming opinion. Here members of synod who are church employees can often fall back on their own network.

In some churches it is usual to have synodal group(ing)s that may be firmly integrated into the running of the session. For example, there are synods that regularly interrupt the plenary if the groups first want to confer

6 Synode der Union der Evangelischen Kirchen von Elsass und Lothringen in Oberbronn (Frankreich) im Juli 2022. | *Assembly of the Union of Protestant Churches of Alsace and Lorraine in Oberbronn (France) in July 2022.*

or vote on a topic. Bilateral talks are also usual outside the plenary in order to weigh up the respective interests regarding individual agenda items or electoral proposals and, as appropriate, decide on mutual support.

The allocation of members to the groups is voluntary. Precisely for inexperienced members of a synod, the sharing of views in the group may be a good opportunity to obtain supplementary information. If the members feel bound to the decisions of the group, the discussion in plenary may be considerably shortened. On the other hand, aspects of a topic discussed in a group that do not gain a majority often remain unheard in the plenary.

In many synods such group(ing)s are most unusual. They attach great importance to the principle that individual members are autonomous. The way majorities form depends on the case, which can then lead to surprising results.

In particular, amendments that have not already been discussed in committees but only in the plenary can, if supported by strong opinion leaders, give decisions a completely new twist.

The presiding officer will endeavour to ensure, as far as possible, that all the pros and cons of the issue are raised and that the main speakers for and against are not the only ones to present their views. Occasionally the lay members will need to be explicitly encouraged to speak if the clergy are the most frequent to take the floor, and are often very eloquent advocates of a certain outcome. The aim of synodal decision-making is not to push through particular interests but to achieve a voting result that is as close to a consensus as possible. Precisely if, as indicated above, completely new aspects are introduced by means of amendments, this can considerably prolong the length of the discussion until a sufficiently large majority is achieved. Unlike in a state parliament, a synod is not about pushing through specific interests, regardless of whether this is by a professional group or a congregation, but about governing the church in the service of the Lord. Despite all efforts, it is still not always possible to take consensual, let alone unanimous decisions.

Cooperation between the synod, church executive board and church administration

Since a synod convenes only once or twice a year, the implementation of its decisions, and perhaps of further decisions that have come up meanwhile, lies in the hands of the church board and administration.

As the highest church body, a synod can check on, and also correct, all the instructions given or action taken by its officers – that is the legal, theoretical principle. In practice, the cooperation between synod, the church board and the administration is often difficult. The church administration, in particular, occasionally has difficulty in accepting decisions of a synod that would lead to considerable changes in the usual procedures or competences.

On the other hand, government requirements, for example laws relating to construction and cultural heritage, or tax regulations, may mean that church law has to be adapted. The assembled theological, legal and administrative competence that has grown up in the administration and on the full-time executive board is indispensable for church governance. Without the competent support of professionals in matters of administration and church leadership, it will be very hard for a synod to meet the demands made on such a large institution nowadays. The challenges therefore mainly consist in communication between the governing bodies and their committees. The better that succeeds and trust can be built, the better all actors can do their job of church leadership and thereby exercise their ministry for the church.

7 Um einen möglichst großen Konsens herbeizuführen, wird bei der Vereinigten Reformierten Kirche in Großbritannien die Versammlung gebeten, durch Stimmkarten anzuzeigen, ob sie mit dem zur Entscheidung stehenden Vorschlag »warm« (orange) oder »kalt« (blau) ist. Wenn nur noch eine kleine Zahl von Teilnehmenden die blaue Karte zeigt, werden diese einzeln gebeten, ihre Einwände vorzutragen. | *In order to obtain as much consensus as possible, the United Reformed Church asks the assembly to use voting cards to indicate whether they are »warm« (orange) or »cold« (blue) to the proposal being voted on. If only a small number of delegates still show the blue card, they are asked to present their objections individually.*

Decision-making in times of declining resources

The tasks of a synod are manifold. When passing church legislation including responsibility for adopting the budget, a synod makes important policy decisions. Nowadays, in view of a clear decline in staff and – almost everywhere – in financial resources, too, this is causing massive cuts in almost all areas of church life. In order to be able to justify them, Synod relies on competent preliminary work from the administration with exact data and analyses. This calls for intensive consultations, and frequently a participation process of more levels or bodies is necessary in order to achieve understanding for the cuts. Both the falling numbers of theology students and the drop in membership of some churches are cause to rethink existing parish models. And in the context of these decision-making processes, which are apparently purely about policy and structure, the theological questions directly related to them must not be neglected.

Synods as mirrors of societal reality

Besides the topics deeply concerning their own churches, synods deal with the questions raised in society as a whole, and on which it is important to reach a substantiated Protestant position. That applies, for example to the topic of mitigating climate change, which is frequently dealt with from primarily market-economy perspectives. It is important to broaden horizons and recall our mission as human beings to care for creation.

In most churches, the issue of whether to conduct blessings or weddings of same-sex couples is leading – or has already led – to deep-seated theological debates. Further, the recent argument about peace ethics that has – sadly – flared up again challenges every synod, but it will have to confront it. With these topics, in particular, it proves especially beneficial when youth representatives and more seasoned members, pastors and lay people, can feed their respective standpoints into the discussion and listen attentively to the arguments of their fellow members. Unlike in a parliament it is not about convincing others of personal opinions but of coming up with as whole-hearted a consensus as possible, after friendly debates.

Apart from the duties mentioned above, synods can have historical powers that have grown up over time. For instance, the General Assembly of the Church of Scotland also functions as a court and in spiritual matters it is the highest authority.

Characteristic of social reality are a great diversity of opinion, fake news and a lack of orientation regarding vital issues. The public mission of the church and therefore also of synods has great importance when the governing body of the church takes up current social-welfare concerns, for instance whether to conduct blessings or marriages for same-sex couples, or matters affecting the whole of society, such as appropriate action against climate change. A synod deals with a topic independently of the Zeitgeist against the backdrop of church confessions and their significance for the present. How these issues are interpreted by the different synods will differ sometimes considerably, depending on a church's theological approach. But regardless of how the decision turns out in the respective case, each of these decisions is intended to do justice to the mission of the church. Making these decisions known and thereby feeding them into the general process of opinion formation is no small challenge in view of the flood of news. It is therefore no surprise that the press only reports on synods when they are in session, in other words, once or twice a year.

Acceptance of synodal decisions

It is, however, possible to obtain comprehensive, in-depth information via church and social media. Members of synod should always be fundamentally aware of the relevance of their decisions for the ›public‹, first the church public and then the public at large.

Precisely the decisions directly affecting congregational life – through a change in financial rules or staffing decisions — must be communicated in an understandable way. Merely referring to the legal competence and responsibility of a body is not sufficient in any area in the 21st century. Furthermore, the members of synod, unlike members of parliament, cannot appeal to a majority vote by the electorate since they have, almost everywhere, been elected by only a small share of church members or appointed by an even smaller group.

8 Mehrheitsentscheidungen werden in der Vereinigten Reformierten Kirche in Großbritannien wie in anderen Kirchen auch durch klassische Stimmkarten herbeigeführt. | *Majority decisions in the United Reformed Church, as in other churches, are made using traditional voting cards.*

9 In der Vereinigten Reformierten Kirche in Großbritannien werden die Delegierten während den Verhandlungen regelmäßig gebeten, in Kleingruppen einzelne Aspekte des Themas zu diskutieren. | *In the United Reformed Church, delegates are regularly asked to discuss individual aspects of the topic under discussion in small groups.*

Hence when justifying decisions, it should always be clear what counts is not the interest of individuals or even of whole groups; rather, every decision must benefit the church and safeguard its mission of pastoral care, proclamation and serving the neighbour. That applies also, indeed particularly, in times in which church membership is no longer the norm, and synodal decisions are likewise the subject of critical questioning. Consequently it is essential to explain how the available funds are used.

Conclusion

Protestant synods express the fact that, in the Protestant understanding, guiding the church is a matter for the whole church. The joint church leadership is a precious good and cannot be left to an individual or a small body. The work of synod calls for responsibility, but also enables all church stakeholders to have their say in a mature way. The current issues confronting synods and every individual member of synod are diverse, and are challenges in the best sense of the word. But these challenges can be overcome – in cooperation with the other staff or volunteers in the different governing bodies and in the administration, and trusting in the Holy Spirit.

---

1 Wolfgang Huber, Synode und Konziliarität. Überlegungen zur Theologie der Synode, in: Gerhard Rau/Hans-Richard Reuter/Klaus Schlaich (eds), Das Recht der Kirche Bd. III: Zur Praxis des Kirchenrechts (Gütersloh: 1994), 319–348, 335.

2 Constitution of the Evangelical Lutheran Church of Saxony, 1950, §20(1).

Italien
Italy
Italia

1689 1939
NOI GIVRIAMO E PROMETTIAMO AL COSPETTO
DELL'IDDIO VIVENTE DI MANTENERE TRA NOI
L'VNIONE E L'ORDINE... GIVRIAMO FEDELTÀ FINO
ALL'VLTIMA GOCCIA DEL NOSTRO SANGVE

SII FEDELE FINO ALLA MORTE...

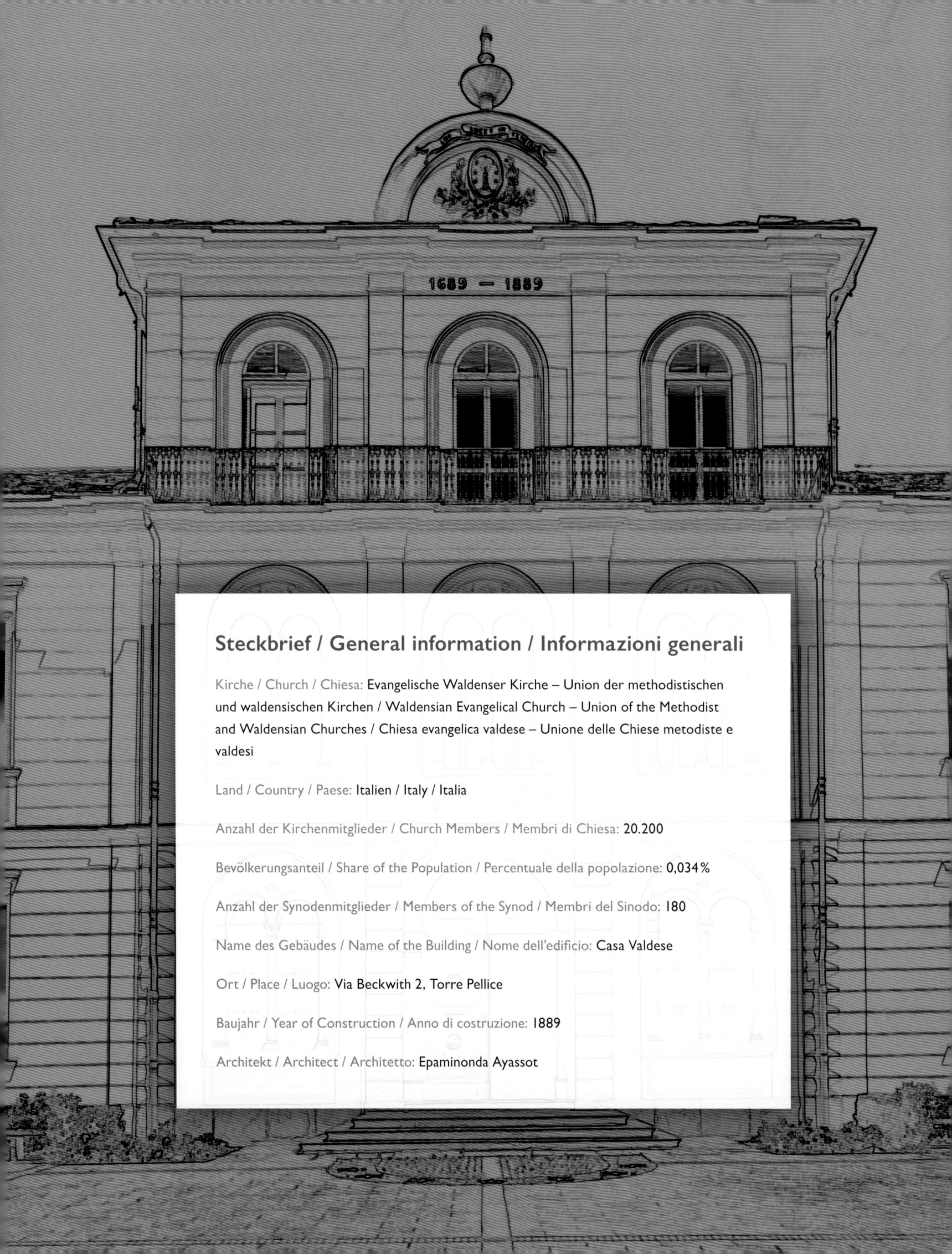

Steckbrief / General information / Informazioni generali

Kirche / Church / Chiesa: **Evangelische Waldenser Kirche – Union der methodistischen und waldensischen Kirchen / Waldensian Evangelical Church – Union of the Methodist and Waldensian Churches / Chiesa evangelica valdese – Unione delle Chiese metodiste e valdesi**

Land / Country / Paese: **Italien / Italy / Italia**

Anzahl der Kirchenmitglieder / Church Members / Membri di Chiesa: **20.200**

Bevölkerungsanteil / Share of the Population / Percentuale della popolazione: **0,034 %**

Anzahl der Synodenmitglieder / Members of the Synod / Membri del Sinodo: **180**

Name des Gebäudes / Name of the Building / Nome dell'edificio: **Casa Valdese**

Ort / Place / Luogo: **Via Beckwith 2, Torre Pellice**

Baujahr / Year of Construction / Anno di costruzione: **1889**

Architekt / Architect / Architetto: **Epaminonda Ayassot**

Gabriella Ballesio · Simone Baral

Der Synodensaal der Evangelischen Waldenserkirche

Die jährliche Synode der Evangelischen Waldenser- und Methodistenkirche in Italien findet in Torre Pellice in einem 1889 erbauten Saal in der *Casa Valdese* (Waldenserhaus) statt (Abb. 1). Die *Casa Valdese* wurde vom Architekten Epaminonda Ayassot (1866–1941) entworfen. Im Unterschied zum Gebäude, dessen Geschichte und Charakteristika im Laufe der Jahrzehnte Gegenstand diverser Forschungen und Darstellungen[1] waren, wurde dem Synodensaal bisher kein besonderes Interesse entgegengebracht und der vorliegende Text ist das Ergebnis unveröffentlichter Recherchen, die auf schriftlichen Dokumenten und mündlichen Überlieferungen beruhen.

Ein Zuhause für die Synode und die »Waldenserfamilie«

Der Synodensaal war Teil eines großangelegten architektonischen Projekts, das auch eine Bibliothek, ein Archiv, ein Museum, Büros und einen Sitzungssaal für die *Tavola Valdese*, also die Kirchenleitung, umfassen sollte. Die Idee eines »Hauses«, das nicht nur ein Verwaltungsgebäude, sondern ein »sichtbares Zeichen der Einheit der Waldenserfamilie«[2] sein sollte, entstand auf der Synode von 1880[3]. Dies war zumindest teilweise eine Reaktion auf die von der *Tavola Valdese* getroffene Entscheidung, das Obergeschoss einer 1879 fertiggestellten Turnhalle des *Collegio Valdese*, das 1836 errichtete Jungengymnasium, als Synodensaal zu nutzen. Dieser Entschluss war ohne Rücksprache mit der Synodenversammlung getroffen worden. Die mangelnde Stabilität des Fußbodens und die großen Fenster, die zu viel Licht und Wärme hereinließen, überzeugten schließlich die Delegierten von der Notwendigkeit, einen geeigneteren und festen Sitz für die für das kirchliche Leben so wichtige Institution zu errichten.

Was den Standort des Synodensaals in Torre Pellice betrifft, so ist erwähnenswert, dass die Synode sich bis zur Mitte des 19. Jahrhunderts abwechselnd in verschiedenen Kirchengebäuden in den drei Tälern, in denen es Waldensergemeinden gab, versammelte. Die letzte Synode außerhalb des Pellice-Tals fand im Jahr 1860 statt. Seit 1866 bis heute ist Torre Pellice ständiger Sitz der Synode. Diese kam zunächst in der alten Kirche im Stadtviertel Coppieri zusammen, und von 1867 bis 1879 sowie von 1881 bis 1888 im *Temple Neuf*, dem 1852 im Stadtzentrum erbauten neuen Gotteshaus. Obwohl einige den Ort der Synode lieber in Turin oder Florenz gesehen hätten, um zu zeigen, dass die Waldenserkirche nun eine landesweite Kirche sei, war Torre Pellice seit Jahrzehnten als faktische »Hauptstadt« der Waldenser anerkannt und daher der einzig geeignete Ort für die Synodenversammlungen.

Die Entwürfe und ihre Planer

Ein erster Entwurf für die *Casa Valdese* wurde im Jahre 1883 vom Londoner Architekten und Ingenieur William Allen Boulnois (1823–1893) vorgelegt, der als ausländischer Gast im Namen der *Presbyterian Church of England* an der Synode von 1880 teilgenommen hatte. Das Projekt, dessen Pläne noch erhalten sind, sah zwei unterschiedliche Hauptgebäude vor, die durch einen überdachten Durchgang miteinander verbunden waren: In einem der beiden Flügel sollten sich die Sitzungsräume des Verwaltungsapparats, das Archiv und die Bibliothek befinden, im anderen ein achteckiger Synodensaal (Abb. 2).

Der Entwurf des achteckig geplanten Synodensaals scheint von der *Round Church* (Abb. 3) in Cambridge inspiriert gewesen zu sein, die aus dem 12. Jahrhundert stammt und damit aus der Zeit des Petrus Valdes von Lyon, jener historischen Persönlichkeit, auf die Ursprung und Name der piemontesischen reformierten Waldenserkirchen zurückgehen. Die *Round Church* war Boulnois, der in der Universitätsstadt Cambridge studiert hatte, vertraut. Zugleich scheinen seine Pläne auf einige bei der Synode von 1879 geäußerten Wünsche einzugehen, dass zusätzlich zum Synodensaal auch eine Bibliothek, ein Museum und ein Archiv gebaut werden sollten. Dies war ein Jahr vor Beginn des Bauvorhabens. Geplant war »ein Gebäude im gotischen Stil, der für die lange Tradition und Stabilität unserer Kirche steht und eine Garantie für ihre Zukunft ist. Es umfasst ein Geschoß, das groß genug für mindestens 500 Personen ist und dennoch über eine gute Akustik und Anordnung der Plätze verfügt, damit es weder Redner noch Zuhörer ermüdet; […] ein Gebäude, an das ein Saal für die Versammlungen der Pfarrerschaft und ein anderer für die der Synodalausschüsse angeschlossen ist«[4] (Abb. 4).

Das Projekt von Boulnois wurde allerdings wegen der exorbitanten Kosten aufgegeben, welche die finanziellen Möglichkeiten der Kirche gesprengt hätten. Die *Tavola Valdese* griff stattdessen auf einen Fachmann vor Ort zurück, den jungen Architekten Ayassot, der bereits für andere öffentliche sowie private Gebäude im Pellice-Tal verantwortlich gezeichnet hatte (Abb. 5).

Damit entschied man sich für einen finanziell und architektonisch weniger ehrgeizigen Bau, der stärker dem

1 Die Casa Valdese zum Zeitpunkt ihrer Einweihung im Jahre 1889. | *The Casa Valdese at the time of its inauguration in 1889.* | *La Casa Valdese al momento della sua inaugurazione nel 1889.*

lokalen Baustil entsprach. Von Ayassot liegen zwei unterschiedliche Projektentwürfe vor, von denen einer die Idee von Boulnois aufgriff, das Gebäude in zwei unterschiedliche Bereiche zu unterteilen und so den Synodensaal räumlich von den für andere Tätigkeiten vorgesehenen Räumen abzugrenzen. Der zweite Entwurf, welcher eine Gebäudestruktur skizzierte, die der später realisierten ähnelte, beschrieb demgegenüber ein einziges Gebäude, das so homogen gestaltet war, dass es nicht möglich war, die Innenräume von außen voneinander zu unterscheiden (Abb. 6). Letzteres sollte dem Gedanken von der Einheit von Kirche und Volk, von Geschichte und Glauben entsprechen, wie er in den Synodendebatten geäußert worden war.

Für den Neubau wurde ein Grundstück gegenüber dem *Collegio Valdese* bzw. neben dem Pfarrhaus und der Kirche von Torre Pellice ausgewählt, was als ein weiterer Baustein zur Errichtung des sogenannten »Waldenserviertels« beitrug, welches zu Beginn des 20. Jahrhunderts mit der Eröffnung des CVJM-Hauses und des Jungeninternats seine Vollendung fand (Abb. 7).

Sobald die Finanzierung des Vorhabens durch Kollekten und private Spenden sichergestellt war, wurden am 25. Juli 1888 in einem feierlichen Festakt zwei Grundsteine gelegt. Am 2. September 1889 schließlich wurde die *Casa Valdese* eingeweiht. Noch im selben Jahr fanden darin die Synode sowie die Feierlichkeiten zum 200. Jahrestag des 1689 erfolgten *Glorioso Rimpatrio* – der »glorreichen Rückkehr« der Waldenser ins Piemont nach ihrem Schweizer Zwangsexil – statt.

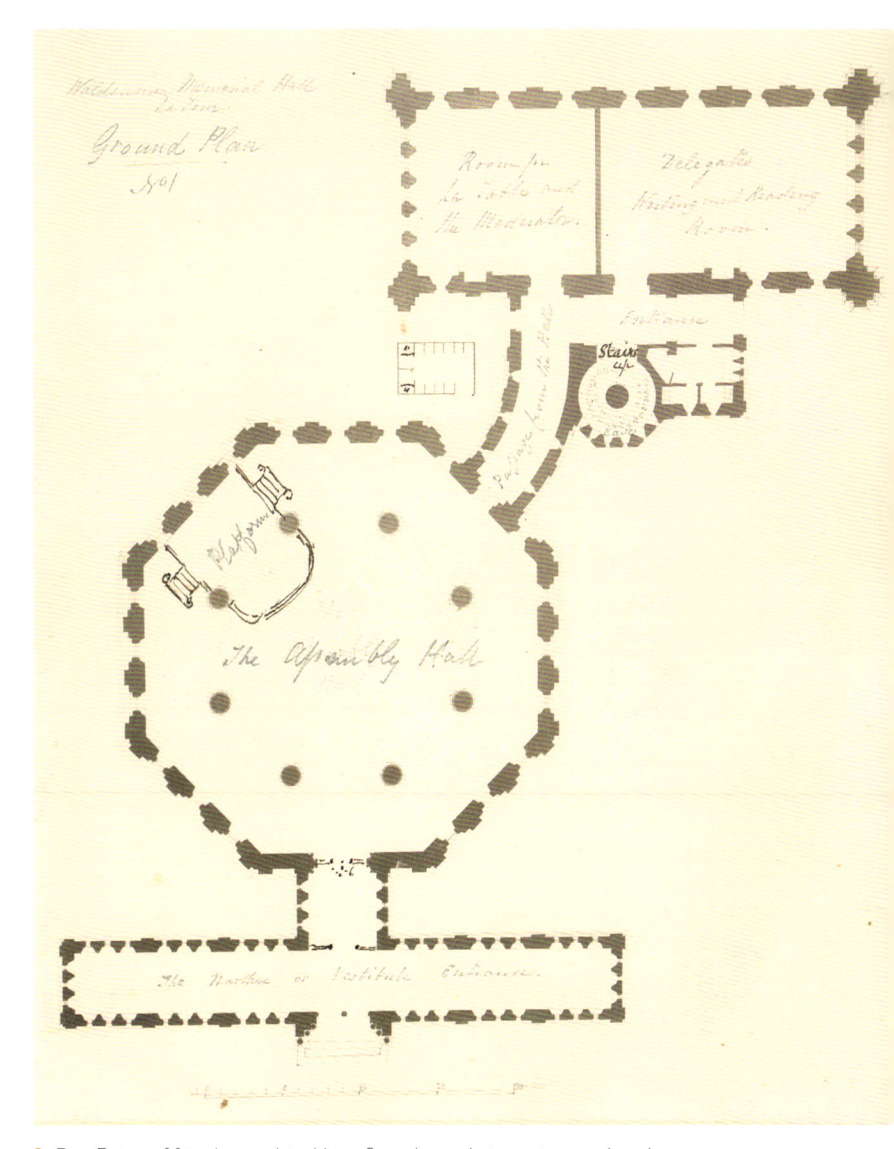

2 Der Entwurf für einen achteckigen Synodensaal stammte vom Londoner Architekten William Allen Boulnois. | *London architect William Allen Boulnois designed the octagonal synod hall.* | *Il progetto dell'aula sinodale ottagonale è dell'architetto londinese William Allen Boulnois.*

Architektur und Ausgestaltung

Vergleicht man Ayassots Entwürfe, historische Fotos und die heutige Ausführung der *Casa Valdese* wird ersichtlich, dass das Projekt in seiner äußeren Gestalt fast vollständig wie geplant realisiert wurde, abgesehen von einigen Details wie der Anzahl und Form einiger Fenster, der Lage der Balkone und dem Dach des mittleren Gebäudeteiles. Was den Innenraum des Synodensaals betrifft, zeigt ein Vergleich der Entwürfe, dass der Architekt bei beiden Projekten einen rechteckigen Raum dafür vorsah, inklusive einer Apsis auf der dem Eingang gegenüberliegenden Schmalseite und einer hufeisenförmigen Empore (Abb. 8). Die größten Unterschiede finden sich bei der Aufteilung der Räumlichkeiten für die Verwaltung und andere Aufgaben.

Den wenigen in Text- oder Bildform vorliegenden Beschreibungen des Saales in seiner ursprünglichen Gestalt entnehmen wir, dass sich in der Apsis ein Porträtfoto und eine Büste von Umberto I., dem König von Italien zur Zeit der Einweihung der *Casa Valdese*, befand (Abb. 9). Er war übrigens der einzige italienische Monarch, der jemals den Synodensaal besuchte. Dies geschah im Jahr 1893.[5] Wir wissen, dass diese Huldigungssymbole an die Monarchie mindestens bis Mitte der 1920er Jahre zu sehen waren.

3 Die *Round Church* in Cambridge diente wahrscheinlich als Inspiration für den nie realisierten Entwurf eines achteckigen Synodensaals. | *The Round Church in Cambridge probably served as inspiration for the design of an octagonal Synod Hall, which was never realised.* | *La Round Church di Cambridge probabilmente servì da ispirazione per il progetto di un'aula sinodale di forma ottagonale mai realizzato.*

Was die Ausschmückung des Saals betrifft, so wurden die ursprünglich die Innenwände zierenden Blumenmotive und die *trompe l'oeil* in *grisailles* im Jahr 1939 durch eine einheitliche Farbe (dunkler als das heutige Pastellgelb) ersetzt. Dadurch wurde das allegorische Gemälde in der Apsis optisch hervorgehoben. Es stammt von dem waldensischen Künstler Paolo Antonio Paschetto (1885–1963), der später für den Entwurf des Wappens der Republik Italien berühmt wurde. Das Gemälde stellt eine große Eiche, deren Wurzeln im Felsen verankert sind, vor dem Hintergrund einer Berglandschaft dar; die Zweige des Baumes tragen eine aufgeschlagene Bibel mit einem Zitat aus Offenbarung 2,8–11: »Sei treu bis an den Tod.« (Abb. 10). Darunter wird ein Auszug aus dem Treueschwur zitiert, den die waldensischen Soldaten und Kommandeure in Sibaud (Bobbio Pellice) einander bei ihrer Rückkehr aus dem Exil leisteten: »Wir schwören und geloben vor dem lebendigen Gott, untereinander Einheit und Ordnung zu bewahren. Wir schwören Treue bis zum letzten Tropfen unseres Blutes.« Dieses Zitat wird von den Jahreszahlen 1689 und 1939 flankiert.

Die Auswahl der Zitate sowie einige Bildelemente – die abgeschnittenen Zweige und die in sich geschlossene Eichenkrone – sind nur im historischen Kontext der Entstehungszeit zu verstehen. Dies waren ohne Frage die Feierlichkeiten zum 250. Jahrestag der Glorreichen Rückkehr, vor allem aber auch die tiefgreifenden sozialen, politischen und kulturellen Probleme kurz vor Ausbruch des Zweiten Weltkriegs. Wie Giorgio Rochat betont, bringt Paschettos künstlerische Gestaltung in diesem Zusammenhang »letzten Endes das Bild einer bedrängten und isolierten Kirche zum Ausdruck, die nach außen hin abgeschirmt ist, ein Bewusstsein für die eigene Stärke hat und dazu entschlossen ist, mit ihrer vielgerühmten Geschlossenheit und Tradition im Rücken, Widerstand zu leisten«[6]. An den Seitenwänden über der Empore vervollständigen zwei Inschriften in Großbuchstaben die Ausgestaltung des Saals: ein Bibelvers (»Schaut den Fels an, aus dem ihr gehauen seid«, Jesaja 51,1) sowie ein Zitat aus den »Militärischen Anweisungen« Giosué Gianavellos, eines nach Genf verbannten Waldenserveteranen und Vordenkers der Glorreichen Rückkehr: »Nichts sei stärker als euer Glaube.« Beim Eingang über der Empore prangt eines der fünf Sola: »Gott allein sei die Ehre«.

Das Mobiliar und seine Anordnung

Ein großer Teil des ursprünglichen Mobiliars aus rotem Lärchenholz wurde 1974 umgestaltet und in jüngerer Vergangenheit restauriert. Die Anzahl der Sitzplätze wurde reduziert, die Anordnung gleichförmiger Bänke in Reihen entlang dreier Seiten des Saals für die Delegierten und auf der Empore für die Öffentlichkeit hingegen wurde beibehalten. Die leicht erhöhte Apsis war für das Präsidium der Synode sowie für die scheidende *Tavola Valdese* vorgesehen (Abb. 11).

Es wurden keine schriftlichen Dokumente gefunden, die Aufschluss darüber geben, ob die Kirche oder ihre Verwaltungsorgane dem Architekten klare Anweisungen für die Innenausstattung gaben. Es lässt sich aber feststellen, dass bei der Innengestaltung auf die überarbeitete Waldensische Kirchenordnung aus dem zweiten Viertel des 19. Jahrhunderts eingegangen wurde. Als Beispiel sei die Synode von 1848 erwähnt. Sie war nach der Erlangung bürgerlicher und politischer Freiheiten für die waldensische Bevölkerung im Königreich Sardinien die erste, die der jahrhundertealten Tradition ein Ende bereitete, wonach die *Tavola Valdese* unter der Leitung des Moderators auch in der Synode den Vorsitz innehatte. Von der darauffolgenden Synode (1851) an wurde die Eröffnung jeweils dem Dekan der Pastoren anvertraut, woraufhin dann ein

4 Bei diesem Entwurf war ein achteckiger Synodensaal geplant, im hinteren Trakt Bibliothek und Archiv. | *The synod hall was planned to be in the octagonal hall, with the library and archives in the rear wing.* | *La sala sinodale era prevista nella sala ottagonale, con la biblioteca e gli archivi nell'ala posteriore*

5 Der Architekt Epaminonda Ayassot (Zweiter von rechts) plante das realisierte Gebäude der *Casa Valdese*. | *Architect Epaminonda Ayassot (second from the right) planned the building that was finally constructed.* | *Il geometra Epaminonda Ayassot (secondo a destra) progettò l'edificio che fu infine realizzato.*

Präsidium zur Leitung der Versammlung ernannt wurde. In der Apsis befindet sich deshalb an zentraler Stelle der Platz für das Präsidium mit Sitz und Pult des Präsidenten samt dem für den Sekretär (Abb. 12, 13, 14).

Seitlich befinden sich an die Wand der Apsis angepasste halbrunde Bänke, auf denen die scheidende *Tavola Valdese* Platz nimmt, deren Vorrechte für die Dauer der Synode außer Kraft gesetzt sind, die aber, gewissermaßen vor der Versammlung sitzend, für ihre jährliche Arbeit Rechenschaft abzulegen hat (Abb. 15).

Was die anderen Bankreihen anbelangt, so gibt es zwischen ihnen keine Rangordnung; ebenso wenig gibt es Regeln oder Gebräuche, die den Delegierten eine strikte Sitzordnung vorschreiben. Die einzige Ausnahme bilden die der Apsis am nächsten gelegenen Bänke: Auf der Bank links vom Vorsitz sitzt die Prüfungskommission, ein Gremium, das 1833 zu dem Zweck gegründet wurde, die inhaltliche und wirtschaftliche Tätigkeit der *Tavola Valdese* zu überprüfen. Sie legt der versammelten Synode einen Bericht vor, der eine Art »Zweitstimme« zum vom Verwaltungsapparat der Kirchenleitung selbst vorgelegten Bericht darstellt. Auf der rechten Seite hingegen sitzen die nach und nach eingesetzten Kommissionen, deren Aufgabe es ist, sich mit spezifischen Themen und Bereichen des kirchlichen Lebens zu befassen und der Synode jeweils Bericht zu erstatten. Schließlich stellt die Empore, die ausdrücklich für die Teilhabe des Publikums gebaut wurde, ein wesentliches Element des synodalen Lebens dar (Abb. 16).

In einer Chronik der Synode von 1931 heißt es: »Wie jedes Publikum, das etwas auf sich hält, schweigt es manchmal, oft schaudert es, und am Ende bricht es in Tränen aus.«[7] Außer in Fällen, in denen der Synodenvorsitz beschließt, bestimmte Themen nicht-öffentlich hinter verschlossenen Türen zu behandeln, nimmt das Publikum ganz und gar nicht passiv an der Arbeit der Synode teil, sondern beteiligt sich, indem es applaudiert, Unmut zum Ausdruck bringt, den Geschehnissen lauscht und durch die bloße Anwesenheit die *Performance* der Redner beeinflusst.

Ein »Mehrzweck«-Saal

Bis heute ist die *Casa Valdese* jedes Jahr Sitz der Synode und beherbergt einen Teil der Büros der kirchlichen Verwaltung, während die kulturellen Veranstaltungen und Einrichtungen vor einigen Jahrzehnten in die Räumlichkeiten des nahegelegenen ehemaligen Waldenser-Konvikts verlegt wurden. Eine Ausnahme bilden die Räume der alten Bibliothek, die nach wie vor als Aufbewahrungsort für einige Bestände und für gelegentliche Einzelveranstaltungen genutzt werden. Der Synodensaal selbst wird seit seiner Erbauung auch für andere Zwecke zur Verfügung gestellt. Schon zwei Tage nach der Einweihung, am Abend des 4. September 1889, fand im überfüllten Saal die achte Versammlung der *Société d'Histoire Vaudoise* (der heutigen *Società di Studi Valdesi*) statt, und wenn man alte Zeitschriften durchblättert, erfährt man, dass der Raum, ohne seinen ureigenen Charakter zu verlieren, im Laufe der Jahrzehnte nicht nur für Pfarrkonferenzen, Gottesdienste und Weihnachtsfeiern mit Christbaum genutzt, sondern auch für nichtkirchliche Veranstaltungen wie Konzerte, Konferenzen und Tagungen zur Verfügung gestellt wurde. Neue Technologien und unvorhersehbare Situationen wie etwa die Covid-19-Pandemie, die die ganze Welt getroffen hat, trugen dazu bei, den Garten rund um die *Casa Valdese* vermehrt zur Begegnung miteinzubeziehen, indem dort Zelte und Bildschirme aufgestellt werden, damit sowohl die Synodalen selbst als auch die Öffentlichkeit die Arbeit der Synode leichter verfolgen können (Abb. 17).

Raum, Synodalität, Identität

Befragt man Menschen mit langjähriger Synodenerfahrung, so stößt man auf die weit verbreitete Meinung, die räumliche Gestaltung des Saales erinnere an diejenige des Unterhauses des britischen Parlaments. Untermauert wird diese Meinung dadurch, dass die viktorianische Kirche und Gesellschaft großen Einfluss auf die Waldenserkirche des 19. Jahrhunderts hatten. Bis 1974 waren die Bänke grün gepolstert, also in der Farbe wie im Saal des Westminster-Palasts. Dann wurde die alte Lederpolsterung durch eine modernere dunkelbraune aus synthetischem Material ersetzt. Vergleicht man jedoch den waldensischen Synodensaal mit dem äußeren Erscheinungsbild anderer Synoden, die im Laufe der Jahrhunderte in Europa abgehalten wurden, wird ziemlich schnell deutlich, wie sich seine Gestaltung – insbesondere die Anordnung der Sitzplätze – in die Tradition der europäischen reformierten Kirchen einfügt. Dies wird zum Beispiel an Darstellungen der französisch-reformierten Synode von Montpellier im Jahr 1598 oder des Innenraumes des einige Jahrzehnte später für die Dordrechter Synode verwendeten *Kloveniersdoelen* erkennbar.

Gleichzeitig deutet die Existenz der Apsis darauf hin, dass sich Ayassot auch an kirchlichen, für liturgische Zwecke genutzten Gebäuden mit parallelen Reihen einander zugewandter Kirchenbänke orientiert hat, wie sie insbesondere in der anglikanischen Welt verbreitet sind (Abb. 18). Wie Gélineau und Reymond[8] unterstreichen, begünstigt dieses Modell räumlicher Aufteilung einerseits die Dimension der »Begegnung zur Feier der Verbundenheit« und demonstriert andererseits – wie aus seiner Verwendung im Bereich der Politik des Vereinigten Königreiches hervorgeht – seine Brauchbarkeit auch für Zusammenkünfte ohne liturgischen Charakter.

Mehr als 130 Jahre nach ihrer Einweihung scheinen die *Casa Valdese* und der Synodensaal auch heute sowohl innerhalb als auch außerhalb der Kirche die Orte zu sein, die die aktuelle Bedeutung der Waldensergemeinden am besten symbolhaft veranschaulichen. Während die Synode das Ereignis ist, zu dem das Gremium zusammentritt, um Entscheidungen von gesamtkirchlichem Interesse zu treffen, bildet der Saal, der die Synode beherbergt, die alljährliche Bühne für dieses Geschehen, das Menschen zusammenbringt.

6 Dieser Entwurf von Ayassot wurde schließlich mit geringen Abweichungen realisiert. | *The design was finally implemented by Ayassot with slight deviations.* | *Il progetto fu infine realizzato con piccole modifiche.*

---

1 Vgl. Paolo Paschetto (1885–1963): Torre Pellice, Società di Studi Valdesi, 1985; B. Peyrot: La memoria costruita sul »Glorioso Rimpatrio«, in: Albert de Lange (Hg.): Dall'Europa alle Valli valdesi, Torino, Claudiana, 1990, 523–546; G. Rochat: Il contesto delle celebrazioni del Rimpatrio nel 1939, in: Ebd., 573–590; Samuele Tourn Boncoeur: Musei storici, in: Daniele Jalla (Hg.): Héritage(s). Formazione e trasmissione del patrimonio culturale valdese, Torino, Claudiana, 2009, 95–98.

2 »Le Tëmoin«, a. XIV, n. 43, 26. Oktober 1888.

3 »Art. 31. Le Synode charge la future administration de faire préparer, pour le présenter au prochain Synode, le plan, avec les devis y relatifs, d'un édifice destiné à server de local pour la tenue des Synodes, les réunions de la Table, les archives de l'Église, la bibliothèque pastorale et le musée«, *Synode der Evangelischen Waldenserkirche vom 6.–10. September 1880 in Torre Pellice.*

4 *Relation de la Commission examinatrice de l'activité de la Table vaudoise au Synode de 1879,* Archiv der *Tavola Valdese.*

5 »Le Tëmoin«, a. XIX, n. 37. 14. September 1893.

6 Rochat: *Il contesto* (wie Anm. 1), 587.

7 »L'Echo des Vallées«, a. LXVII, n. 36, 11. September 1931.

8 Vgl. Bernard Reymond: *L'architecture religieuse des protestants: histoire, caractéristiques, problèmes actuels,* Genève, Labor et Fides, 1996, 153–154.

Gabriella Ballesio · Simone Baral

The Synod Hall of the Waldensian Evangelical Church

The annual synod of the Waldensian and Methodist Churches takes place in a hall built in Torre Pellice in 1889, at the same time as the building that houses it, the »Waldensian House« (*casa valdese*) (Fig. 1), designed by the surveyor Epaminonda Ayassot (1866–1941). Unlike the Waldensian House as a whole, whose history and characteristics have been the subject of research and descriptions[1] over the decades, the Synod Hall has not aroused specific interest and the present text is the result of unpublished research based on documentation and oral memory.[2]

A House for the Synod and the »Waldensian family«

The Synod Hall was part of a larger architectural project, which also included a library, archives, museum, offices and a meeting room for the Waldensian Board, the executive and representative body of the church. The idea of a »house« that was not only for the assembly but a »visible symbol of the union of the Waldensian family«[3] emerged during the Synod of 1880.[4] It was, at least in part, a response to the decision taken autonomously by the Waldensian Board without consulting the assembly, to take advantage of the construction, in 1879, of a gymnasium for the Waldensian College (a boys' high school founded in 1836) in order to build a hall for the Synod as a second storey. The precarious stability of the flooring and the large windows, which let in too much light and heat, convinced the members of the need to build a suitable and definitive venue to host the most important moment in the life of the church.

Until the mid-19th century, the assembly had been held in rotation in different churches in the three valleys where the Waldensian communities resided. The last Synod held outside the Pellice Valley had been in 1860, however, and in 1866 Torre Pellice had become the permanent seat of the assembly, first held in the old church located in the Coppieri district, then, from 1867 to 1879 and from 1881 to 1888, in the *temple neuf*, the new church built in 1852 in the town centre. Although some would have preferred to locate the synod site in Turin or Florence, to show that the Waldensian Church was now a national church, Torre Pellice had been recognised for decades as the de facto Waldensian ›capital‹ and, therefore, the only suitable place to host the synodal assemblies.

Projects and designers

An initial project for the Waldensian House was delivered in 1883 by the London architect and engineer William Allen Boulnois (1823–1893), who was present during the Synod of 1880 as a guest from the Presbyterian Church of England. The project, the plans of which are preserved, envisaged two distinct main buildings connected by a covered passageway: on the one hand, the wing dedicated to the meeting rooms of the administrative bodies, the archive and the library, on the other, the octagonal Synod Hall (Fig. 2). The latter seems to have been inspired by the Round Church in Cambridge (Fig. 3), a building contemporary with the events around Valdes of Lyon (the historical figure after whom the Piedmontese Reformed churches are named) in the 12th century. Boulnois was familiar with the Round Church, having studied in

7 Das Waldenserviertel umfasst (von links nach rechts) im Norden die Lehrerhäuser, die Kirche, das Pfarrhaus und die Casa Valdese; im Süden das Haus des Christlichen Vereins junger Menschen (CVJM), das ehemalige Schülerinternat (das heute ein Archiv, eine Bibliothek und ein Museum beherbergt) und das Gymnasium. | *The Waldensian Quarter comprises (from left to right) the teachers' houses, church, parsonage and the Casa valdese, to the north; the YMCA building, the former school dormitory (today home to the archive, library and museum) and the grammar school to the south.* | *Il quartiere valdese comprende (da sinistra verso destra) a nord, le case dei professori, il tempio, il presbiterio e la Casa valdese; a sud, la Casa dell'Associazione cristiana dei giovani, il Convitto maschile (oggi sede di archivio, biblioteca e museo) e il liceo.*

Cambridge. At the same time, the plans for the hall seem to respond to some of the requirements expressed at the Synod in 1879, a year before the project acquired a broader scope, including premises for a library, museum and archive: »a building in Gothic style, an image of the age and solidity of our Church and a pledge for its future, rising at most to the height of a ground floor, large enough to contain at least 500 people, but whose acoustics would be good and whose seating arrangement would not tire either speakers or listeners; […] a building to which would be attached a room for the meetings of pastors and another for those of the Synod committees«[5] (Fig. 4).

Boulnois's project ended up being abandoned, however, due to its exorbitant costs compared to the church's financial resources. The Waldensian Board turned to a local professional, the young surveyor Ayassot (Fig. 5), responsible for other public and private buildings in the Pellice Valley, opting for a less ambitious construction, both economically and architecturally, as it was more in line with local building styles. Two different designs by Ayassot are available, one of which took up Boulnois's idea of dividing the building into two distinct bodies, spatially distinguishing the Synod Hall from the rooms intended for other activities; the second set of drawings, with a structure similar to the one that was later realised, depicted a single, homogenous building – seen from outside, it was not possible to distinguish the internal spaces (Fig. 6). This building rendered more clearly the idea of the unity of church and people, of history and faith, that had emerged from the Synod debate. A plot of land in front of the Waldensian College and next to the manse and church of Torre Pellice was chosen for the new building, contributing a further piece to the progressive constitution of what came to be called the »Waldensian quarter«, completed at the beginning of the 20th century with the inaugurations of the YMCA building and the boys' boarding school (Fig. 7).

Having financed the work thanks to collections, donations from private individuals and public subscriptions, two cornerstones were solemnly laid on 25 July 1888, while the Waldensian House was inaugurated on 2 September 1889, hosting the Synod of that year and the

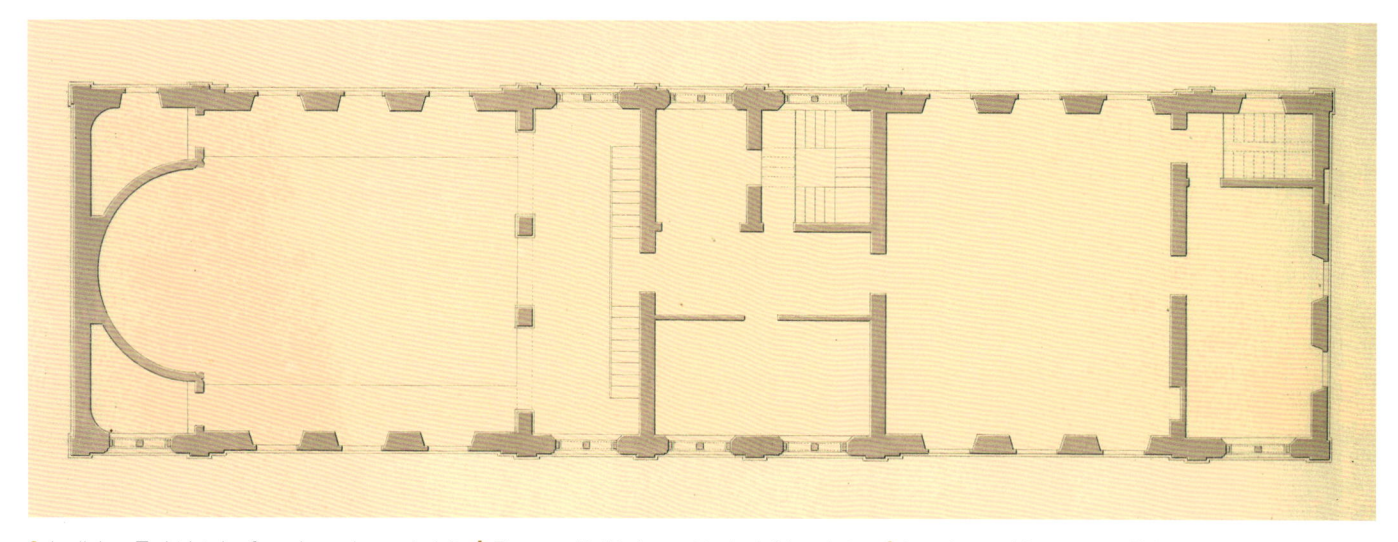

8 Im linken Trakt ist der Synodensaal angesiedelt. | *The synod hall is located in the left-hand wing.* | *La sala sinodale si trova nell'ala sinistra.*

celebrations for the Bicentenary of the *Glorious Return*, that is, of the return of the Waldensians to Piedmont in 1689 after their forced exile in Switzerland.

The architecture and decorations

By comparing Ayassot's preparatory drawings, period photographs and the current shape of the Waldensian House, we can see that the plans for the exterior were realised almost in their entirety except for a few details, such as the number and shape of some windows, the positioning of the balconies and the roof of the central portion of the building. For the interior of the Synod Hall, on the other hand, a comparison with the plans shows that the surveyor had in mind, in both projects, a rectangular hall ending, on the short side facing the entrance, with an apse, and a horseshoe-shaped gallery (Fig. 8); the most significant differences concern the organisation of the service areas and those for other activities.

Based on the rare textual and iconographic descriptions of the original hall, we know that the apse contained a photographic portrait and a bust of Umberto I, King of Italy at the time of the inauguration of the Waldensian House and the only Italian monarch to visit the Synod Hall in 1893;[6] we know that these symbols of reverence for the monarchy remained on display until at least the mid-1920s (Fig. 9). From a decorative point of view, the floral motifs and *trompe l'oeil* in *grisailles* that originally adorned the interior walls were replaced in 1939 with a uniform colour (darker than the current pastel yellow), in order to highlight the new allegorical painting in the apse by the Waldensian artist Paolo Antonio Paschetto (1885–1963), who later became famous for designing the coat of arms of the Republic of Italy. His painting depicts a large oak tree sinking its roots into the rock, against the backdrop of the Pellice Valley mountain landscape; the branches of the tree support an open Bible with the quotation »Be faithful until death« (Rev 2: 8–11) (Fig. 10), while at the foot of the painting the dates 1689 and 1939 enclose an excerpt from the oath of mutual solidarity recited by Waldensian soldiers and commanders at Sibaud (Bobbio Pellice), on their return from exile »We promise before the living God to maintain union and order among us. We promise allegiance to the last drop of our blood«.

To fully understand the choice of quotations, as well as certain pictorial elements such as the cut branches and the foliage of the oak tree closed in on itself, it is necessary to remember the era in which they were made: a time certainly of celebrations for the 250th anniversary of the Glorious Return, but above all a time of profound social, political and cultural difficulties around the outbreak of the Second World War. As historian Giorgio Rochat has pointed out, in this context, Paschetto's decoration »effectively expresses the image of a besieged and isolated church, with no openings to the outside world, confident of its strength and determined to resist by exalting compactness and tradition«.[7] On the side walls, above the gallery, two inscriptions in capital letters complete the decoration of the hall: a biblical verse, »Look to the rock from which you were cut« (Isaiah 51:1), and a quotation (»Let nothing be stronger than your faith«) taken from the *Military Instructions* of Josué Janavel, a veteran Waldensian combatant banished to Geneva and inspirer of the return to the valleys. One of the five *solae* is inscribed on the entrance wall, above the gallery: »Glory to God alone«.

The furnishings and their arrangement

The majority of the original furnishings, in European larch, were restored in 1974 and in more recent years, reducing the number of seats, but maintaining the arrangement in rows of equal benches along three sides of the hall (for the members of synod) and in the gallery (for the public), reserving the slightly raised apse for the presidency of the assembly and the »outgoing« Waldensian Board (Fig. 11). In the absence of any documents indicating a clear wish of the church or its administrative bodies to give instructions to the interior designer, it is notable how some elements of the furnishings respond to needs arising from innovations introduced in the Waldensian ecclesiastical order in the second quarter of the 19th century.

The Synod of 1848, for example, the first one following the granting of civil and political rights for the Waldensian population of the Kingdom of Sardinia, had put an end to the ancient tradition that saw the Waldensian Board, led by the Moderator, also preside over the synodal assembly. As of the following Synod (1851), its opening was entrusted to the dean of pastors, followed by the appointment of an office to chair the assembly. The presiding officer sits in the apse, in a central position, where the seat and desk of the president and the secretaries' table are situated (Fig. 12, 13, 14).

On the sides, against the apsidal wall, are the semi-circular benches accommodating the outgoing Waldensian Board, whose prerogatives are suspended for the duration of the Synod, but who must answer for their year's work, sitting in front of the assembly (Fig. 15). There are no distinguishing features among the other benches, just as there are no rules or practices describing a strict order in which members must take their seats. The only exception are the benches closest to the apse: the one to the left of the presidency is occupied by the Scrutiny Committee, a body established in 1833 with the task of examining the moral and economic performance of the Waldensian Board, then presenting a report to the assembly to critique the report of the executive body. On the right are the policy reference committees that were set up over time, tasked with dealing with specific themes and areas of the life of the churches.

Finally, the gallery, expressly built to accommodate the public (complete with »leg covers« on the railing to prevent the ladies from being the object of prying eyes), constitutes an indispensable element of »synod life« (Fig. 16). As recalled in a chronicle of the Synod of 1931, »like any self-respecting audience, sometimes it is silent, often it murmurs, and sometimes explodes«.[8] Except in cases where the presidency of the assembly decides to deal with certain topics behind closed doors, in the absence of the public, the latter does not attend the synod proceedings

9 Bis zur Renovierung des Saales 1939 waren die Innenwände mit Trompe l'oeil-Malereien dekoriert. Die Büste des italienischen Königs Umberto I. war bis in die 1920er Jahre aufgestellt. | *Until the renovation of the hall in 1939 the interior walls were decorated with trompe-l'œil paintings. The bust of King Umberto I of Italy stood there into the 1920s.* | *Fino alla ristrutturazione della sala, avvenuta nel 1939, le pareti interne erano decorate con dipinti trompe l'oeil. Il busto del re italiano Umberto I fu esposto fino agli anni Venti.*

passively but participates with applause, expressing discontent, listening and having an effect on the speakers' performances with its presence.

A »multi-purpose« Hall

Today, the Waldensian House continues to host the annual Synod and some of the church's administrative offices while, several decades ago, the cultural services and institutions were moved to the premises of the nearby former Waldensian boarding school. An exception is the rooms of the old library, which continue to hold some collections and are used for occasional initiatives.

From the time of its construction, the Synod Hall itself was made available for other purposes. Two days after its inauguration, on the evening of 4 September 1889, the packed hall hosted the eighth assembly of the *Société d'Histoire Vaudoise* (today's Society of Waldensian Studies). And leafing through the periodicals we find news of how this space, while maintaining its design over the decades, has also been used for pastoral meetings, worship, Christmas activities (complete with a decorated fir tree), but also made available for events unrelated to the ecclesiastical sphere, such as concerts, conferences and conventions. New technologies and contingencies (such as the Covid 19 pandemic that struck the entire world) have also made it possible to bring the Synod Hall into greater dialogue with the garden surrounding the Waldensian House, by setting up marquees and monitors so that the assembly and the public can follow the synod proceedings in greater safety and comfort (Fig. 17).

10 Die von Paschetto gemalte Eiche kann als allegorische Darstellung der Waldenserkirche in den Jahren des Faschismus interpretiert werden. | *Paschetto's painting of the oak can be interpreted as an allegorical depiction of the Waldensian Church during the Fascist years.* | La quercia disegnata dal pittore Paschetto può essere letta come rappresentazione allegorica della Chiesa valdese negli anni del fascismo.

11 Der Synodensaal von der Galerie aus betrachtet. | The synod hall as seen from the gallery. | L'aula sinodale vista dalla galleria.

Space, synodality, identity

Interviews of people with long experience of synods revealed a widespread opinion that the spatial form of the hall is reminiscent of the House of Commons in the British Parliament, an idea corroborated by the important influence that the Victorian churches and society had on the 19th century Waldensian Church. Until 1974 the benches were also green, the same colour as in Westminster Palace Hall; then the old leather upholstery was replaced by a more modern dark brown artificial material. However, comparing the Waldensian Synod Hall with the iconography relating to synods held in Europe over the centuries, it is quite evident how its shape – and in particular the seating arrangement of the assembly – is rooted in the tradition of the European Reformed churches, as can be seen in the images of the French Reformed Synod of Montpellier in 1598 or the interior of the *Kloveniersdoelen* used a few decades later for the Synod of Dordrecht. At the same time, the presence of the apse makes it plausible to assume that Ayassot also took his cue from church buildings used for liturgical purposes that were particularly widespread in the Anglican world, with parallel rows of pews facing each other (Fig. 18). As Gélineau and Reymond point out, this model of spatial organisation favours the dimension of the »meeting to celebrate the Covenant«,[9] but, at the same time, as its use in British politics shows, it also proves effective for non-liturgical meetings.

More than one hundred and thirty years after their inauguration, the Waldensian House and the Synod Hall still seem to constitute, both inside and outside the church, the main iconographic elements with which to

12 In der leicht erhöhten Apsis nehmen der Synodenvorsitz (Präsidium und Sekretär) und die *Tavola Valdese* Platz. | *The slightly raised apse is reserved for the synod chair (presidium and secretary) and the Tavola Valdese.* | *Il Seggio del Sinodo (presidenza e segreteria) e la Tavola valdese uscente sono seduti nell'abside leggermente rialzata.*

illustrate the relevance of the Waldensian communities. The Synod, on the other hand, represents the moment in which the body that takes decisions of general interest for the churches comes together, while the hall that hosts sets the scene for the union between these groups and the encounter of the people who are part of them every year.

---

1 Cf. *Paolo Paschetto 1885–1963*, Torre Pellice, Società di Studi Valdesi, 1985, B. Peyrot, *La memoria costruita sul »Glorioso Rimpatrio«*, in Albert de Lange (a cura di), *Dall'Europa alle Valli valdesi*, Torino, Claudiana, 1990, pp. 523–546, G. Rochat, *Il contesto delle celebrazioni del Rimpatrio nel 1939*, in ibid., pp. 573–590, Samuele Tourn Boncoeur, *Musei storici*, in Daniele Jalla (a cura di), *Héritage(s). Formazione e trasmissione del patrimonio culturale valdese*, Torino, Claudiana, 2009, pp. 95–98
2 We thank Nicky Raddon and David Milne for their assistance with the English translation.
3 »Le Témoin«, year XIV, no 43, 26 October 1888.
4 Art. 31. »The Synod instructs the future administration to have prepared, for presentation to the next Synod, a plan, with related estimates, for a building to serve as a venue for Synods, Board meetings, Church archives, pastoral library and museum,« *Synod of the Waldensian Evangelical Church held at Torre Pellice from 6 to 10 September 1880*.
5 *Relation de la Commission examinatrice de l'activité de la Table vaudoise au Synode de 1879*, Archive of the Waldensian Board.
6 »Le Tèmoin«, year XIX, no 37. 14 September 1893.
7 Rochat, *Il contesto*, op. cit., p. 587.
8 »L'Echo des Vallées«, year LXVII, no 36, 11 September 1931.
9 Cf. Bernard Reymond, *L'architecture religieuse des protestants: histoire, characteristiques, problèmes actuels*, Genève, Labor et Fides, 1996, pp. 153–154.

Gabriella Ballesio · Simone Baral

L'aula sinodale della Chiesa evangelica valdese

L'annuale Sinodo delle Chiese valdesi e metodiste si svolge in una sala edificata nel 1889 a Torre Pellice, contestualmente all'edificio che la ospita, la cosiddetta «Casa valdese» (fig. 1), progettato dal geometra Epaminonda Ayassot (1866–1941). A differenza della Casa valdese nella sua globalità, la cui storia e le cui caratteristiche sono state oggetto nel corso dei decenni di alcune ricerche e descrizioni[1], l'aula sinodale non ha goduto di interesse specifico e il presente testo è frutto di ricerche inedite sulla documentazione e nella memoria orale.

Una casa per il sinodo e la «famiglia valdese»

L'aula sinodale venne inserita in un progetto architettonico più ampio, comprendente anche la biblioteca, gli archivi, il museo, gli uffici e una sala per le riunioni della Tavola valdese, l'organo amministrativo e rappresentativo della Chiesa. L'idea di una «Casa» che fosse non solo locale di servizio ma «simbolo visibile dell'unione della famiglia valdese»[2], emerse nel corso del Sinodo del 1880[3]; si trattò, quanto meno in parte, di una risposta alla decisione presa in autonomia dalla Tavola valdese senza consultare l'assemblea, di approfittare della costruzione, nel 1879, di una palestra per il Collegio valdese (un liceo maschile fondato nel 1836) al fine di realizzarvi, al piano superiore, una sala per il Sinodo: la precaria stabilità del pavimento e le grandi finestre che facevano filtrare troppa luce e calore, convinsero i deputati della necessità di costruire una sede idonea e definitiva per ospitare l'importante momento di vita della Chiesa e non solo.

13 Der Sitz des Präsidenten, darüber das Bibelzitat »Das Licht leuchtet in der Finsternis.« | *The seat of the president, above the Bible verse »The light shines in the darkness«.* | *La sedia del presidente, con sopra la citazione biblica «La luce brilla nelle tenebre».*

Rispetto alla località nella quale situare l'aula sinodale, Torre Pellice, occorre ricordare come sino a metà Ottocento l'assemblea si fosse tenuta a rotazione in diversi templi delle tre vallate in cui risiedevano le comunità valdesi; l'ultimo Sinodo svoltosi fuori dalla val Pellice era però stato nel 1860 e sin dal 1866 Torre Pellice era divenuta la sede stabile dell'assemblea, prima riunita presso l'antico tempio in località Coppieri, quindi, dal 1867 al 1879 e dal 1881 all'1888, all'interno del *temple neuf*, il nuovo locale di culto costruito nel 1852 nel centro abitato. Anche se alcuni avrebbero preferito collocare la sede del sinodo a Torino o a Firenze, per dimostrare che la Chiesa valdese era ormai una chiesa nazionale, Torre Pellice era stata riconosciuta per decenni come la «capitale» valdese de facto e, quindi, l'unico luogo adatto a ospitare l'assemblea sinodale.

Progetti e progettisti

Un primo progetto di Casa valdese fu consegnato nel 1883 dall'architetto e ingegnere londinese William Allen Boulnois (1823–1893), presente ai lavori del Sinodo del 1880 come invitato straniero della Chiesa presbiteriana d'Inghilterra. Il progetto, di cui si conservano le tavole, prevedeva due distinte costruzioni principali collegate tra loro tramite un passaggio coperto (Fig. 2): da un lato l'ala dedicata alle sale per le riunioni degli organi amministrativi, l'archivio e la biblioteca, dall'altro l'aula sinodale di forma ottagonale, che sembra prendere ispirazione dalla *Round Church* di Cambridge (Fig. 3), edificio coevo alle vicende di Valdo da Lione nel XII secolo (il personaggio storico a cui si riconducono l'origine e il nome delle chiese riformate piemontesi) e che Boulnois conosceva avendo studiato in tale cittadina universitaria.

Allo stesso tempo, i disegni dell'aula paiono rispondere ad alcune delle esigenze espresse in sede sinodale nel 1879, un anno prima quindi che il progetto acquistasse una portata più ampia, prevedendo anche i locali per biblioteca, museo e archivio: «une construction en style gothique, image, tout à la fois, de l'ancienneté et de la solidité de notre Église et gage de son avenir, s'élevant tout au plus à la hauteur d'un rez-de-chaussée, assez vaste pour contenir au moins 500 personnes, mais dont l'acoustique serait assez bonne et la disposition des places assez heureuse pour qu'il ne fatiguât ni orateurs ni auditeurs; [...] bâtiment auquel se rattacherait une salle pour les réunions du Corps des pasteurs et une autre pour celles des commissions synodales»[4] (Fig. 4).

Il progetto di Boulnois, tuttavia, finì per essere abbandonato per i costi esorbitanti rispetto alle disponibilità finanziarie della Chiesa: la Tavola valdese ripiegò su un professionista locale, il giovane geometra Ayassot (Fig. 5), responsabile di altri edifici sia pubblici che privati in val Pellice, optando per una costruzione meno ambiziosa, tanto dal punto di vista economico, che stilistico,

14 Der Eingang in den Synodensaal. | *The entrance to the synod hall.* | L'ingresso dell'aula sinodale.

15 Die scheidende Tavola Valdese legt von diesen Bänken aus Rechenschaft für die Arbeit der vergangenen Periode ab. | *From these benches, the retiring Tavola Valdese gives an account of its work during the past period.* | Seduti su questi banchi, i membri uscenti della Tavola Valdese rispondono alle domande sui lavori passati.

16 Der Sichtschutz entlang des Geländers wurde angefertigt, um die Beine der weiblichen Zuschauer zu verdecken. | The screen along the rail was made to cover the legs of the female spectators. | Il paravento lungo la ringhiera è stato realizzato appositamente per coprire le gonne del pubblico femminile.

in quanto più in linea con l'edilizia locale. Si dispone di due diversi progetti di Ayassot, di cui uno riprendeva l'idea di Boulnois di suddividere la costruzione in due distinti corpi di fabbrica, distinguendo spazialmente l'aula sinodale dai locali destinati ad altre attività; il secondo insieme di disegni, che presentano una struttura simile a quella poi realizzata, descriveva invece un edificio unico e omogeneo, in cui dall'esterno non era possibile distinguere gli spazi interni e che rendeva maggiormente l'idea di unità di chiesa e popolo, di storia e fede che era emerso dal dibattito sinodale (Fig. 6). Per il nuovo edificio fu scelto, inoltre, un appezzamento di terra di fronte al Collegio valdese e a fianco della casa pastorale e del tempio di Torre Pellice, contribuendo come ulteriore tassello alla progressiva costituzione del cosiddetto «quartiere valdese», completato a inizio Novecento con le inaugurazioni della Casa dell'Associazione cristiana dei giovani e del Convitto maschile (Fig. 7).

Finanziata l'opera grazie a collette e a doni di privati, furono posate solennemente due pietre angolari il 25 luglio 1888, mentre la Casa valdese venne inaugurata il 2 settembre 1889, ospitando il Sinodo di quell'anno e i festeggiamenti per il Bicentenario del Glorioso Rimpatrio, cioè del rientro dei valdesi in Piemonte nel 1689 dopo l'esilio forzato in Svizzera.

L'architettura e le decorazioni

Mettendo a confronto i disegni preparatori di Ayassot, le foto d'epoca e la conformazione attuale della Casa valdese, è possibile notare come all'esterno il progetto fu realizzato pressoché integralmente, fatto salvo per alcuni dettagli, come il numero e la forma di alcune finestre, il posizionamento dei balconi e il tetto della porzione centrale del fabbricato (Fig. 8). Per gli interni dell'aula sinodale, invece, un raffronto con le planimetrie mostra come il geometra avesse in mente, in entrambi i progetti, una sala rettangolare terminante, sul lato corto prospicente l'ingresso, con un'abside, e una galleria a ferro di cavallo; le differenze più rilevanti riguardano invece l'organizzazione degli spazi di servizio e per le altre attività.

Sulla base delle rare descrizioni testuali e iconografiche dell'aula originale, sappiamo che nell'abside trovavano posto un ritratto fotografico e un busto di Umberto I, Re d'Italia al momento dell'inaugurazione della Casa valdese e unico monarca italiano a visitare l'aula sinodale nel 1893[5]; sappiamo che questi simboli di omaggio per la monarchia rimasero esposti almeno sino alla metà degli anni '20 del Novecento (Fig: 9). Dal punto di vista decorativo, i motivi floreali e i *trompe l'oeil* in *grisailles* che ornavano originariamente le pareti interne furono sostituiti nel 1939 con una tinta uniforme (più scura del giallo pastello attuale), al fine di far risaltare il nuovo dipinto allegorico realizzato nell'abside dall'artista Paolo Antonio Paschetto (1885-1963): una grande quercia che affonda le radici nella roccia, sullo sfondo di un paesaggio montano; i rami dell'albero sostengono una Bibbia aperta con una citazione[6] dall'Apocalisse (2, 8–11), mentre ai piedi del dipinto le date 1689 e 1939 racchiudono uno stralcio[7] del giuramento di solidarietà reciproca recitato da soldati e comandanti valdesi a Sibaud (Bobbio Pellice), al rientro dall'esilio (Fig. 10). Per comprendere sino in fondo la scelta delle citazioni, nonché di alcuni elementi pittorici come i rami tagliati e la chioma della quercia richiusa su se stessa, occorre ricordare l'epoca nel quale fu realizzato: un momento certamente di festeggiamenti per il 250° anniversario del Rimpatrio, ma soprattutto di profonde difficoltà sociali, politiche e culturali a ridosso dello scoppio del secondo conflitto mondiale; come sottolineato da Giorgio Rochat, in tale contesto la decorazione di Paschetto «esprime efficacemente l'immagine di una chiesa assediata e isolata, senza aperture verso l'esterno, sicura della sua forza e decisa a resistere esaltando compattezza e tradizione»[8]. Sulle pareti laterali, sopra la galleria, due iscrizioni in caratteri capitali completano la decorazione dell'aula: un versetto biblico[9] (Isaia 51, 1) e una citazione[10] tratta dalle *Istruzioni militari* di Giosué Gianavello, anziano valdese bandito a Ginevra e ispiratore del Rimpatrio.

L'arredo e la sua disposizione

La gran parte dell'arredo originale, in larice rosso, fu rimaneggiata nel 1974 e restaurata in anni più recenti, riducendo il numero di posti a sedere, ma mantenendo la disposizione in file di panche uguali lungo tre lati della sala (per i deputati) e nella galleria (destinata al pubblico), riservando alla presidenza dell'assemblea e alla Tavola valdese «uscente» l'abside (Fig. 11), leggermente sopraelevata. In assenza di documenti che indichino una chiara volontà della Chiesa o dei suoi organi amministrativi di dare disposizioni al progettista riguardo alla disposizione degli arredi, è possibile notare come alcuni elementi dell'arredo rispondano a esigenze nate da innovazioni introdotte nell'ordinamento ecclesiastico valdese nel secondo quarto dell'Ottocento. Il Sinodo del 1848, ad esempio, il primo successivo all'ottenimento delle libertà civili e politiche per la popolazione valdese del Regno di Sardegna, aveva posto fine alla tradizione secolare che vedeva la Tavola valdese, guidata dal moderatore, presiedere anche l'assemblea sinodale: dal Sinodo successivo (1851), la sua apertura fu affidata al decano dei pastori, seguita dalla nomina di un ufficio di presidenza dell'assemblea. Nell'abside, in posizione centrale, trova dunque posto il seggio di presidenza, col sedile e la cattedra del Presidente e il tavolo dei segretari (Fig. 12, 13, 14); sui lati, addossati alla parete absidale, sono invece presenti le panche ad andamento semicircolare che ospitano la Tavola valdese uscente, le cui prerogative sono sospese per la durata del Sinodo, ma che deve rispondere del proprio operato annuale, sedendo di fronte all'assemblea (Fig. 15).

Per quanto concerne le altre panche, non vi sono tra esse elementi distintivi, così come non esistono regole o prassi che descrivano un ordine rigoroso nel quale i deputati debbano prendere posto. L'unica eccezione è costituita dalle panche più vicine all'abside: quella a sinistra

17 Auch der Garten dient als Begegnungsort. | *The garden is another place to meet people.* | Il giardino funge anche da luogo di incontro.

18 Die Synodalen sitzen einander gegenüber. | *The members of the synod sit opposite each other.* | *I membri del Sinodo siedono uno di fronte all'altro.*

della presidenza è occupata dalla Commissione di esame, organo istituto nel 1833 col compito di esaminare l'operato morale ed economico della Tavola valdese, quindi di presentare un rapporto all'assemblea che costituisce un «contro-canto» rispetto alla relazione proposta dall'organo amministrativo. A destra, invece, siedono le commissioni *ad referendum* via via istituite, con l'incarico di occuparsi di temi e ambiti specifici della vita delle chiese. La galleria, infine, espressamente costruita per ospitare il pubblico (con tanto di «copri-gambe» sulla ringhiera, onde evitare che le signore fossero oggetto di sguardi indiscreti) (Fig. 16), costituisce un elemento imprescindibile della «vita sinodale».

Come ricordato in una cronaca del Sinodo del 1931, «comme tout public qui se respecte, il se tait quelquefois; souvent il frémit, et, à l'issue, il éclate»[11]; salvo i casi in cui la presidenza dell'assemblea decida di affrontare taluni argomenti a «porte chiuse», in assenza di pubblico, quest'ultimo non assiste cioè passivamente ai lavori sinodali ma vi partecipa con applausi, manifestando malumori, ascoltando e condizionando con la propria presenza le *performance* degli oratori.

Un'aula «polivalente»

Oggi la Casa valdese continua a ospitare annualmente il Sinodo e parte degli uffici amministrativi della Chiesa, mentre da alcuni decenni le funzioni e le istituzioni di carattere culturale sono state traslocate nei locali del vicino ex-Convitto valdese, fatta eccezione per le sale dell'antica biblioteca che continuano a essere utilizzate come deposito di alcune collezioni e per occasionali iniziative. Sin dalla sua costruzione, la stessa aula sinodale fu messa a disposizione per altri scopi; a due giorni dall'inaugurazione, la sera del 4 settembre 1889, la sala gremita ospitò l'ottava assemblea della *Société d'Histoire Vaudoise* (l'attuale Società di Studi Valdesi) e sfogliando i periodici si trova notizia di come questo spazio, pur mantenendo la sua conformazione, nel corso dei decenni sia stato utilizzato anche per riunioni pastorali, culti, feste dell'albero di Natale (con tanto di abete addobbato), ma anche messo a disposizione per eventi slegati dalla sfera ecclesiastica, come concerti, conferenze e convegni. Le nuove tecnologie e situazioni contingenti (come la recente pandemia che ha colpito tutto il mondo) hanno inoltre permesso di mettere maggiormente in dialogo l'aula sinodale con il giardino circostante la Casa valdese, allestendo tensostrutture e schermi affinché l'assemblea e il pubblico possano seguire i lavori sinodali in maggiore sicurezza e agio (Fig. 17).

Spazio, sinodalità, identità

Interrogando alcune persone che possono vantare lunghe esperienze sinodali, è emersa l'opinione diffusa che la conformazione spaziale dell'aula ricordi quella della Camera dei Comuni del Parlamento britannico, un'idea corroborata dall'importante influenza che le chiese e la società vittoriane ebbero sulla Chiesa valdese ottocentesca, nonché dal colore verde che le panche dell'aula condividevano con quelle della sala del Palazzo di Westminster sino al 1974, quando la vecchia imbottitura in pelle fu sostituita con una più moderna e sintetica, di colore marrone scuro. Tuttavia, mettendo a confronto l'aula sinodale valdese con l'iconografia relativa a sinodi svoltisi in Europa nel corso dei secoli, appare piuttosto evidente come la sua conformazione – e in particolare la disposizione dei posti a sedere dell'assemblea – affondi nella tradizione delle chiese riformate europee, come emerge dalle immagini del Sinodo riformato francese di Montpellier del 1598 o dell'interno del *Kloveniersdoelen* utilizzato pochi decenni più tardi per il Sinodo di Dordrecht. Al tempo stesso, la presenza dell'abside rende plausibile ipotizzare come Ayassot abbia preso spunto anche da edifici ecclesiastici utilizzati per scopi liturgici, particolarmente diffusi nel mondo anglicano, con file parallele di banchi rivolti gli uni verso gli altri (Fig. 18). Come sottolineato da Gélineau e Reymond[12] questo modello di organizzazione spaziale favorisce la dimensione dell'«incontro per celebrare l'Alleanza», ma, al tempo stesso, come emerge dal suo uso in ambito politico britannico, dimostra la sua efficacia anche per incontri non di carattere liturgico.

A oltre centotrent'anni dalla loro inaugurazione, la Casa valdese e l'aula sinodale sembrano ancora oggi costituire, sia all'interno che all'esterno della Chiesa, i principali elementi iconografici con i quali illustrare l'attualità delle comunità valdesi. Il Sinodo, d'altro canto, rappresenta sì il momento in cui si riunisce l'organo che prende le decisioni di interesse generale delle chiese, ma l'aula che lo ospita è lo scenario nel quale ogni anno si sostanzia l'unione e l'incontro di queste realtà e delle persone che ne fanno parte.

---

1 Cfr. *Paolo Paschetto 1885–1963*, Torre Pellice, Società di Studi Valdesi, 1985, B. Peyrot, *La memoria costruita sul «Glorioso Rimpatrio»*, in Albert de Lange (a cura di), *Dall'Europa alle Valli valdesi*, Torino, Claudiana, 1990, pp. 523–546, G. Rochat, *Il contesto delle celebrazioni del Rimpatrio nel 1939*, in ivi, pp. 573–590, Samuele Tourn Boncoeur, *Musei storici*, in Daniele Jalla (a cura di), *Héritage(s). Formazione e trasmissione del patrimonio culturale valdese*, Torino, Claudiana, 2009, pp. 95–98.
2 «Le Témoin«, a. XIV, n. 43, 26 ottobre 1888.
3 «Art. 31. Le Synode charge la future administration de faire préparer, pour le présenter au prochain Synode, le plan, avec les devis y relatifs, d'un édifice destiné à server de local pour la tenue des Synodes, les réunions de la Table, les archives de l'Église, la bibliothèque pastorale et le musée», *Sinodo della Chiesa evangelica valdese tenuto a Torre Pellice dal 6 al 10 settembre 1880*.
4 *Relation de la Commission examinatrice de l'activité de la Table vaudoise au Synode de 1879*, Archivio della Tavola valdese.
5 «Le Tèmoin», a. XI X, n. 37. 14 settembre 1893.
6 «Sii fedele fino alla morte».
7 «Noi giuriamo e promettiamo al cospetto dell'Iddio vivente di mantenere tra noi l'unione e l'ordine. Giuriamo fedeltà fino all'ultima goccia del nostro sangue».
8 Rochat, *Il contesto*, cit., p. 587.
9 «Riguardate alla roccia onde foste tagliati».
10 «Nulla sia più forte della vostra fede».
11 «L'Echo des Vallées», a. LXVII, n. 36, 11 settembre 1931.
12 Cfr. Bernard Reymond, *L'architecture religieuse des protestants: histoire, caracteristiques, problemes actuels*, Genève, Labor et Fides, 1996, pp. 153–154.

Schottland
Scotland

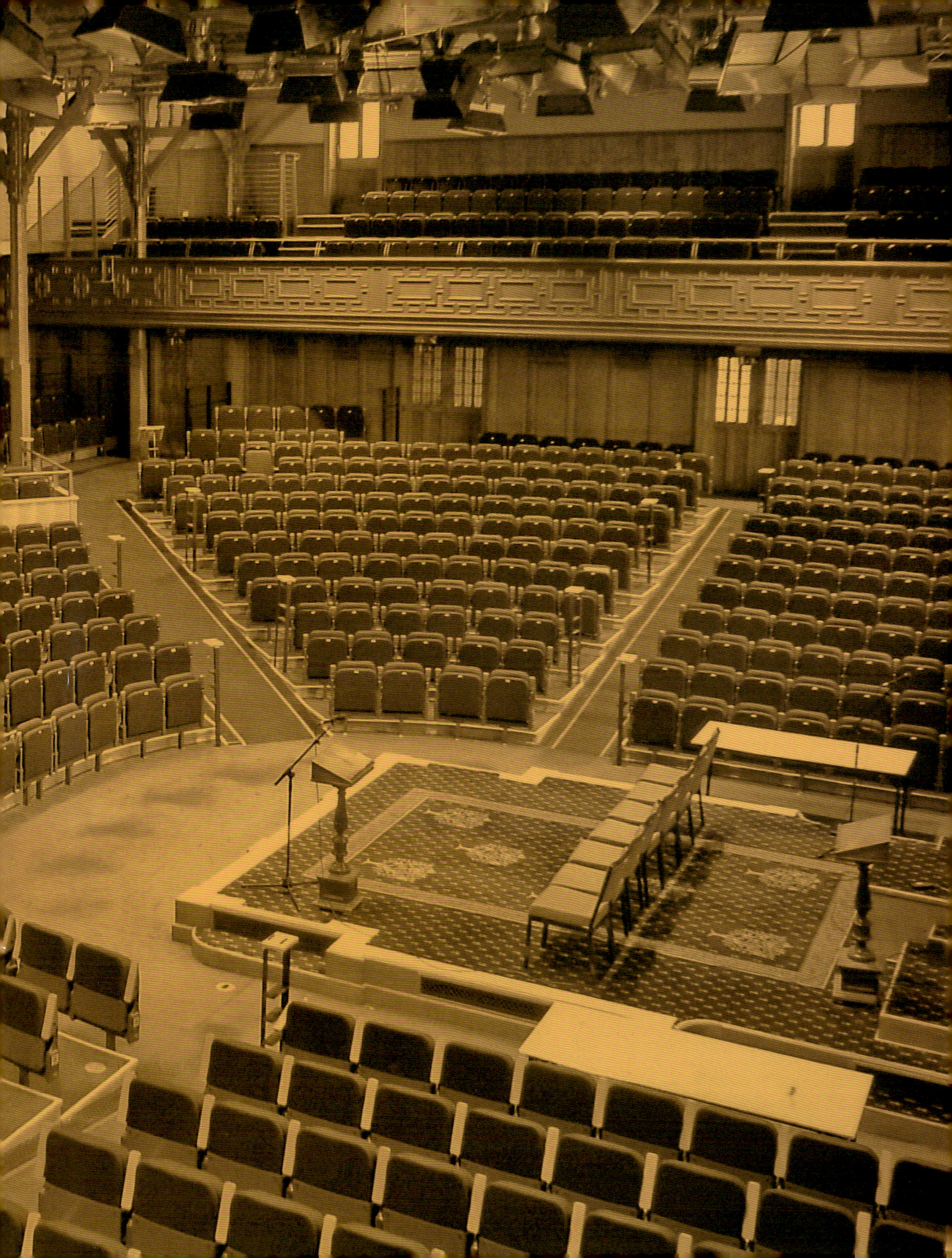

Steckbrief / General information

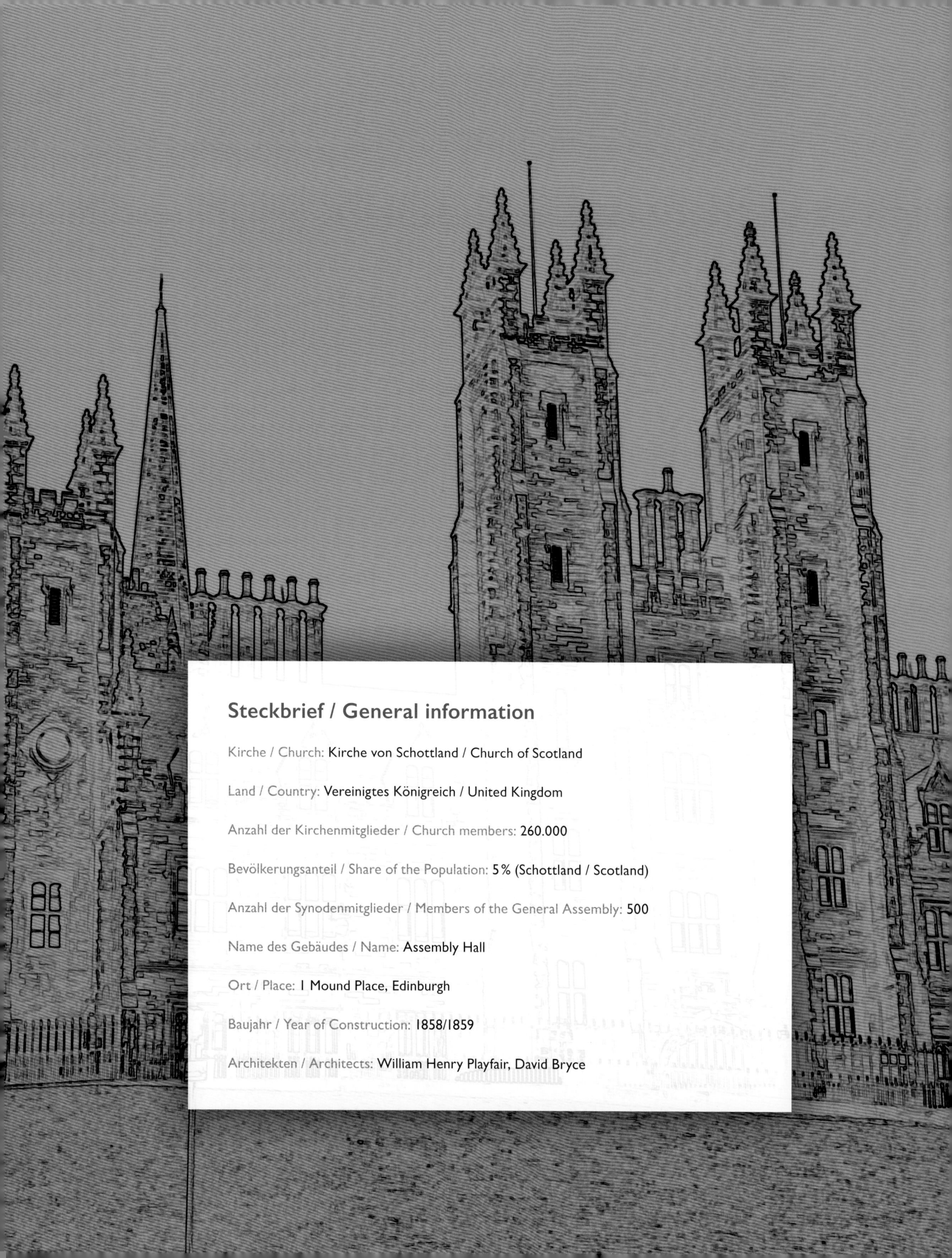

Kirche / Church: **Kirche von Schottland / Church of Scotland**

Land / Country: **Vereinigtes Königreich / United Kingdom**

Anzahl der Kirchenmitglieder / Church members: **260.000**

Bevölkerungsanteil / Share of the Population: **5 % (Schottland / Scotland)**

Anzahl der Synodenmitglieder / Members of the General Assembly: **500**

Name des Gebäudes / Name: **Assembly Hall**

Ort / Place: **1 Mound Place, Edinburgh**

Baujahr / Year of Construction: **1858/1859**

Architekten / Architects: **William Henry Playfair, David Bryce**

Rosalind Taylor

Das Assembly Building der Kirche von Schottland

Einführung

Das *Assembly Building* der Kirche von Schottland wird alljährlich für die *General Assembly*, die Generalversammlung aller Delegierten aus den Gemeinden und Bezirken, genutzt. Das Gebäude, oft nur als »The Hall« bezeichnet, wurde 1858 an einem zentralen Ort in Edinburgh erbaut und hat einen Grundriss, der den Gedanken der Synodalität architektonisch zur Geltung bringt.

Die Kirche von Schottland, häufig schlicht »The Kirk« genannt, gehört der presbyterianischen Konfession an, bei der der Grundsatz gilt, dass keiner über dem anderen steht. Dieses Prinzip wird gewahrt durch eine Reihe von Gerichten (*Courts*), die in den Jahren 1560 bis 1690 im Zuge der Reformation entwickelt wurden.

Auf lokaler Ebene gibt es bis heute für jede Gemeinde die *Kirk Session*, auf Bezirksebene die *Presbyterien* mit Vertretern aus jeder Gemeinde. Auf der nächstgrößeren Ebene, als Repräsentanz der Presbyterien einer Region, versammelten sich die *Synoden*. Diese wurden jedoch 1990 abgeschafft, weil die direkte Verbindung zwischen den Presbyterien und der Generalversammlung intensiviert worden war und Synoden als Zwischeninstanz nicht mehr nötig waren. Die Generalversammlung hat die Befugnis, Gesetze zu erlassen, die die Arbeits- und Verhaltensweise der Kirche von Schottland festlegen. Soll eine neue oder innovative Richtung eingeschlagen werden, hat sie die Pflicht, vorher umfangreiche Konsultationen durchzuführen wie dies im *Barrier Act*[1] von 1697, der die presbyterianischen Grundsätze der Kirche festlegte, verankert ist.

Die *Assembly Hall* der Kirche von Schottland am Mound Place 1 in Edinburgh verkörpert die Hoffnungen und Absichten, die in der Planungs- und Bauphase in den 1850er Jahren bestanden. Bis zur Mitte des 19. Jahrhunderts hatte die Generalversammlung keinen für ihre Zwecke eigenen Raum, sondern nutzte über die Jahre verschiedene Veranstaltungsorte.

Geschichtlicher Hintergrund

Im September 1842 wurde der Grundstein für die *Victoria Hall* gelegt. Die *Victoria Hall*, später als *Tolbooth Church* (Abb. 1) bezeichnet und heute als *The Hub* bekannt, wurde von James Gillespie Graham (1776–1855), einem bekannten schottischen Architekten, in Zusammenarbeit mit seinem Freund Augustus Welby Northmore Pugin (1812–1852), einem der führenden britischen Architekten seiner Zeit, entworfen. Die beiden Architekten waren auch für die Errichtung des Westminster-Palasts in London verantwortlich. Das auffälligste Merkmal des Hub-Gebäudes ist der gotische Turm, der mit 72 Metern den höchsten Punkt der Stadt darstellt.

Das Gebäude wurde vom Stadtrat von Edinburgh mitfinanziert und für Leitungsversammlungen der Kirche von Schottland genutzt. Unter anderem tagten darin die Synode von Lothian, das Presbyterium von Edinburgh und die Generalversammlung. Der Standort befindet sich am oberen Ende der High Street in Edinburgh auf der Südseite des Lawnmarket. *The Hub* liegt somit direkt unterhalb des Schlosses von Edinburgh, einem weithin sichtbaren Wahrzeichen der Stadt (Abb. 2 und 3).

Unabhängig hiervon führten etwa zur gleichen Zeit (1843) unterschiedliche Themen zu einer zunehmenden Unzufriedenheit innerhalb der Kirche von Schottland. Der Konflikt entbrannte vor allem an der Frage, ob statt der

Gemeindeglieder weiterhin die Grundbesitzer als Patrone das Recht haben sollten, den Pfarrer einer Gemeinde zu bestimmen, wobei die Regierung in London die Position der Grundbesitzer unterstützte. 1843 verließen Hunderte von Pfarrern und Älteste die bestehende Kirche und gründeten die *Free Church of Scotland* (Freie Kirche von Schottland), ein Ereignis, das als *Disruption* (Kirchenspaltung) bekannt wurde. Diese neue *Free Church* (Abb. 4) sollte eine vollständige Ersatzorganisation sein mit dem Ziel, in jeder Gemeinde eine neue Kirche zu bauen und schließlich auch ein neues Gebäude für ihre beschlussfassenden Versammlungen.

Die Kirchenspaltung führte deshalb in Schottland zu einer Hochzeit der Kirchenneubauten, wobei die Mittel für die neuen Gebäude meistens durch Mitgliedsbeiträge aufgebracht wurden. Für die *Free Church of Scotland* wurden aber nicht nur Gemeindekirchen benötigt, sondern auch Colleges und ein eigenes Versammlungsgebäude. Erst 1858 wurde mit dem Bau einer *Assembly Hall* begonnen. Der Standort befand sich im Herzen des neuen *Free Church Theological College* in Edinburgh.

Als die Kirchenspaltung 1929 durch die Vereinigung der beiden Kirchen beendet wurde und man nur noch einen Ort für die Leitungsversammlungen der Kirche benötigte, einigte man sich auf die Nutzung der *Assembly Hall* der *Free Church*, die bis heute Tagungsort der Generalversammlung der *Church of Scotland* ist.

Das New College Gebäude

Die *Free Church* hatte bereits 1845 mit dem Bau ihrer neuen theologischen Hochschule begonnen. Sie wurde ebenfalls am oberen Ende der High Street direkt unterhalb des Schlosses, jedoch gegenüber der *Victoria Hall* bzw. *The Hub*, auf der Nordseite des Lawnmarket errichtet. Auf diesem steil abfallenden Gelände befanden sich noch einige Überreste des ehemaligen Palastes der Maria von Guise, Mutter der schottischen Königin Maria Stuart (Abb. 5). Das Gebäude des *New College* war nach Norden ausgerichtet und überblickte die Neustadt von Edinburgh. Die Neustadt, die seit den 1770er Jahren rasant wuchs, bildete städtebaulich eine neue, moderne Gesellschaft ab, deren geistige Begründer David Hume und Adam Smith waren. Symbolisch war das neue College also der Zukunft zugewandt und von den breiten Straßen der Neustadt aus gut sichtbar (Abb. 6).

Der Architekt war William Henry Playfair (1790–1857), der auch für die Terrassen der East New Town, die *St. Stephen's Church*, das *Royal College of Surgeons* und die nur einen Steinwurf entfernte National Gallery of Scotland am Fuße des Mound verantwortlich zeichnete (Abb. 7). Er war ein herausragender Architekt seiner Zeit, ehrgeizig und erfolgreich. Obwohl Playfair nach der Kirchenspaltung von 1843 der *Free Church* beigetreten war und von ihren Anliegen überzeugt gewesen sein muss, erfolgte seine Beauftragung nicht deswegen, sondern nach einer öffentlichen Ausschreibung.

Da das *New College* ähnlich wie die Colleges in Oxford und Cambridge um einen Innenhof im Tudor-Stil angelegt ist, liegt die Vermutung nahe, dass Playfair sich an der Architektur der berühmten Universitätsstädte orientiert hat. Als Standort für das *Assembly Building* wählte man das Herzstück des Innenhofs an der Südseite.

Der Turm des *Hub* wird vom *New College* perfekt eingerahmt. Von der Kreuzung George Street und Hanover Street aus sehen das College und die Turmspitze so aus, als bildeten sie am oberen Ende der Altstadt ein einziges Gebäude (Abb. 8).

Das Bauensemble mit der *Assembly Hall* im Zentrum war vermutlich das bedeutendste seiner Zeit in Edinburgh. Am Ende der Mound, einer imposanten, bergauf verlaufenden Straße, die 1830 als Verbindung zwischen Alt- und Neustadt angelegt wurde, betritt man das *New College* durch ein gewölbtes Portal, quert den viereckigen Hof und geht dann die Treppe hinauf zum Eingang des Gebäudes, das stets vom Turm des *Hub* dominiert wird.

Die Finanzierung der Assembly Hall

Die Kosten für die *Assembly Hall* beliefen sich auf 7.000 Pfund, eine für die damalige Zeit enorme Summe, die vollständig von den Frauen der *Free Church of Scotland* aufgebracht wurde. Dies sagt einiges über das Wesen dieser neuen Kirchenorganisation aus, bei der die Mitarbeit der Frauen offensichtlich auch auf Leitungsebene miteinbezogen war. Abbildungen aus jener Zeit zeigen dennoch, dass die überwiegende Mehrheit der Teilnehmer an den Leitungsversammlungen Männer waren.

| In der Tolbooth Church fanden zunächst die Versammlungen der Church of Scotland statt. | *General Assemblies of the Church of Scotland were first held in Tolbooth Church.*

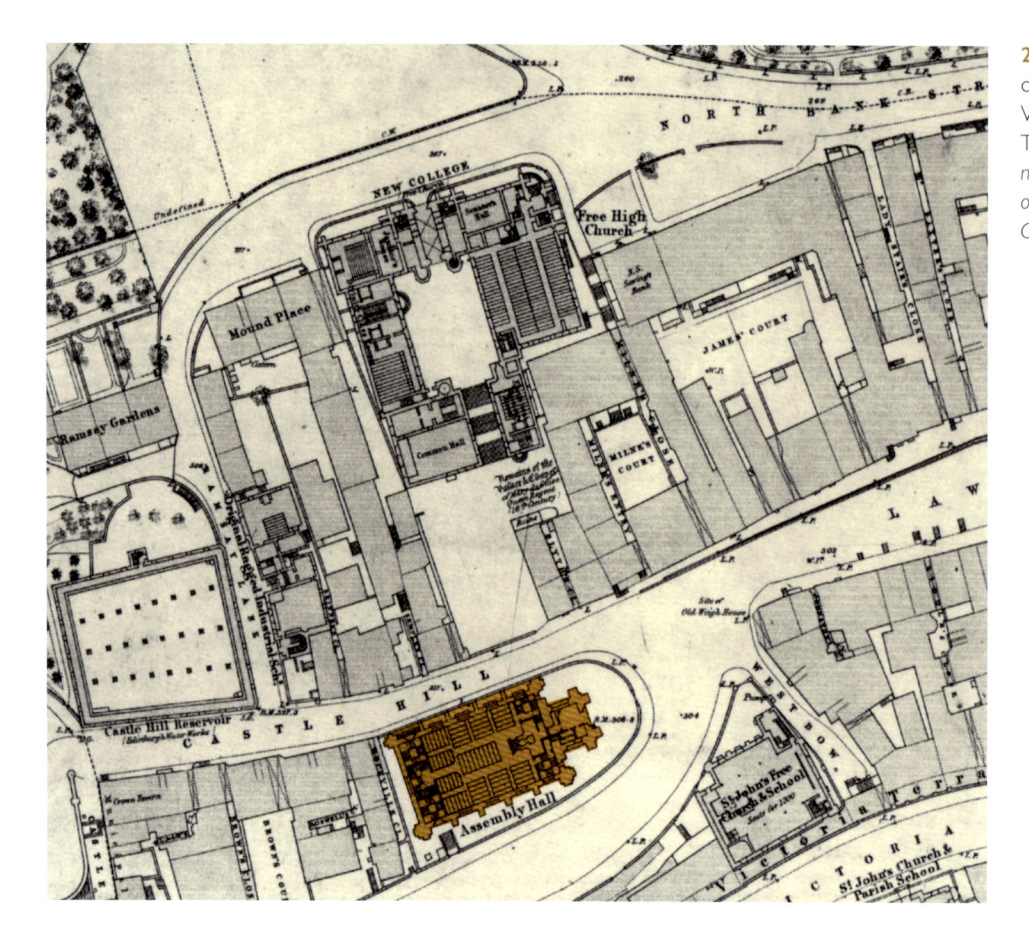

2 Die Karte von 1849 zeigt den Standort des früheren Versammlungssaals in der Tolbooth Church. | *The 1849 map shows the original location of the Assembly Hall in Tolbooth Church.*

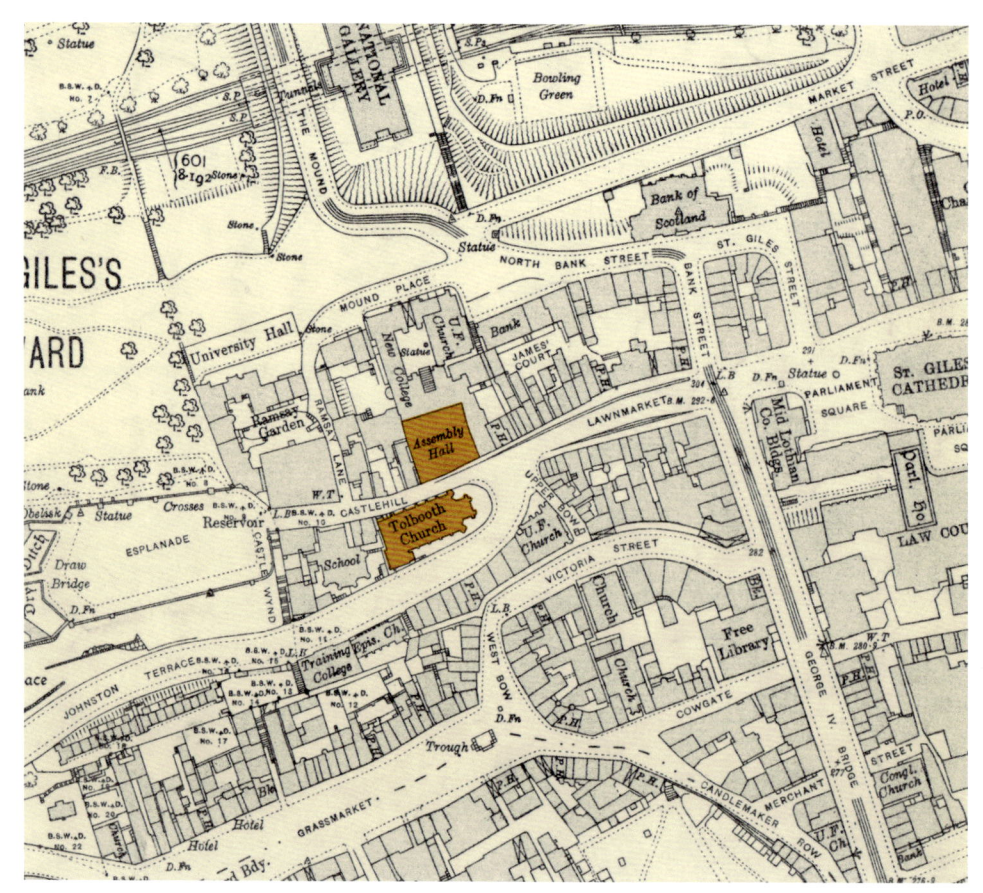

3 Entgegen ursprünglicher Planungen wurde die Assembly Hall der Free Church auf der gegenüberliegenden Straßenseite der Tolbooth Church im New College eröffnet. | *Contrary to original plans, the Assembly Hall of the Free Church was opened across the road from Tolbooth Church in New College.*

4 Die erste Generalversammlung der Free Church of Scotland im Jahr 1843. | *The first General Assembly of the Free Church of Scotland in the year 1843.*

Die solide Finanzierung dieses wichtigsten Gebäudes könnte auch die Wahl des Architekten beeinflusst haben: Während die Wohnung für den Moderator in der südöstlichen Ecke des Hofes des *New Colleges* von Playfair entworfen wurde, fiel sie für die *Assembly Hall* auf den in damaliger Zeit berühmten David Bryce (1803–1876). Er entwickelte und perfektionierte den schottischen Baronialstil und war besonders geschickt in Innenraumplanung und Raumnutzung. Viele Landhäuser wie *Torosay Castle* auf der Insel Mull oder das *Edinburgh Royal Infirmary* wurden von ihm entworfen. Sein bekanntestes Gebäude ist wahrscheinlich auch heute noch das *Fettes College* in Edinburgh.

Der Entwurf der Assembly Hall

Die Ausschreibung sah einen Versammlungsraum vor, in welchem Gleichrangige vor Gott zusammenkommen. 1.500 Teilnehmer sollten untergebracht werden können mit leicht zugänglichen Plätzen für die Delegierten, den Moderator, die Öffentlichkeit und den *Lord High Commissioner* als Vertreter der Monarchie. Ein solches Gebäude auf einem abschüssigen Gelände zu errichten, war eine herausfordernde Aufgabe, die Bryce sicherlich sehr gereizt hat (Abb. 9).

In seiner Entstehungszeit hatte das Innere der *Assembly Hall* die landesweit größte Dachspannweite; sie ermöglichte von allen vier Galerien und von der Erdgeschossebene aus einen uneingeschränkten Blick in den Raum. Um dies verwirklichen zu können, verwendete Bryce, der ein sehr innovativer Architekt war, hohe mit einem Holzmaserungseffekt lackierte gusseiserne Säulen, die das schwere Holzdach stützten.

Klug konzipiert waren auch die Korridore auf zwei Ebenen, die sich die Hanglage zunutze machten. Sie ermöglichen einen guten Zugang zu den Galerien und zum Saal. Der repräsentative Haupteingang vom Innenhof des Colleges aus erfolgt über eine beeindruckende Freitreppe. Vom Eingang aus gelangt man über den charakteristischen Schwarz-Weiß Korridor in den Saal im Erdgeschoss. Das in den Raum hineinragende Podium, von wo aus die Versammlungen geleitet werden, befindet sich auf der Nordseite; die Nordgalerie ist ebenfalls über den schwarz-weißen Korridor zu erreichen. Zugang zu den Galerien im Süden, Westen und Osten hat man über den Lawnmarket.

Die *Hall* ist ein großer, fast quadratischer Raum von 35 × 27 Metern an der breitesten Stelle mit leicht aufsteigend verlaufenden Sitzplätzen sowie den Galerien an vier Seiten. Klarglaskuppeln und Dachlaternen ermöglichten schon damals eine gleichmäßige und natürliche Beleuchtung, während die Raumform und die verwendeten Wandoberflächen eine hervorragende Akustik für alle Teilnehmenden erzeugten – noch bevor es Elektrizität und Tonanlagen gab.

In diesem wundervollen Raum verstellen keine Säulen die Sichtachsen und auch von den Galerien aus kann man alles gut überblicken. Die Decke ist hoch, eben und aus Eichenholz. Von der Außenwelt kaum berührt, strahlt der Saal trotz seiner Größe eine unerwartete Stille und Nähe aus.

Die schlichte Eichenholzvertäfelung hinter dem Podium ist typisch für die einfachen, schmucklosen, aber hochwertigen Materialien, die für die Ausstattung der *Hall* verwendet wurden. Ohne überflüssigen Zierrat heben sie die Bedeutung des Raumes hervor. Im Gegensatz dazu sind die anderen Innenräume des *New College* häufig mit mehr dekorativen Details versehen, was den eigenen Charakter der *Hall* noch zusätzlich unterstreicht.

Die Form der *Assembly Hall* ging von der ihr bestimmten Funktion aus und sollte gewährleisten, dass die über 1.300 Teilnehmenden sich sowohl vom Plenum als auch von den Galerien aus uneingeschränkt sehen und hören konnten (Abb. 11). Dahinter stand die Überzeugung, dass alle vor Gott gleich sind. Diese Anordnung unterschied sich deutlich von den Kirchenplänen der damaligen Zeit, die in der Regel lange, rechteckige Räume mit nach vorne ausgerichteten Bänken vorsahen. Die Gemeinde sollte sich auf das gesprochene Wort, das von der Kanzel aus gepredigt wurde, konzentrieren; Redebeiträge von anderen Gemeindegliedern waren nicht vorgesehen.

Die Innenausstattung der Assembly Hall

Die Bestuhlung des Saals bestand bis 1999 aus langen, grün gepolsterten Holzbänken auf drei Seiten und einem Podium für den Moderator und die Repräsentantinnen und Repräsentanten der Kirchenverwaltung auf der Stirnseite, so dass eine runde Anordnung der Plätze entstand.

Die Nordgalerie hinter dem Moderator ist für den *Lord High Commissioner* reserviert, der die Monarchie jedes Jahr bei der Generalversammlung vertritt (Abb. 10). Diese Galerie hat einen separaten Zugang, um zu unterstreichen, dass die Versammlung von der Moderatorin oder dem Moderator geleitet wird und der *Lord High Commissioner* zwar anwesend ist, aber nicht an Debatten oder Entscheidungen teilnimmt.

Über dem Podium befindet sich ein kleines Buntglasfenster mit der Darstellung des brennenden Dornbuschs. Seit 1691 ist der brennende Dornbusch ein Symbol der Kirche von Schottland, häufig untertitelt mit dem lateinischen Text *Nec Tamen Consumebatur*. Der Satz bezieht sich auf das Buch Exodus, wo Mose einem brennenden Dornbusch begegnete. Wie sehr der Busch auch brannte, er wurde nicht von den Flammen verzehrt. Alle anderen Fenster sind aus Klarglas mit Ausnahme eines Fensters hinter der nördlichen Empore, das König David zeigt. Dieses Glasfenster von Douglas Strachan wurde 1929 anlässlich der Vereinigung der *Free Church* und der *Church of Scotland* hinzugefügt, als die *Hall* die *Assembly Hall* der ganzen Kirche wurde.

5 Foto aus den 1840er Jahren mit Resten des alten Palastes von Maria von Guise im Vordergrund und der Turmspitze der Tolbooth Church im Hintergrund. | *Photograph from the 1840s showing some details of Mary La Guise's Palace and the spire of Tolbooth Church.*

6 Auf dem Gelände des ehemaligen Palastes der Maria von Guise wurde das New College errichtet. | *The New College was built on the site of the former Mary La Guise's Palace.*

Umbauten an der Assembly Hall

Sydney Mitchell (1856–1930) fügte 1899 an Stelle des offenen Kreuzgangs das Eingangsvestibül und den Schwarz-Weiß-Korridor hinzu. Er hatte bereits viele Gebäude für die *Free Church* entworfen, darunter die *New Restalrig Parish Church* und die *Polwarth Parish Church*. Über den Eingangstüren zum Vestibül wurden die den Zweck der *Assembly Hall* unterstreichenden Worte eingemeißelt: PRAISE HIM IN THE ASSEMBLY OF THE ELDERS.

Eines der auffälligsten Merkmale des Gebäudes wurde der Schwarz-Weiß-Korridor (Abb. 12). Er wurde nicht nur für formelle Treffen und Fernsehübertragungen, sondern auch als Filmkulisse genutzt. In dem Film »Looking after Jojo« mit Robert Carlyle in der Hauptrolle war das Gebäude Drehort für die Gerichtsszenen, wobei die dramatischen Auseinandersetzungen im Schwarz-Weiß-Korridor stattfanden.

Sydney Mitchell setzte den Tudor Collegiate-Stil im Schwarz-Weiß-Korridor mit dem namensgebenden Schachbrettmuster aus schwarzem, grauem und weißem Marmor fort. Als die *Assembly Hall* von 1999 bis 2004 zum Sitzungssaal des schottischen Parlaments wurde, inspirierte dieses Muster den Architekten Enric Miralles (1955–2000) ebenfalls einen schwarz-weißen Flur in das am 9. Oktober 2004 eröffnete neue schottische Parlamentsgebäude einzubauen (Abb. 13).

Sydney Mitchells letztes größeres Werk war das Büro der *Church of Scotland* in der George Street 121, das 1908 ursprünglich für die *United Free Church of Scotland* errichtet wurde. Für dessen Eingangsbereich wählte er erneut einen schwarz-weißen Bodenbelag.

7 Bronzestatue des Architekten William Playfair. | *Bronze of the architect William Playfair.*

Nutzung der Assembly Hall

Die Generalversammlung findet gewöhnlich im Mai statt. Die daran teilnehmenden Delegierten sind größtenteils Älteste und Pfarrerinnen und Pfarrer aus den Gemeinden. Die Generalversammlung dauert etwa eine Woche, sie ist sowohl eine Gelegenheit für Debatten und Diskussionen, als auch für Beschlussfassungen und Abstimmungen über gemeinsame Maßnahmen. Die Versammlung wählt jährlich einen Moderator als Vorsitzenden.

Dieser sowie der *Principal Clerk* als Leitungsperson der Versammlungsadministration und weitere funktionstragende Personen sitzen auf dem Podium an der Nordseite des Saals mit der Galerie für den *Lord High Commissioner* dahinter. Ehemaligen Moderatoren, ausländischen Delegierten und zusätzlichen Personen werden ebenfalls Sitzplätze zugewiesen, wodurch jedoch keine hierarchische Rangordnung ausgedrückt werden soll.

Mitglieder von Kommissionen sitzen wie die delegierten Pfarrerinnen und Pfarrer und Ältesten unten und auf der West- und Südgalerie. Sie haben das Recht zu reden und abzustimmen. Die Ostgalerie ist für die Öffentlichkeit und für Besucher reserviert, die in der Regel in der Reihenfolge der Anmeldungen zugelassen werden. Besucherinnen und Besucher sind nicht stimmberechtigt.

Als Teil des *New College* ist die *Assembly Hall* durch den Schwarz-Weiß-Korridor mit den Unterkünften der Universität im Osten und der *Rainy Hall* im Westen verbunden. Während der Generalversammlung werden die *Rainy Hall* und andere Räume, die normalerweise von der Universität genutzt werden, für organisatorische und Versorgungszwecke verwendet. Der Innenhof ist bei den Versammlungen und bei anderen Veranstaltungen ebenfalls ein wichtiger Raum, sowohl für informelle Treffen als auch für festliche Zusammenkünfte. Auch der Hof diente schon als Filmkulisse: Im Film »Chariots of Fire« eilt Eric Liddell, gespielt von Ian Charleston, über den Hof und läuft die Treppe zum Gebäude hinauf.

Auf einem Sockel an der Ostseite des Hofes steht eine von John Hutchison (1832–1910) im Jahr 1895 angefertigte Bronzestatue von John Knox (Abb. 14). Sie ist in den letzten Jahren zu einer großen Touristenattraktion geworden und wird häufig fotografiert.

Abgesehen von der Nutzung für die Generalversammlung der Kirche von Schottland im Mai und für einige andere ofizielle Treffen hat sich die *Assembly Hall* auch für andere Veranstaltungen als geeignet erwiesen und wird an Gruppen und Organisationen vermietet, wie z.B. für Schulpreisverleihungen oder Konferenzen.

Während des *Edinburgh Festivals* wird der Raum seit vielen Jahren erfolgreich als Theaterspielstätte für das *Fringe* genutzt. Dafür wird auf dem in den Raum hineinragenden Podium eine Bühne errichtet, so dass ein runder Theaterraum entsteht (Abb. 15).

8 Der Treppenaufgang zur Assembly Hall wird von zwei Türmen flankiert und optisch von der Turmspitze der Tolbooth Church dominiert.
The staircase to the Assembly Hall is flanked by two towers and visually dominated by the spire of Tolbooth Church.

Der größte moderne Eingriff in die *Assembly Hall* erfolgte in den späten 1990er Jahren, als das Gebäude vorübergehend dem neu gegründeten schottischen Parlament zur Verfügung gestellt wurde. Das neue Parlamentsgebäude wurde damals am Fuß der *Royal Mile* erbaut. Die dichtgedrängten kirchenbankartigen Sitzreihen wurden durch auf das Podium ausgerichtete geschwungene Theatersitzreihen ersetzt. Die Sichtachsen wurden dabei sorgfältig beibehalten, denn es sollte gewährleistet bleiben, dass jede und jeder Anwesende von allen anderen gesehen und befragt werden kann. Die Tatsache, dass nur minimale Änderungen erforderlich waren, um das Gebäude als nationales Parlament nutzen zu können, ist ein Beweis für die Qualität des ursprünglichen Entwurfs und seiner schon damals gefundenen modernen Lösungen.

Die Aussenansicht der Assembly Hall

Von der Straße aus ist die *Assembly Hall* kaum sichtbar. Am Lawnmarket zeigt sich die Südfront als eine unscheinbare zweistöckige Steinfassade mit einfachen Holztüren. Die Westseite des Gebäudes grenzt fast vollständig an das *New College*. An der Ostseite befindet sich das Studierendenwohnheim *Mylne's Court*. Auch dort ist die Außenfassade der *Hall* schlicht und fensterlos. Nur die nördliche Fassade der *Assembly Hall* hat aufgrund der Eingangstreppe und des Vestibüls, gerahmt von den beiden Playfair-Innentürmen, Strahlkraft. Die hohen Fenster an der Nordseite des Saals sind von außen nicht sichtbar. Diese Schlichtheit scheint ungewöhnlich für ein Versammlungsgebäude, von dem man eine öffentliche Sichtbarkeit erwarten könnte. Stattdessen fügt sich die *Assembly Hall* in die Fassade des *New College* ein und nutzt deren Eingangstorbogen zum eleganten Innenhof, der von der Statue von John Knox dominiert wird.

Resümee

Die *Assembly Hall* ist in der Öffentlichkeit kaum bekannt – nicht zuletzt deswegen, weil sie von der Straße aus nicht auffällt. Besucherinnen und Besucher, die das Gebäude zum ersten Mal betreten, sind über die Größe des Saals umso erstaunter. Als die *Hall* vor mehr als 150 Jahren gebaut wurde, war sie ein außergewöhnlicher, ganz für ihre Zweckbestimmung entworfener Raum. Auch die Lage am Anfang der High Street mit Blick auf die Princes Street war beeindruckend. Wie jedes Gebäude musste die *Assembly Hall* weiterentwickelt und stetigen Veränderungen angepasst werden. Durch die Installation von Beleuchtungen für Videokonferenzen, Wi-Fi und Streamingmöglichkeiten ist sie auch heute noch ein geeigneter Ort für Versammlungen.

---

1 Der Barrier Act besagt: »Bevor die Generalversammlung dieser Kirche Gesetze beschließen kann, die für die Kirche verbindlich sind, müssen diese zuerst der Versammlung als Entwurf vorgelegt werden. Nach der Beschlussfassung müssen die verschiedenen Presbyterien der Kirche die beschlossenen Gesetze nochmals prüfen. Deren Meinungen und Zustimmung müssen von ihren Beauftragten an die nächste Generalversammlung berichtet werden. Nur wenn die große Mehrheit der Kirche zugestimmt hat, dürfen die Gesetze in Kraft gesetzt werden.« https://www.churchofscotland.org.uk/about-us/church-law.

Rosalind Taylor

The Assembly Building of the Church of Scotland

Introduction

The Assembly Building of the Church of Scotland is used annually for its General Assembly. Often known affectionately only as The Hall, this was built in 1858, on a central site in Edinburgh, with a striking plan form to suit the synodality of the meetings it was designed to serve.

The Church of Scotland is a Presbyterian denomination, and as such no individual should have more influence than any other, with this principle being upheld by a series of courts which have developed from the pattern laid down between 1560 and 1690 following the Reformation. At local level, for each parish there is a Kirk Session, at district level there are the Presbyteries with representatives attending from each parish. Synods representing regional groups of Presbyteries were the next level until 1990 when these were abolished, having largely become redundant as the relationship between the Presbyteries and the General Assembly had grown. The General Assembly has the power to make laws determining how the Church of Scotland operates. The requirement for it to consult widely before any new or innovative direction is taken, is enshrined in the Barrier Act[1] of 1697, a fundamental Church of Scotland act confirming the Presbyterian principles of the Church.

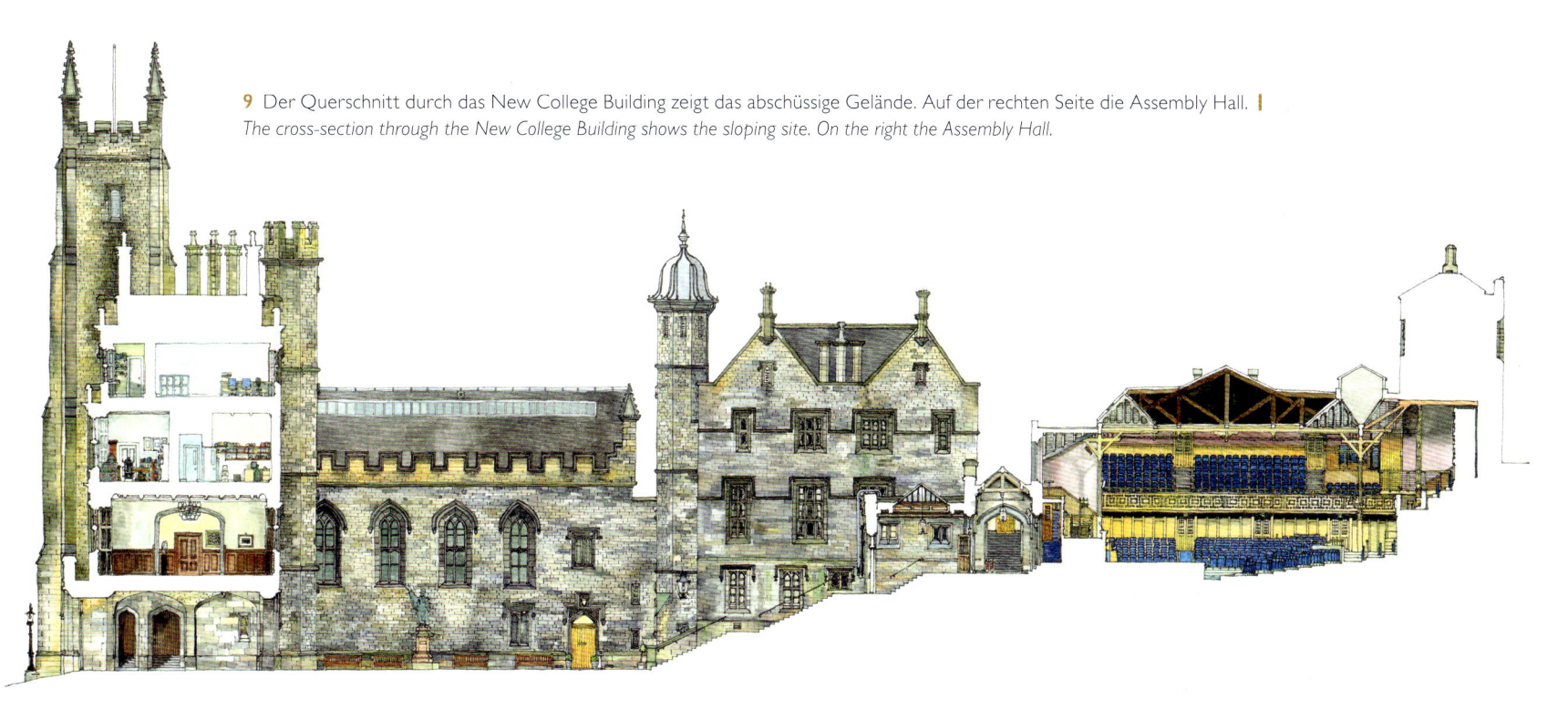

9 Der Querschnitt durch das New College Building zeigt das abschüssige Gelände. Auf der rechten Seite die Assembly Hall.
The cross-section through the New College Building shows the sloping site. On the right the Assembly Hall.

The Church of Scotland Assembly Building at 1 Mound Place in Edinburgh embodies the original hopes and intentions from the 1850s when it was conceived and built. Before the mid-19th century there was no purpose-built Hall in which the General Assembly met, various different venues having been used over the years.

Historical background

In September 1842 the foundation stone was laid for the Victoria Hall. The Victoria Hall, later known as the Tolbooth Church (Fig. 1), and now as the Hub, was designed by James Gillespie Graham (1776–1855), a prominent Scottish architect, in collaboration with his friend, Augustus Welby Northmore Pugin (1812–1852) one of the foremost British architects of his day. Indeed, the partnership of Gillespie Graham and Pugin would go on to work on the Palace of Westminster in London. The most striking feature of the Hub building is its Gothic spire, 72 metres tall, the highest point in the city.

This building was partly funded by the Edinburgh City Council, and was to be used for the Church of Scotland assemblies, including the Synod of Lothian, the Presbytery of Edinburgh and the General Assembly of the Church of Scotland. The location was at the top of the High Street in Edinburgh, where it is known as the Lawnmarket, on the South side. This is just below Edinburgh Castle; a landmark visible for miles around (Fig. 2 and 3).

Meanwhile, quite unrelated, discontent erupted within the Church of Scotland over various matters, including who was able to select the minister for a congregation. The conflict was largely over whether landowners should have a right to continue to select a parish minister rather than the members of the congregation doing so, with the landowners' position being supported by the government in London. In 1843 hundreds of ministers and elders left the established church to form the Free Church of Scotland, an event known as the Disruption. This new Free Church (Fig. 4) was to be a complete replacement body with the aim to build a new free church building in every parish and eventually a new assembly hall.

The Disruption was therefore the catalyst for a great period of church building in Scotland, with funds for the new buildings often raised by subscription from members. It was not only parish churches that were needed, there were also to be colleges, and a purpose-built assembly building. It was 1858 before a start was made on the new assembly hall. The site was at the heart of the new Free Church Theological College in Edinburgh. Following the union of 1929, when the Church of Scotland joined with the United Free Church of Scotland, only one assembly hall was needed and it is the Free Church assembly hall that is now used.

The New College building

The Free Church had lost no time in building its new theological college, which was begun in 1845. Again, at the top of the High Street in Edinburgh, just below the castle, but across the road from the Victoria Hall or Hub, on the North side of the Lawnmarket. This steeply sloping site still had some remains of the former palace of Mary of Guise, the mother of Mary Queen of Scots (Fig. 5). The new college was going to present a northward face (Fig. 6), looking over the new town of Edinburgh, the embodiment of a new society based upon the philosophies of David Hume and Adam Smith, which had been developing fast since the 1770s. Symbolically the new college was going to be facing the future, and in turn was highly visible from the wide streets of new town Edinburgh.

The architect was William Henry Playfair (1790–1857), also responsible for the terraces of the East New Town, St Stephen's Church, the Royal College of Surgeons, and the National Gallery of Scotland at the foot of the Mound sited just a stone's throw away (Fig. 7). He was an outstanding architect of his time, ambitious and successful. Although Playfair had joined the Free Church following the Disruption of 1843, and must have believed in the cause, his appointment followed a public competition.

He is said to have been inspired by the Colleges of Oxford and Cambridge to create his New College around a Courtyard in a Tudor Gothic Collegiate style. The site for the Assembly Building was the centre piece of the Courtyard on its South side.

The spire of the Hub is perfectly framed by the New College. From George Street at its junction with Hanover Street, the New College and the spire of the Hub are aligned to appear as one building at the top of the Old

10 Blick auf die Nordgalerie und das Podium. | *View on the North Gallery and the apron platform.*

Town, possibly the most important one at that time in Edinburgh with the Assembly Hall at the heart of it. The approach is, up the Mound, a broad street created by 1830 to link the old and new towns of Edinburgh, through the arched pend from the Mound, across the quadrangle and up the stairs to the entrance, with the spire always dominating from its position overhead (Fig. 8).

The Assembly Hall – funding

The cost of the Assembly Building was to be £7,000, a huge sum at the time, and raised entirely by the women of the Free Church of Scotland. This surely tells us something about the nature of the new organisation where the assembly must have been seen as integral to the working of the church by the women, even though illustrations of the time confirm that the vast majority of the participants in the assemblies were men. The funding for this most important of buildings may also have influenced the choice of architect, for although the Moderator's suite in the southeast corner of the New College quadrangle is by Playfair, the design of the hall itself was not his, but by David Bryce (1803–1876), responsible for many country houses such as Torosay Castle on Mull, the Edinburgh Royal Infirmary, but perhaps best known for Fettes College in Edinburgh. He developed and mastered the Scots Baronial style, being particularly skilled in his internal planning and use of space.

The Assembly Hall – design

The brief called for a bespoke space to hold an assembly of equals meeting before God. 1500 participants would need to be accommodated with good access for commissioners, the Moderator, the public and the Lord High Commissioner as the representative of the monarch. The challenge of creating such an assembly hall on this sloping site is certainly something that Bryce would have relished (Fig. 9).

At the time of its building, the interior of the Assembly Hall had the widest span roof in the country, to give clear uninterrupted views across the chamber from all four galleries and the main hall. To achieve this, Bryce, who was a very innovative architect, adopted tall cast-iron columns, painted with a wood grain effect, to support the heavy timber roof.

His cleverly conceived corridors, with an upper and lower corridor each side of the chamber, make use of the sloping site to give good access to the galleries and hall. The main ceremonial entrance from the college quadrangle is via an impressive, if not imposing, flight of steps.

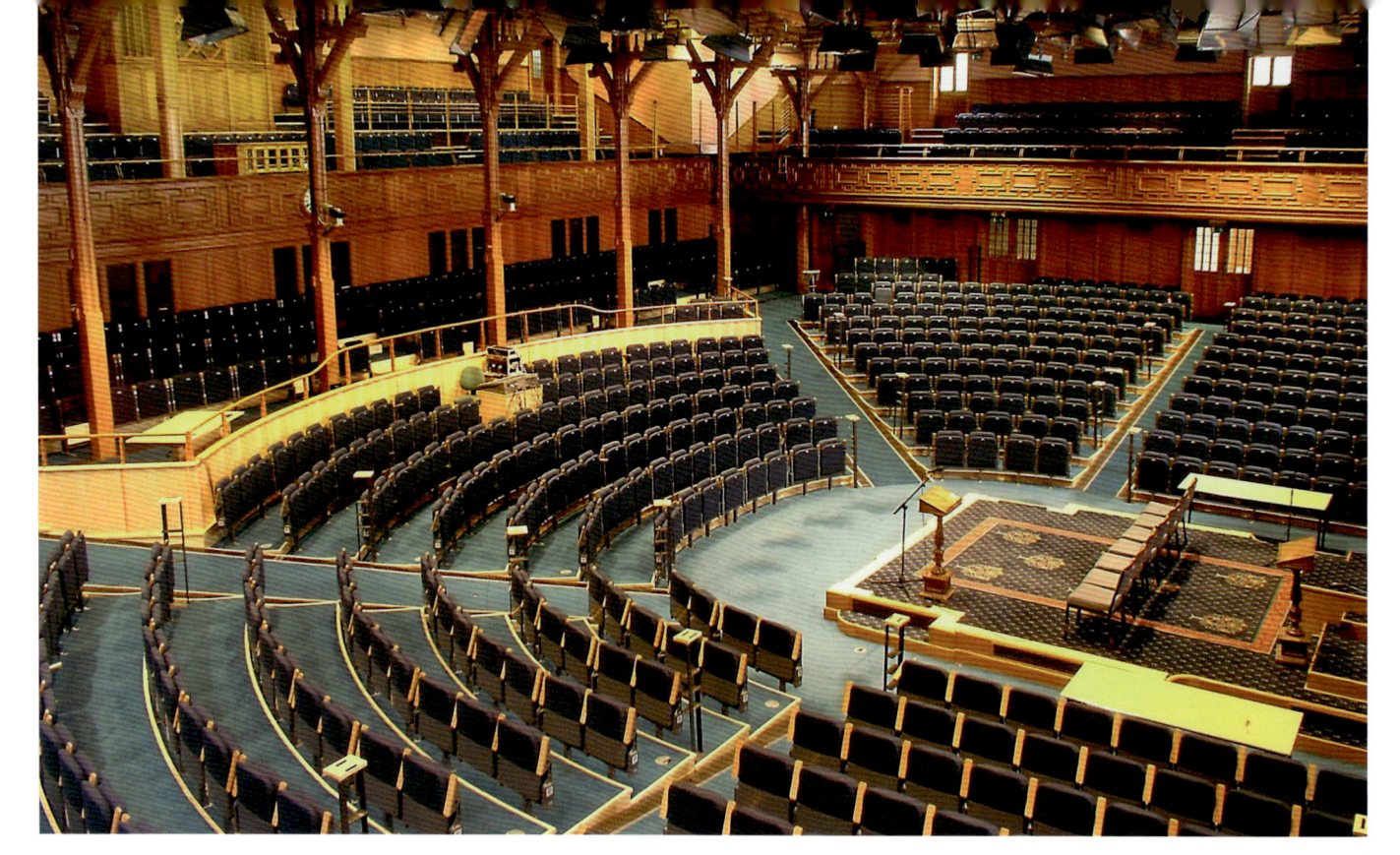

11 Keine Säulen verstellen die Sichtachsen im Saal, sodass man von überall einen guten Blick hat. | *No pillars obstruct the lines of sight inside the Hall, so everyone has a good view from everywhere.*

From this entrance, access to the ground floor debating chamber is across the iconic Black and White corridor. The apron platform from which the business of the Assembly is conducted is on the North side, the North Gallery is also reached from the Black and White corridor. From the pavement on the Lawnmarket level to South of the whole, direct entry is gained to the South, West and East galleries.

The Hall is a large, almost square space, 35 m × 27 m at the widest, with slightly raked seating and galleries on four sides. Making use of a series of clear glass cupola and roof lanterns, the hall was evenly and naturally lit, while the form of the space and the wall surfaces created excellent acoustics for participation by all, even before the use of electricity and sound systems.

It is a wonderful space with a raked floor towards the platform, no columns to obscure the sight lines on the ground floor level and good views from the galleries. The ceiling is high, level and of oak. The outside world does not impinge at all, giving the space a stillness, an intimacy and a simultaneous sense of space, which is unexpected.

The plain oak panelling behind the platform is typical of the simple, unadorned but high quality materials that were used in the finishes of the Hall, and which contribute to the sense of significance without superfluous show. This is somewhat different from the other parts of the interior of New College which tend to have more ornate detailing and decoration, giving the Hall a quite distinct character.

The shape of the Hall was dictated by the functionality required for over 1300 participants to be able to see and hear one another on an equal basis, thus a large square open space with galleries on all four sides (Fig. 11). The overarching concept is one of all being equal before God and all being able to see and hear one another. This arrangement was quite different from the church plans of the period which tended to be long, rectangular spaces with pews all facing the front to allow the congregation to focus on the spoken word from the figure in the pulpit, and with no expectation that members of the congregation would speak.

The Assembly Hall – interior

The layout of the seating in the hall, until 1999, was of long wooden benches with green upholstery set on three sides, with a platform for the Moderator and the functionaries of the church administration on the fourth side, so a meeting in the round, with the Moderator acting as the convenor or chair.

The North Gallery behind the Moderator is reserved for the Lord High Commissioner who represents the monarch at the General Assembly each year (Fig. 10). This gallery is entered separately to confirm the fact that the Assembly is chaired by the Moderator and the Lord High Commissioner, although present, does not participate in any debates or decision-making.

Above the platform there is a small stained-glass window with the Burning Bush, a symbol of the Church of Scotland. Since 1691 the Burning Bush has been used as a symbol, often with the Latin text *Nec Tamen Consumebatur*. The wording refers to the Book of Exodus when Moses encountered the burning bush. No matter how much it burned, it was never consumed by the flames. All the other windows are clear glass except for one behind the North gallery by Douglas Strachan, which shows David; the stained glass was added when the Free Church and Church of Scotland united in 1929 and the building became the Assembly Building of the Church of Scotland.

Alterations to the Assembly Building

The entrance vestibule and Black and White corridor were added by Sydney Mitchell (1856–1930) in 1899, replacing an open-air cloister; the Black and White corridor providing one of the most memorable features of the building (Fig. 12). This iconic space has been used for formal meetings, televised events and as a film set. In the film »Looking after Jo Jo«, which starred Robert Carlyle, the court scenes make use of the building, with dramatic exchanges taking place in the Black and White corridor.

Sydney Mitchell had designed many buildings for the Free Church, including New Restalrig Parish Church and Polwarth Parish Church. Above the entrance doors to the vestibule the following words are carved, PRAISE HIM IN THE ASSEMBLY OF THE ELDERS, confirming the purpose of the Hall.

Sydney Mitchell continued the Tudor Collegiate style in the Black and White corridor with its floor finish of black, grey and white marble in a diagonal chequered pattern, giving the name. When the Assembly Building was used by the Scottish Parliament from 1999 until 2004 this

12 Der Schwarz-Weiß-Korridor diente als Filmkulisse und inspirierte das Foyer des schottischen Parlaments. | *The Black and White corridor served as a film set and inspired the foyer of the Scottish Parliament.*

13 Der schwarz-weiße Korridor im schottischen Parlament. | *The Black and White corridor in the Scottish Parliament.*

14 Die Statue von John Knox dominiert den Innenhof. | *John Knox's statue dominates the courtyard.*

flooring reportedly inspired the architect Enric Miralles to incorporate a Black and White hallway in the New Scottish Parliament building opened 9 October 2004 (Fig. 13).

Sydney Mitchell's last major work was the Church of Scotland offices at 121 George Street, in 1908 originally for the United Free Church of Scotland, where Black and White flooring was once more adopted for the entrance.

Use of the chamber

The Moderator is selected annually to chair the General Assembly. This is a meeting now normally in May attended by commissioners who are largely elders and ministers of the Kirk. The General Assembly lasts for approximately a week and is an opportunity for debate and discussion, as well as for decisions to be taken and actions agreed upon.

The Moderator, the Principal Clerk and other officials sit on the platform at the North side of the Hall with the Lord High Commissioner's gallery behind. Seats are allocated to former Moderators, overseas delegates, and others, but this is for convenience rather than to signify any hierarchy.

Commissioners, who are ministers and elders, are seated in the ground floor of the hall and the West and South galleries. They are able to speak and to vote. The East gallery is reserved for members of the public and visitors normally on a first-come-first-served basis. Visitors are not able to vote.

As part of the New College the Hall is linked at either end of the Black and White corridor to what is now University accommodation to the East and to the Rainy Hall at the West. During the General Assembly, the Rainy Hall and other rooms normally in use by the University are used for circulation, cloak room, office and refreshments. The outside courtyard space is also important during the General Assembly and other events for both informal meetings and ceremonial gatherings.

It memorably appeared in the film »Chariots of Fire« when Eric Liddell, played by Ian Charleston, is seen hurrying across the courtyard, up the steps into the building.

The bronze statue of John Knox by the artist John Hutchison (1832–1910) from 1895 stands on a plinth at the East side of the quadrangle (Fig. 14). This has proved in recent years to be a great tourist attraction, frequently sought out and photographed.

Apart from being used for the Church of Scotland General Assembly in May and for a few other formal meetings the Hall has proved suitable for other gatherings and is let out to groups and organisations, such as for school prize-givings and conferences.

During the Edinburgh Festival it has been used successfully for many years as a theatre venue for the Fringe. For this, a stage is built up above the assembly apron platform to create a theatre in the round (Fig. 15).

The largest modern intervention to the hall came in the late 1990s when the building was seconded to the newly formed Scottish parliament as its temporary home while the new Scottish Parliament Building was being constructed down the hill at the foot of the Royal Mile.

The serried ranks of pew-like benches were replaced by arcs of theatre-style seats focused onto the apron area with the sightlines being carefully maintained to ensure the same sense that each participant should be subject to the oversight and questioning of all the other members. The fact that only minimal changes were needed to allow the building to function as a national Parliament is an indication of the quality of the original design and the modernity of the solution formed a century and a half earlier.

The exterior

The exterior of the hall is barely visible in the streetscape. On the Lawnmarket, the South elevation is an unassuming two-storey stone facade with plain timber doors. The West side of the building almost entirely abuts New College. The East abuts the Mylne's Court student accommodation with only a single plain unfenestrated wall along the Mylne's courtyard itself. The North alone has any presence, and this is restricted to the entrance steps and vestibule, framed by the Playfair inner towers. High-level windows in the North wall of the Hall are concealed from view. This seems to be unusual for an Assembly building, which might be expected to have a public face. Instead, the Assembly Hall borrows the impressive front elevation of the New College, and its entrance archway to the fine quadrangle, dominated by a statue of John Knox.

In short

Easily missed from the street, the Hall is not very well known. The exterior is in fact so minimal that new visitors are astonished at the size of the chamber, hardly able to believe that such a generous space could exist there. When it was built more than 150 years ago, it was an exceptional space, most particularly designed for its purpose, and located very significantly at the head of the High Street overlooking Princes Street in Edinburgh. Like any building it has had to evolve to suit the many and constant changes that go on around us. Broadcast lighting, Wi-Fi and streaming facilities are now installed to make it suitable for an assembly today.

15 Für das Festival wird die Assembly Hall in einen Theatersaal umgewandelt. | *The Assembly Hall is transformed into a theatre for the Festival.*

---

1 The Barrier Act states: »The General Assembly … do … declare that, before any General Assembly of this Church shall pass any Acts which are to be binding Rules and Constitutions to the Church, the same Acts [shall] be first proposed as overtures to the Assembly, and, being by them passed as such, be remitted to the consideration of the several Presbyteries of this Church, and their opinions and consent reported by their commissioners to the next General Assembly following, who may then pass the same in Acts, if the more general opinion of the Church thus had agreed thereunto.« https://www.churchofscotland.org.uk/about-us/church-law.

Ungarn
Hungary
Magyarország

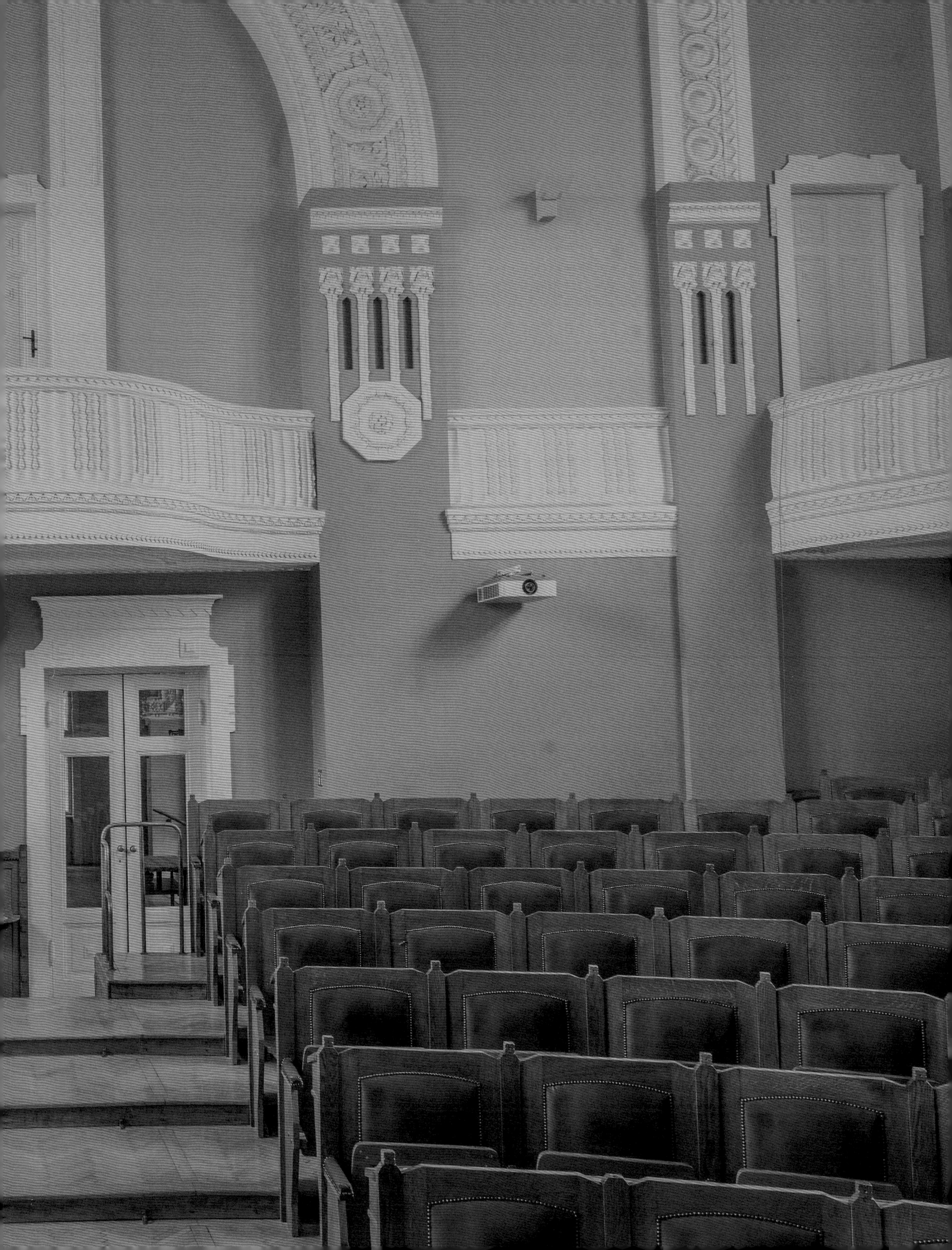

Steckbrief / General information / Általános információk

Kirche / Church / Egyház: Reformierte Kirche in Ungarn / Reformed Church in Hungary / Magyarországi Református Egyház

Land / Country / Ország: Ungarn / Hungary / Magyarország

Anzahl der Kirchenmitglieder / Church Members / Egyháztagok száma: 944.000

Bevölkerungsanteil / Share of the Population / Népességarányosan: 9,83 %

Anzahl der Synodenmitglieder / Members of the Synod / A zsinati tagok száma: 100

Name des Gebäudes / Name of the Building / Az épület megnevezése:
Magyarországi Református Egyház Zsinati Székháza

Ort / Place / Hely: Abonyi utca 21, Budapest

Baujahr / Year of Construction / Építés éve: 1908/1909

Architekten / Architects / Építészek: Alfréd Hajós, János Villányi

Máté Millisits · András Czanik

Das Synodengebäude der Reformierten Kirche in Ungarn

Die Geschichte der Synode

In Ungarn hielten während der Zeit der Habsburger Herrschaft die zum Landtag versammelten evangelischen Stände bereits ab dem 17. Jahrhundert eigene Tagungen ab, die sogenannten Konvente. 1715 aber wurden kirchliche Versammlungen, die keine königliche Erlaubnis hatten, gesetzlich verboten. Außerdem durften Beschwerden von evangelischer Seite, die die Religionsausübung betrafen, nicht mehr vor den Landtag gebracht werden. Von da an traf sich die Kirchenleitung der reformierten Kirche bei anderen Anlässen, wie zum Beispiel bei der Weinlese in Tokaj oder während der Prüfungen des Reformierten Kollegiums in Sárospatak, um aktuelle Themen zu besprechen. Die Bezeichnung »Konvent« ging auf diese Versammlungen über. Auch wenn die reformierte und die lutherische Kirche kein gemeinsames Exekutivorgan hatten, ernannten beide ab 1710 jeweils Beauftragte, die von der Regierung anerkannt wurden. Diese hatten die Aufgabe, Beschwerden und allgemeine kirchliche Angelegenheiten vor die Ungarische Hofkanzlei in Wien oder vor den Statthalterrat in Bratislava, der später nach Buda übersiedelte, zu bringen.

Ab 1791 war es den Reformierten erneut gestattet, Versammlungen abzuhalten. Bereits im September desselben Jahres tagte die Synode in Buda. Sie beschloss die Einrichtung eines Hauptkonsistoriums und des Amtes eines leitenden Kurators. Doch die dafür notwendige Anerkennung durch die Krone blieb aus. Der Generalkonvent in Pest und Debrecen, der 1821/1822 stattfand, trat hingegen ausdrücklich auf königlichen Erlass zusammen, um einige kontroverse Fragen zu klären.

Der österreichisch-ungarische Ausgleich im Jahr 1867 brachte eine große Veränderung: Die Religionsgleichheit, die schon während der Revolution und des Unabhängigkeitskriegs 1848-49 für kurze Zeit in Kraft gewesen war, wurde dauerhaft etabliert. Beim Konvent von Pest 1867 verabschiedete man daraufhin Reformen, die ihn mit gesetzgebenden und Verwaltungsbefugnissen ausstattete. Im November 1881 konnte die Ungarische Reformierte Kirche auf der Synode in Debrecen eine einheitliche reformierte Landeskirche schaffen. Auf dieser Synode wurden die wichtigsten Grundsätze der Kirchenverfassung festgelegt. Das Prinzip der Parität, d. h. der gleichen Beteiligung von ordinierten und nicht ordinierten Vertretern, wurde für alle Entscheidungsorgane – von der Gemeindeebene bis hin zur Synode – beschlossen. Die Synode sollte alle zehn Jahre zusammentreten. Der Generalkonvent wurde als höchstes Leitungsgremium der Kirche eingerichtet. Er war für die Verwaltung der kirchlichen Angelegenheiten zwischen den Synodentagungen, die Umsetzung der Beschlüsse der Synode und die formelle Vertretung der Kirche gegenüber dem Staat und anderen Institutionen zuständig. Außerdem wurde ein Finanzfonds eingerichtet, um gemeinsame Anliegen innerhalb der Kirche, wie z. B. Pensionszahlungen für Geistliche und die Versorgung von Armen und Waisen, finanziell abzudecken.

Die Baugeschichte des Synodengebäudes

Der Generalkonvent entschied 1897, ein Gebäude zu errichten, das Platz für Synodensitzungen, Komitees und Büros bieten sollte. Um die nötigen Vorbereitungen zu treffen, stellte das Konventspräsidium ein Komitee auf, dessen Vorsitz Dr. Dezső Bánffy innehatte. Ernő Dókus wurde zum Referenten des Komitees gewählt. Die Vorbereitungen dauerten mehrere Jahre. Über den Fortschritt wurde regelmäßig Bericht erstattet.

1903 beschloss die Synode, dass das neue Gebäude nicht nur einen Sitzungssaal für die Synode und Büros für die zentrale Kirchenverwaltung beherbergen solle, sondern auch einen Festsaal und Unterkünfte für Theologiestudenten. Gleichzeitig wurde für die Ausschreibung des imposanten Gebäudes ein Budget von 310.000 Kronen (entspricht heute ca. 600 Mio. Forint bzw. 1,5 Mio. Euro) beschlossen. Schon zu Beginn zeichnete sich klar ab, dass dafür ein Baukredit notwendig war. An der späteren Abbezahlung des Kredites beteiligten sich alle Kirchendistrikte der Reformierten Kirche Ungarns.

Bei der Suche nach einem geeigneten Standort war die ursprüngliche Idee, das Gebäude in zentraler Lage neben der reformierten Kirche am Kálvin-Platz zu errichten (Abb. 1).

Dieser Platz ist heute ein Verkehrsknotenpunkt und wegen seiner Nähe zum ungarischen Nationalmuseum bekannt. Dort sollte das so genannte »Calvineum« als ein zentrales Gebäude der Kirchenleitung der Reformierten Kirche Ungarns entstehen. In diesem Gebäude waren nicht nur der Sitzungssaal der Synode und die mit der Arbeit des Generalkonvents verbundenen Büros geplant, sondern auch eine theologische Akademie (Fakultät), eine Bibliothek, ein modernes Studentenwohnheim, die Wohnung und das Büro des Bischofs sowie des Pfarrers der örtlichen Gemeinde. Diese Idee konnte jedoch mangels Unterstützung nicht verwirklicht werden. 1905 fand man einen geeigneteren Standort in der Nähe der Thököly Straße auf Höhe der Szabó József Gasse. So wurde das Gebäude schließlich etwas weiter vom Stadtzentrum entfernt in einem Villenviertel in der Nähe des Stadtparks (Városliget) errichtet (Abb. 2).

| Ursprünglich war das Synodengebäude am Kálvin-Platz geplant. | *The synod building was originally planned for Kálvin Square.* | A zsinati épületet eredetileg a Kálvin térre tervezték.

2 Das schließlich realisierte Gebäude war das Ergebnis eines Architekturwettbewerbs, an dem neunzehn Architekturbüros teilnahmen. | *The building that was finally realised was the result of a construction tender in which 19 architectural firms took part.* | *A végül megvalósult épület egy építési pályázat eredménye, amelyen 19 építésziroda vett részt.*

1907 schrieb das Präsidium des Generalkonvents einen Architekturwettbewerb aus. Neunzehn Entwürfe wurden eingereicht. Den ersten Platz erhielten Alfréd Hajós (1878–1955) und János Villányi (1874–1924) für ihren Entwurf »Ein' feste Burg«. Der zweite Platz ging an einen Entwurf mit der Bezeichnung »Klarheit«. Realisiert wurde schließlich eine Kombination aus den mit den beiden ersten Plätzen ausgezeichneten sowie drei weiteren ausgewählten Entwürfen (Abb. 3 und 4). Mit der Errichtung des Gebäudes wurden die beiden Architekten Hajós und Villányi beauftragt.

Alfréd Hajós (Abb. 5) war ein berühmter ungarischer Sportler. 1896 errang er bei den Olympischen Spielen in Athen über 100 Meter Freistil die erste Schwimm-Olympiamedaille der Neuzeit und die erste olympische Goldmedaille für sein Heimatland Ungarn. Am selben Tag gewann er auch den Wettbewerb über 1200 Meter Freistil.

»Der ungarische Delphin« – wie er genannt wurde – gewann später noch weitere nationale Leichtathletikwettbewerbe. 1907 gründete er gemeinsam mit János Villányi ein eigenes Architekturbüro.

Die Ausstattung des Synodengebäudes

Die Bauarbeiten für das Synodengebäude begannen am 16. März 1908. Die Übergabe erfolgte am 5. April 1909, im 400. Geburtsjahr Johannes Calvins. Der Sitzungssaal für die Synode, der auch als Festsaal genutzt wird, umfasst 222 Sitzplätze. Das Podium des Präsidiums ist von runden Bankreihen umgeben (Abb. 6). Die Synode als höchstes Beratungs- und Entscheidungsorgan wird quasi als »Parlament der Kirche« angesehen. Dies spiegelt auch die Anordnung der Sitzplätze wider, da in den meisten Parlamentsgebäuden die Sitze zur Förderung der Debattenkultur im Halbkreis angeordnet sind.

Eine vorgegebene Sitzordnung für die Synodalen gibt es außer für die Präsidien der einzelnen Kirchendistrikte, die in der ersten Reihe sitzen, nicht. Sonderplätze haben leitende Mitarbeitende des Synodenbüros und ständige Gäste (Abb. 7 und 8). In den Sitzungssaal gelangt man über eine Treppe (Abb. 9 und 10). An drei Seiten des Saals befinden sich Galerien, auf denen Sitzplätze für Gäste und extra Plätze für Journalisten vorgesehen sind.

3 Das 1909 eröffnete zentrale Synodengebäude der reformierten Kirche in Ungarn | *Headquarters of the Reformed Church in Hungary, opened in 1909* | *A Magyarországi Református Egyház 1909-ben átadott főépülete*

Im Erdgeschoss und im Kellergeschoss des Gebäudes befinden sich die Büros des Generalkonvents, des nationalen reformierten Fonds, die Waisen- und Pensionskasse, das Archiv, die Bibliothek und der Sitzungsraum des Konvents. Im ersten Stock befand sich vor der Renovierung im Jahr 2003 eine Mietwohnung mit 6 Zimmern und im zweiten Stock eine Wohnung für den Sekretär des Generalkonvents.

Das Grundstück und der Bau des Gebäudes samt Inneneinrichtung kosteten damals 525.000 Kronen, was heute etwa dem Betrag von 1000 Mio. Forint bzw. 2,5 Mio. Euro entspricht.

Die erste Sitzung im neuen zentralen Synodengebäude fand am 21. April 1909 im Rahmen des 400. Jubiläumsjahres der Geburt von Johannes Calvin statt. Dezső Bánffy, Vorsitzender des Konvents, eröffnete das Gebäude mit folgenden Worten:

»[…] Lasst uns hier und jetzt unsere Beratungen zum Wohle unserer ganzen Kirche beginnen, in friedlicher Stimmung danach strebend, dass die vom Gesetz gegebene Autonomie und der Leitungsauftrag unseren Organen nicht wieder genommen wird. Sollte dies geschehen, würden wir schwächer sein und nicht durch dieses uns zugestandene Recht geleitet werden, sondern von einer von Tag zu Tag wechselnden Stimmung, die zwar Revolutionen entfachen kann, aber nicht imstande ist, etwas verlässlich aufzubauen und eine dauerhafte Organisation aufrecht zu erhalten.«

Die Gedenktafel für die Galeerensklaven

Die 1670er Jahre, während der Gegenreformation, waren für die protestantischen Kirchen in Ungarn eine besonders herausfordernde Zeit. Am 5. März 1674 wurden mehr als 700 Protestanten, die sich zu ihrem Glauben bekannten, vor ein Sondergericht nach Bratislava zitiert. Das Gericht beschuldigte sie des Verrats, des Hochverrats und der Beleidigung der katholischen Kirche und verlangte, dass sie ihre ›Sünden‹ bekennen und zum Katholizismus übertreten sollten. Pastoren und Prediger, die nicht bereit waren, ihre Überzeugung aufzugeben, wurden in kleinen Gruppen eingekerkert. Mehr als vierzig von ihnen wurden als Galeerensklaven verkauft und nach Neapel transportiert, von denen nur zweiunddreißig den Transport überlebten. Ihr Schicksal erregte in den protestantischen Ländern Europas großes Aufsehen. Es wurden Kollekten für ihre Befreiung organisiert und nach mehreren Versuchen gelang es dem niederländischen Admiral Michiel de Ruyter am 11. Februar 1676, die Galeerensklaven freizukaufen.

Die Idee zu einer Gedenktafel kam 1933 von Károly Marjai, Pfarrer in Mezőtúr. Er machte dem Konvent den Vorschlag, das Martyrium der Galeerensklaven mit einer Gedenktafel am Gebäude der Kirchenzentrale zu würdigen (Abb. 11). Diese wurde am 6. Mai 1936 im Rahmen eines Festaktes anlässlich des 400-jährigen Jubiläums der ersten Ausgabe von Calvins Hauptwerk »Institutio Christianae Religionis« enthüllt. Neben den Galeerensklaven wurde auf der Tafel auch Admiral Michiel de Ruyter gewürdigt, der sie freigekauft hatte: »Im gesegnetem Gedenken an die Bekennenden und an den Befreier …«.

Die heutige Nutzung des Synodengebäudes

Außer einigen kleineren Instandhaltungen gab es jahrzehntelang keine Umbau- oder Renovierungsarbeiten am Gebäude. Nur die Wohnungen im ersten Stock wurden mit der Zeit in Büroräume umgewandelt. Der letzte bedeutende Umbau des Bürotraktes fand 2003/2004 statt, als alle Spuren der ehemaligen Nutzung als Wohnungen (Fliesen und Waschbecken) aus den Büroräumen entfernt wurden. Der Sitzungssaal wurde 2005 renoviert. Dabei wurden die Möbel originalgetreu nachgebaut und moderne audiovisuelle Technik installiert. Die ursprüngliche Farbgebung und das originale Erscheinungsbild wurden wieder hergestellt. Die alten Möbel fanden, sofern noch möglich, in den Büros und Sitzungsräumen Verwendung. Für die Beleuchtung des Sitzungssaales, eines Besprechungsraums und mehrerer Büros werden immer noch die ursprünglichen Lampen verwendet (Abb. 12 und 13). 2019 begann eine Fassadenrenovierung und 2022 die Umgestaltung und Neubepflanzung des Gartens. Um das Gebäude umweltfreundlicher zu machen, wurde eine Solaranlage installiert.

Zweimal im Jahr hält die Synode als gesetzgebendes Organ der Reformierten Kirche in Ungarn ihre Sitzungen in dem Haus ab. Das Gebäude ist außerdem Sitz des Synodenbüros, das für die Synode, den Synodalrat und das Präsidium der Synode zuständig ist. Im Untergeschoss befinden sich die Pensionskasse für Pfarrerinnen und Pfarrer und das Sekretariat der örtlichen Kirchengemeinde »Budapest – Barossplatz«. Seit 1966 feiert diese reformierte Kirchengemeinde ihre Gottesdienste im Synodensaal und hält für den Gemeindepfarrer ein kleines Büro bereit.

4 Das Gebäude wurde nicht – wie ursprünglich vorgesehen – in zentraler Lage errichtet, sondern in einem Villenviertel in der Nähe des Stadtparks. | The building was not – as originally planned – erected in a central location, but in a residential neighbourhood near the city park. | Az épületet nem – mint eredetileg – központi helyen, hanem egy lakónegyedben, a Városliget közelében emelték.

5 Alfréd Hajós war ein großer Schwimmathlet und Olympiasieger, bevor er Architekt wurde. Gemeinsam mit Villányi gründete er ein Architekturbüro, mit dem er bedeutende Bauprojekte in Ungarn realisierte. | *Alfréd Hajós was a great swimming athlete and Olympic champion before he became an architect. Together with Villányi, he founded an architectural office with which he realised important building projects in Hungary.* | *Hajós Alfréd nagyszerű úszósportoló és olimpiai bajnok volt, mielőtt építész lett. Villányival együtt építészirodát alapított, amellyel jelentős magyarországi építkezéseket valósított meg.*

Berichte aus der Erbauungszeit machen deutlich, dass ursprünglich mit dem Wunsch nach einem Synodengebäude mehr verbunden war als nur ausreichend Platz für die Bedürfnisse des Synodenlebens. Es gab die klare Vorstellung, dass das Gebäude »nicht nur aus Steinen und kunstvollen Verzierungen besteht, sondern etwas von dem bekennenden und kämpfenden Geist der Kirche zeigt (Abb. 14).«

Resümee

Betrachtet man die ursprüngliche Zielsetzung für das Gebäude, nämlich den Versammlungssaal für die Synode und die Büroräume für die administrativen Tätigkeiten in einem einzigen Haus unterzubringen, werden diese Erwartungen heute nur noch beschränkt erfüllt. Durch die Erweiterung des kirchlichen Dienstes sind die Büroräume längst zu klein geworden und mussten vor allem in den letzten Jahren in benachbarte Gebäude verlegt werden. Trotzdem spielt das Gebäude weiterhin eine bestimmende und symbolbehaftete Rolle im Leben der Reformierten Kirche Ungarns. Darüber hinaus bietet es regionalen und internationalen Treffen und Konferenzen Raum für ihre Zusammenkünfte (Abb. 15). In vielerlei Hinsicht symbolisieren das Haus und seine Nutzung, was schon in der Kirchenverfassung formuliert wurde, dass »die Reformierte Kirche in Ungarn Teil der weltweiten Kirche Jesu Christi ist«.

Máté Millisits · András Czanik

The Synod Building of the Reformed Church in Hungary

History of the synod

From the seventeenth century onward, Protestant estates in Hungary held special meetings, called convents in Hungary under the Roman Catholic Habsburg Rule. They often took place during national assemblies known as »Diets«. In 1715, church meetings without special royal permission were outlawed by a new law also prohibiting Protestants to bring any religious concerns they had to the Diet. In response, Protestant church leaders chose to meet in other, more surreptitious settings to discuss current issues, such as at the annual Tokaj-Hegyalja wine harvest, or during the final exam period at the Reformed college in Sárospatak. Even without a formal decision-making body, leaders of the Reformed and Lutheran churches had already begun meeting in the 1710s to appoint representatives (*chargés d'affaires*), who were recognised by the government to administer complaints and various other church affairs before the Hungarian Court Chancellery in Vienna, as well as the Locotenential Council in Bratislava, and later in Buda.

1791, Reformed churches were once again permitted to hold their own Assemblies. They immediately convened the Synod of Buda, and they decided to establish a common General Consistory, as well as the office of Chief Lay President. Unfortunately, this idea did not receive royal approval, but in 1821–1822 the General Convent was able to meet in Pest and Debrecen by royal decree to settle various controversial issues.

In the 1867 Compromise with Austria, a new situation allowed the re-establishment of the principle of religious equality, which had been in place for a brief period after the attempted revolution and freedom fight of 1848–1849. In the Convent in Pest in 1867, reform efforts were supported, according to which the Convent was to be given legislative and administrative powers.

By November 1881, at the Synod in Debrecen, the Hungarian Reformed Church was able to establish a unified national church structure. This Synod set out the main principles of the church constitution, a corporate structure in which the principle of parity or equality between ordained and lay representatives, was designed to be applied and enforced from the local parish level up to the synod level. The Synod was scheduled to meet once every ten years, and the General Convent was established as the highest governing body of the church, with responsibility for administering church affairs between synodical meetings, implementing the laws of Synod, and formally representing the church before the state and other institutions. A common financial fund was set up to meet the needs of common causes within the church, such as pensions of ministers, and the care of the poor and orphans.

How the synod building came about

In 1897 the General Convent decided to construct a building to hold synod meetings and accommodate other Convent-related work. The Presidium duly appointed a committee, which was chaired by convent president Dezső Bánffy and coordinated by Ernő Dókus. The committee worked for several years on the building project, providing regular reports on their work.

In 1903 the committee decided on additional uses for the new building. In addition to the Synod Hall, it

6 Das Pult des Präsidiums mit dem Wappen der Reformierten Kirche Ungarns. | *The lectern of the presidium with the coat of arms of the Reformed Church in Hungary.* | *Az elnökségi emelvény a Magyarországi Református Egyház címerével.*

would include a ceremonial hall, central offices, and residential space for theology students. Secondly, the committee decided to issue a call for tenders, with a total budget of 310,000 crowns (the equivalent of 1.5 million euros in 2022). It was clear from the outset that the large-scale construction project could only be accomplished on credit, and all of the church districts were prepared to finance their share in the repayment.

In the search for a suitable location for the building, the initial idea had been to situate it next to the Reformed Church on Kálvin Square, a central transport hub near many popular destinations, such as the Hungarian National Museum (Fig. 1). The original plans referred to the headquarters as the »Calvineum« and provided for a central building that would house the theological academy, a library, a modern boarding school, the residence and offices of the local bishop, as well as those of the local parish (in addition to the aforementioned Synod Hall, ceremonial hall, etc). Ultimately, this plan for building on Kálvin Square was never realised due to financial constraints, and in 1905 a site was selected near the corner of Thököly and Szabó József streets (Fig. 2).

This new site was located just a little further from the city centre, in a residential area near the City Park.

In 1907 the Presidium of the Convent published a call for tenders, and a total of nineteen architectural plans were submitted. Five design plans were selected from the nineteen submissions. The first prize, designed by

Alfréd Hajós (1878–1955) and János Villányi (1874–1924), was called »A Mighty Fortress« and the second prize went to the submission called »Clarity/Light«. The final plans were a combination of the first and second prize winning submissions, along with three other plans, and the Convent entrusted the architectural work to Hajós and Villányi (Fig. 3 and 4).

Hajós (Fig. 5) had been a very famous Hungarian athlete, winning both the 100-metre and the 1200-metre freestyle swimming in the first modern Olympics in Athens in 1896. Nicknamed the »Hungarian dolphin«, he also won medals in sprints, hurdles and discus. In 1907 he and Villányi founded their own architectural firm.

The interior design of the synod building

Construction work on the secession-style building began on 16 March 1908 and it was opened on 5 April 1909, the 400th anniversary of John Calvin's birth. The Synod Hall (also used as a banquet hall) has 222 seats, with rows of benches surrounding the lectern of the presiding officer in a wide circle. As the highest consultative and decision-making body of the Reformed Church, the Synod is the church's parliament. This is also reflected in the seating arrangement of the main hall, which, like in most parliaments, is semi-circular and well suited for debate (Fig. 6). The members of synod do not have a fixed seating plan. However, in the front row sit the presidents of the church districts and there is a special place for the senior staff of the Synod Office as well as for the permanent invitees (Fig. 7 and 8). A separate staircase leads to the Synod Hall, where three galleries provide seating for guests and journalists (Fig. 9 and 10). The ground floor and the basement house the Convent offices, the national Reformed public fund, the orphans' and pension institutions, the archives, the library, and the Convent's meeting room. A six-room apartment was originally on the first floor, with the offices of the secretary of the General Convent located on the second floor. The total cost for the land and construction, including furnishings, was 525,000 crowns.

At the first synod assembly held (in commemoration of Calvin's 400th anniversary) on 21 April 1909, the chairman of the preparatory committee, Dezső Bánffy, inaugurated the building with the following plea:

»[…] let us begin our assemblies here to the betterment of our universal church in a peaceful manner, with great ambition and the intention not to let the leadership be taken from the hands of our lawful autonomy and the organisations established by it. Because if that happens, we shall become weaker, and instead of the law, temporary moods will control us, which change from day to day and which might result in revolutions, but will not help the gradual growth and the maintenance of a lasting organisation.«

7 Bei der Eröffnung des Gebäudes war der Saal ursprünglich mit *Trompe l'oeil* Malereien dekoriert. | *When the building was opened, the hall was originally decorated with* trompe l'oeil *paintings.* | *Az épület megnyitásakor a termet eredetileg* trompe l'oeil *festményekkel díszítették.*

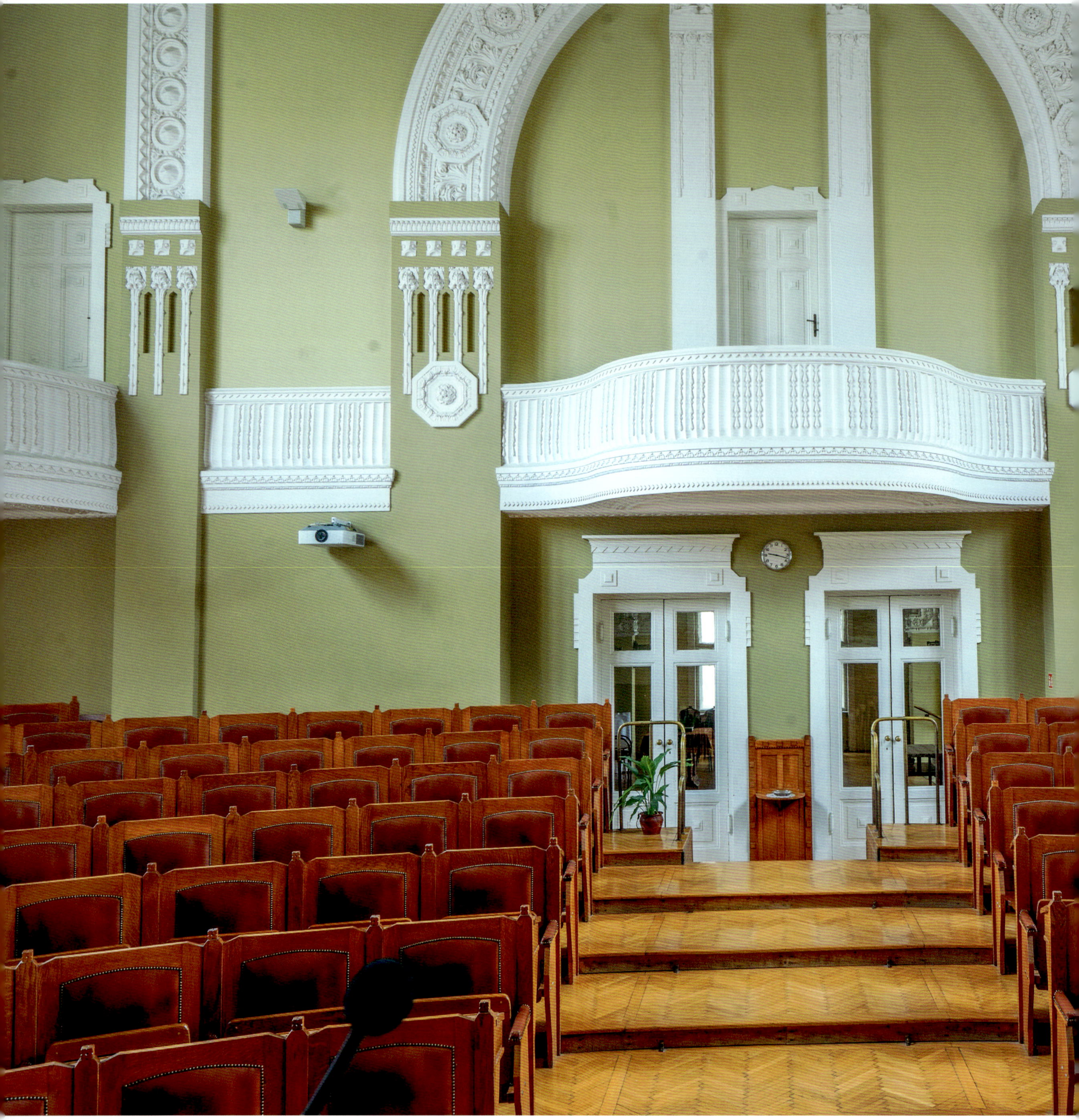

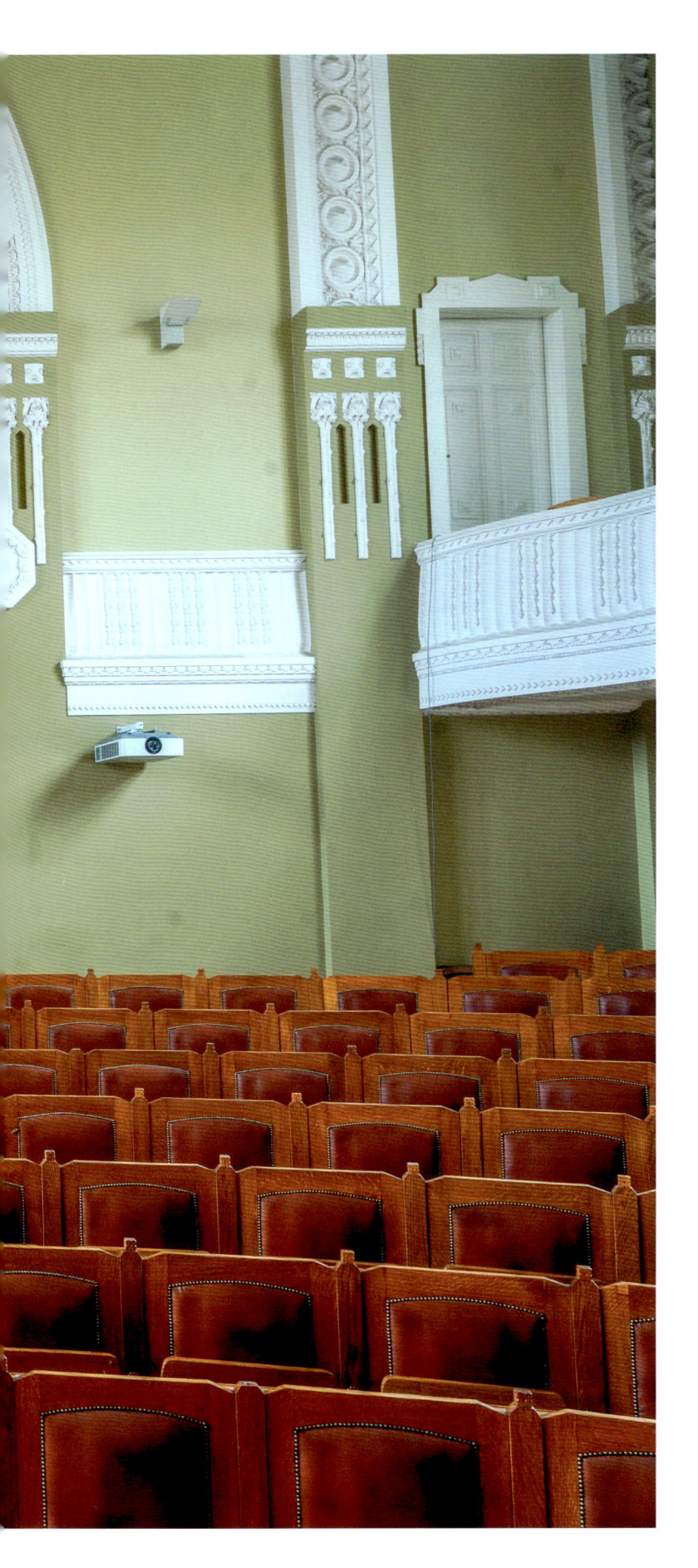

8 Die Bestuhlung wurde originalgetreu nachgebaut, der Saal ist nun aber einfärbig gestaltet. Die Stuckverzierungen werden durch den farblichen Kontrast hervorgehoben. | *The seating has been faithfully reproduced, but the hall is now monochrome. The stucco decorations are emphasised by the colour contrast.* | *Az ülőalkalmatosságokat hűen reprodukálták, de a terem ma már egyszínű. A stukkódíszeket a színkontraszt kiemeli.*

9 Das Treppenhaus, das zum Synodensaal führt, nach der Fertigstellung zu Beginn des 20. Jahrhunderts und der mit Tapeten verzierte Vorraum. | *The staircase leading to the synod hall after its completion at the beginning of the 20th century and the vestibule decorated with wallpaper.* | *A zsinati terembe vezető lépcsőház a 20. század eleji befejezés után és a tapétával díszített előszoba.*

The plaque of the galley slaves

The 1670s were a challenging time for the Protestant churches in Hungary. Inside the assembly hall, there is a memorial tablet commemorating the victims of a violent chapter of the Counter-Reformation. On 5 March 1674, over 700 Protestant confessors of faith were summoned by a special court in Pozsony (Bratislava) and accused of high treason in violation of the Catholic Church. They were ordered to confess their »sins« and to convert to Catholicism. Those not willing to negotiate were imprisoned. Over 40 pastors were forcibly taken to Naples, with only 32 surviving the journey. Those who survived were sold as galley slaves. This injustice created an outcry throughout the Protestant countries of Europe and, in an attempt to free the prisoners, a collection was launched throughout the continent. After several attempts, the Dutch Admiral Michiel de Ruyter set them free on 11 February 1676.

The initiative for the plaque commemorating the martyrdom of the galley slaves came from Károly Marjai, a local Hungarian minister; it was commissioned on 6 May 1936 as part of the celebration of the 400th anniversary of John Calvin's »Institutes of the Christian Religion« (»Institutio Christianae Religionis«). The inscription honours not only the galley slaves but also Admiral Michiel de Ruyter, their liberator: »In the blessed memory of the confessors and the one who liberated them …« (Fig. 11)

The current use of the building

The building itself was not renovated or refurbished for decades, except for a few minor alterations in certain areas. The apartments on the first floor were eventually replaced by offices, with all traces of residential use (sinks, tiles) removed in 2003–2004. The church undertook a major renovation of the Synod Hall in 2005, refurbishing most of the original furniture and installing audio-visual equipment. It was redecorated in the original colour and other decorative elements were restored. Where possible, the original furniture designed by Hajós and Villányi was maintained in certain offices and boardrooms, where original chandeliers and other light fittings are still operational (Fig. 12 and 13). Beginning in 2019, the outside of the building has also seen some renovation, with the small courtyard being redesigned to include some greenery and plants in 2022. A solar panel system was also installed to make the building eco-friendlier.

The Reformed Congregation of Budapest-Baross Square has been worshipping in the Synod Hall every Sunday since 1966, also maintaining a small office for the local minister.

The Synod meets twice a year to perform its role as the legislative governing body of the Reformed Church in Hungary and it also maintains a Synod Office to administer church affairs. The building contains the offices of the Presidium and the General Secretary (Synod Clerk), as well as the following departments: mission, ecumenical and international relations, church law, finance and others.

Early reports from the time of construction make it clear that the original vision for the Synod building went beyond the mere need for more space. There was also the clear idea of a building that would 'not only be brick, not only stone and artistic decoration, but represent also something of the soul and strength of the believing and struggling church' (Fig. 14).

In short

Due to the growth and current complexity of the administration of the denomination and its programmes, the current functions of the Synod building no longer match its original purpose – to house the Synod Hall as well as central church offices in a single building. Offices have had to move to larger spaces in nearby buildings, especially in recent years. Despite this decentralisation, the Synod building continues to serve as a crucial symbol of the unified national church, as well as a venue for regional and international church meetings and conferences (Fig. 15). In many ways it symbolises that – according to its constitution – »the Reformed Church in Hungary shall function as part of Jesus Christ's Universal Church.«

10 Das Treppenhaus, das zum Synodensaal führt, nach der Renovierung. | *The staircase leading to the synod hall after the renovation.* | *A zsinati terembe vezető lépcsőház a felújítás után.*

Máté Millisits · András Czanik

A Magyarországi Református Egyház Zsinati Székháza

A Zsinat története

A Habsburg uralom alatt az országgyűlésekre egybegyűlt protestáns rendek a 17. századtól kezdve gyakran tartottak külön értekezleteket, amelyet »konventnek« neveztek. 1715-ben azonban törvény tiltotta a királyi engedély nélküli egyházi gyűléseket, és azt is, hogy a protestánsok vallási sérelmeiket az országgyűlés elé terjesszék. Ettől kezdve az egyház vezetői más rendezvényekhez kapcsolódóan – például a tokaj-hegyaljai szüretek vagy a sárospataki kollégiumi vizsgák alkalmával – jöttek össze, ott tárgyalták meg az aktuális kérdéseket. Közös végrehajtó szervük nem volt, de a református és evangélikus egyházak az 1710-es évektől a kormányzat által is elismert ügyvivőket állítottak, akik vállalták a panaszok beadását, és az egyház ügyeinek intézését a bécsi Magyar Udvari Kancelláriánál és a pozsonyi, majd budai Helytartótanácsnál.

1791-ben ismét megnyílt a lehetőség a reformátusok előtt, hogy gyűléseket tartsanak. Ezzel éltek is, és 1791 szeptemberében a budai zsinaton elhatározták egy közös főkonzisztórium és egyetemes főgondnoki hivatal létrehozását, ez azonban nem kapott királyi jóváhagyást. Az 1821–1822. évi generális konvent (Pesten és Debrecenben) viszont kifejezetten királyi rendeletre ült össze, hogy elintézzen némely vitás kérdéseket.

Változást az 1867-es kiegyezés hozott, mely – az 1848–1849. évi szabadságharc rövid időszakát követően – ismét érvénybe helyezte a vallásegyenlőség elvét. 1867-ben a pesti konventen támogatták a konvent olyan átalakítását, mely felruházza azt törvényhozó és igazgatási jogokkal.

Végül a magyar reformátusok egységes, országos egyházzá alakulása az 1881 novemberében megtartott debreceni zsinaton valósult meg. Ekkor állapították meg az egyházalkotmány főbb alapelveit: a testületi kormányzást, melyben a paritás elvét az egyházközségektől a zsinatig érvényesítették, amely a lelkészi és nem lelkészi (presbiteri) személyek egyenlő részévételét mondja ki az egyházkormányzásban. Elhatározták, hogy a zsinat tízévente üljön össze, és létrehozták az Egyetemes Konventet, mint a református egyház legfőbb kormányzó testületét, mely képviseli a református egyházat az állam és más testületek felé, továbbá a zsinatok közti időben felelős a zsinati törvények végrehajtásáért és a felmerülő ügyek intézéséért. Felállították a közös pénzügyi alapot, majd később az árva- és nyugdíjintézetet is.

A zsinati székház építésének története

A református egyház országos döntéshozó testülete, az Egyetemes Konvent 1897-ben elhatározta, hogy a zsinati ülések, valamint a konvent munkájához kapcsolódó irodák, bizottságok működésének helyszínéül önálló épületet kell felépíteni. Az előkészületekre a Konvent Elnöksége bizottságot jelölt ki, amelynek elnöke br. Bánffy Dezső volt, konventi előadója pedig Dókus Ernő. Az előkészítés éveken át tartott, munkájukról rendszeresen beszámoltak.

Két dologban már 1903-ban zsinati döntés született: az egyik, hogy olyan új épületre van szükség, amely nem csupán a zsinat üléstermének ad helyet, hanem az elnökségi szalonnak és a központi irodáknak is, valamint teológushallgatók számára diáklakásoknak is. A másik döntés az építési terv pályáztatására vonatkozott: eszerint 310 000 korona (ez 2022-es árfolyamon 600 millió forintnak felel meg) építési összegből kell az impozáns méretű épületet

Die Erinnerungstafel zu Ehren der Pastoren, die als Galeerensklaven verschleppt wurden. | The memorial plaque in honour of the pastors who were deported as galley slaves. | A gályarabként deportált lelkészek tiszteletére állított emléktábla.

kivitelezni. Már a kezdeteknél világosan látszott, hogy a nagyszabású vállalkozást csak hitelből lehet megvalósítani, a törlesztésből pedig minden egyházkerület részt vállalt.

Megfelelő telket keresve az eredeti elképzelés az volt, hogy központi helyszínen, a közlekedési csomópontként és például a Magyar Nemzeti Múzeum közelsége révén turisztikai szempontból is ismertebb Kálvin téri református templom mellett épüljön fel a székház (1. sz. kép). A »Kálvineum«-nak nevezett székház a tervek szerint olyan központi épület lett volna, ahol a zsinati ülésterem, valamint a konvent munkájához kapcsolódó irodák mellett a teológiai akadémia, könyvtár, egy modern internátus, továbbá a püspök lakása és hivatali helyiségei, valamint a helyi egyházközség lelkészének lakása és hivatala is elhelyezhetők lettek volna. Az impozáns terv azonban megfelelő támogatottság hiányában nem valósulhatott meg, és 1905-ben végül a Thököly út és a Szabó József utca sarkához közel sikerült megtalálni a megfelelő telket (2. sz. kép). A székház így végül a városközponttól kicsit távolabb, a Városligethez közeli villanegyedben kapott helyet.

Az építési pályázatot újabb két év múltán, 1907-ben hirdette meg a Konvent Elnöksége. Összesen tizenkilenc terv érkezett. Az első díjat a Hajós Alfréd (1878–1955) és Villányi János (1874–1924) tervezte »Erős várunk« jeligéjű terv kapta, a második helyet a »Világosság« jeligét viselő érdemelte ki. Emellett megvásároltak további három értékes tervet is. Mindezek egybedolgozására és a végleges tervek elkészítésére a konvent a nyertes tervrajzok készítőit, Hajós Alfrédot és Villányi Jánost bízta meg (3. és 4. sz. képek).

Hajós Alfréd (5. sz. kép) híres magyar sportoló volt, aki az 1896-ban Athénban megrendezett első újkori olimpián megnyerte mind a 100 méteres, mind pedig az 1200 méteres gyorsúszószámot. A »Magyar Delfin« becenéven is emlegetett sportoló később síkfutásban, gátfutásban és diszkoszvetésben is szerzett érmeket. 1907-ben Villányi Jánossal együttműködésben alapította meg saját építészirodáját.

Az épület berendezése

Az építkezés 1908. március 16-án kezdődött és az épületet végül – Kálvin születése 400. évfordulójának évében – 1909. április 5-én vehették használatba. A Zsinat ülésterme kétszázhuszonkét ülőhellyel a díszterembe került, ahol a padsorok széles karéjban ölelik körül az elnökségi emelvényt. A Zsinat mint legmagasabb szintű tanácskozó és döntéshozó testület az egyház parlamentje. Ezt tükrözi a székházban található ülésterem székeinek elrendezése is, amely a parlamentek többségéhez hasonlóan félköríves rendszerű és kiválóan megfelel a vita szempontjainak (6. sz. kép). Az zsinati tagoknak nincs meghatározott ülésrendje. Az első sorban az egyházkerületek elnökségei ülnek. Emellett külön helyük van a Zsinati Hivatal vezető beosztású munkatársainak, az állandó meghívottaknak (7. és 8. sz. képek). Az ülésteremhez külön lépcsőház visz, a vendégek három karzaton kaptak helyet, és külön helyük volt az újságíróknak is (9. és 10. sz. képek). A székház földszintjén és a szuterén helyiségben a konventi iroda, a református országos közalap, az árva- és nyugdíjintézet, a levéltár, a könyvtár és a konventi tanácskozóterem nyert elhelyezést. Az első emeleten egy hatszobás bérlakás volt, a második emeleten pedig a konventi előadó lakott. A székház telke és felépítése a berendezéssel együtt 525 000 koronába került.

Az első zsinati ülést az új székházban 1909. április 21-én tartották, megemlékezve Kálvin János születésének 400. évfordulójáról. Bánffy Dezső főgondnok, az előkészítő bizottság elnöke e szavakkal adta át az épületet:

»[…] kezdjük meg itt most már tanácskozásainkat, egyetemes egyházunk javára, békességes hangulatban, nagy törekvéssel és igyekezettel arra, hogy törvényileg biztosított autonómiánk s az ezzel alkotott szervek kezéből ki ne csavartassék a vezetés, mert ha ez megtörténik, akkor bizony gyöngébbek leszünk és nem a törvény fog felettünk állani, csak máról holnapra felhangzó, változó hangulat, mely forradalmakat csinálhat, de építeni fokozatosan és biztosan, állandó szervezetet fenntartani nem képes.«

12 Die Lampen stammen noch aus der Zeit der Errichtung. | *The lighting fixtures date back to the time of construction.* | *A világítótestek az építés idejéből származnak.*

13 An der Gestaltung der Decke zeigt sich das Zusammenspiel von Funktionalität und Schönheit. | *The design of the ceiling demonstrates the interplay of functionality and beauty.* | *A mennyezet kialakítása a funkcionalitás és a szépség kölcsönhatását mutatja.*

A gályarabok emléktáblája

Az 1670-es évek a protestáns egyházak életében a próbatétel évei voltak. A magyarországi ellenreformáció idején, 1674. március 5-én több mint hétszáz protestáns hitvallót idéztek a Pozsonyban felállított különbíróság elé. A bíróság felségsértéssel, hazaárulással, a katolikus egyház megsértésével vádolta őket, egyben követelte »bűneik« beismerését és áttérésüket a katolikus hitre. A beidézett prédikátorok közül azokat, akik semmifajta megalkuvásra nem voltak készek, várbörtönökbe vittek, majd több mint negyven papot Nápolyba hurcoltak, de közülük csak

14 Die Löwen am Eingang sollen die Stärke der Kirche symbolisieren. ǀ *The lions at the entrance symbolise the strength of the church.* ǀ *A bejáratnál lévő oroszlánok az egyház erejét szimbolizálják.*

harminckettő maradt életben, akiket eladtak gályarabnak. Sorsuk nagy visszhangot keltett Európa protestáns országaiban. Gyűjtés indult kiszabadításuk érdekében, és ez többszöri kísérlet után végül a holland Michiel de Ruyter admirálisnak sikerült 1676. február 11-én.

Marjai Károly mezőtúri lelkipásztor tett javaslatot a konventnek, hogy a székházban örökítse meg emléktábla a gályarabok mártíromságát. A táblát 1936. május 6-án avatták fel a központi Kálvin-ünnepség keretében, amit az »Institutio Christianae Religionis« megjelenésének 400. évfordulója alkalmával rendeztek meg. Az emléktáblán a protestáns gályarabok mellett az őket kiszabadító Michiel de Ruyter admirálisról e szavakkal emlékeztek meg: »A hitvallók és a szabadító örökké áldott emlékére …« (11. sz. kép)

A zsinati épület jelenlegi használata

Az épületen jelentősebb átalakítási és felújítási munkák hosszú évtizedekig nem voltak. Az élet és az egyházi szolgálat változásai nyomán a szolgálati lakások helyét fokozatosan átvették az irodák. Az irodaépület utolsó jelentősebb átépítése 2003–2004-ben valósult meg, ekkor tűntek el végleg a lakáshasználatra utaló nyomok (mosdók, csempe) az irodákból. Az ülésterem jelentős felújítására 2005-ben került sor. Ekkor a bútorzat teljes cseréje és a terem modern audiovizuális eszközökkel való ellátása mellett törekedtek az eredeti falszínek és megjelenés visszaadására. Az irodák, tanácstermek bútorzatában, ahol még erre lehetőség volt, az eredeti, ide tervezett darabok vannak használatban. Az ülésterem és tanácsterem, valamint több iroda világítása is még az eredeti csillárokkal és világítótestekkel működik. (12. és 13. sz. kép) 2019-től kezdve a külső homlokzatot újították fel, 2022-ben a kertet tervezték át és ültettek bele új növényeket. Az épület környezetbarátabbá tétele érdekében napelemes rendszert is telepítettek.

1966 óta minden vasárnap a zsinati székház üléstermében tartja istentiszteleteit a Budapest-Baross téri Református Egyházközség, és néhány kisebb iroda is a gyülekezet lelkészének használatában áll.

A Zsinat, a Magyarországi Református Egyház törvényhozó és legfőbb intézkedő testülete évente kétszer e falak között tartja üléseit, az épület ad otthont a Zsinati Hivatalnak – amely a Zsinat, a Zsinati Tanács és a Zsinat Elnöksége hatáskörébe tartozó feladatok ügyintézését végzi –, a Református Lelkészi Nyugdíjintézetnek, valamint az itt működő egyházközség hivatali helyiségeinek is.

Az épülettel kapcsolatos korabeli beszámolók azt fogalmazták meg, hogy az új székház feladata nem csupán az, hogy a tanácskozások számára a korábbi lehetőségeknél alkalmasabb körülményeket biztosítson. Kívánatos lett volna az is, hogy az épület »ne csak tégla volna, ne csak kő és művészi díszítés volna, hanem valami a hívő és küzdő egyház lelkéből, lelkének erejéből is« (14. sz. kép).

Összefoglaló

Ha az építés eredeti célkitűzését vizsgáljuk – a zsinati ülésterem, valamint a hivatali működésekhez kapcsolódó irodák elhelyezése egyetlen épületben –, a székház már csak korlátozottan tud megfelelni ennek az elvárásnak. Az egyházi szolgálat bővülése nyomán az irodák már régen kinőtték az itt rendelkezésre álló helyet, így – főleg az elmúlt években – ezeket közeli épületekben kellett elhelyezni. Mindezekkel együtt az épületnek továbbra is meghatározó és szimbolikus szerepe van az egységes, országos egyház működésében, ugyanakkor helyet ad regionális, valamint nemzetközi találkozóknak és konferenciáknak is (15. sz. kép). Sok tekintetben azt szimbolizálja, hogy – ahogy alkotmánya fogalmaz – »a Magyarországi Református Egyház Jézus Krisztus Egyetemes Anyaszentegyházának része«.

15 Das Synodengebäude der reformierten Kirche in Ungarn ist nach wie vor Veranstaltungsort für regionale und internationale Treffen und Konferenzen. | *The building of the Reformed Church in Hungary continues to be the venue for regional and international meetings and conferences.* | *A Magyarországi Református Egyház épülete ma is regionális és nemzetközi találkozók, konferenciák helyszíne.*

Irland
Ireland

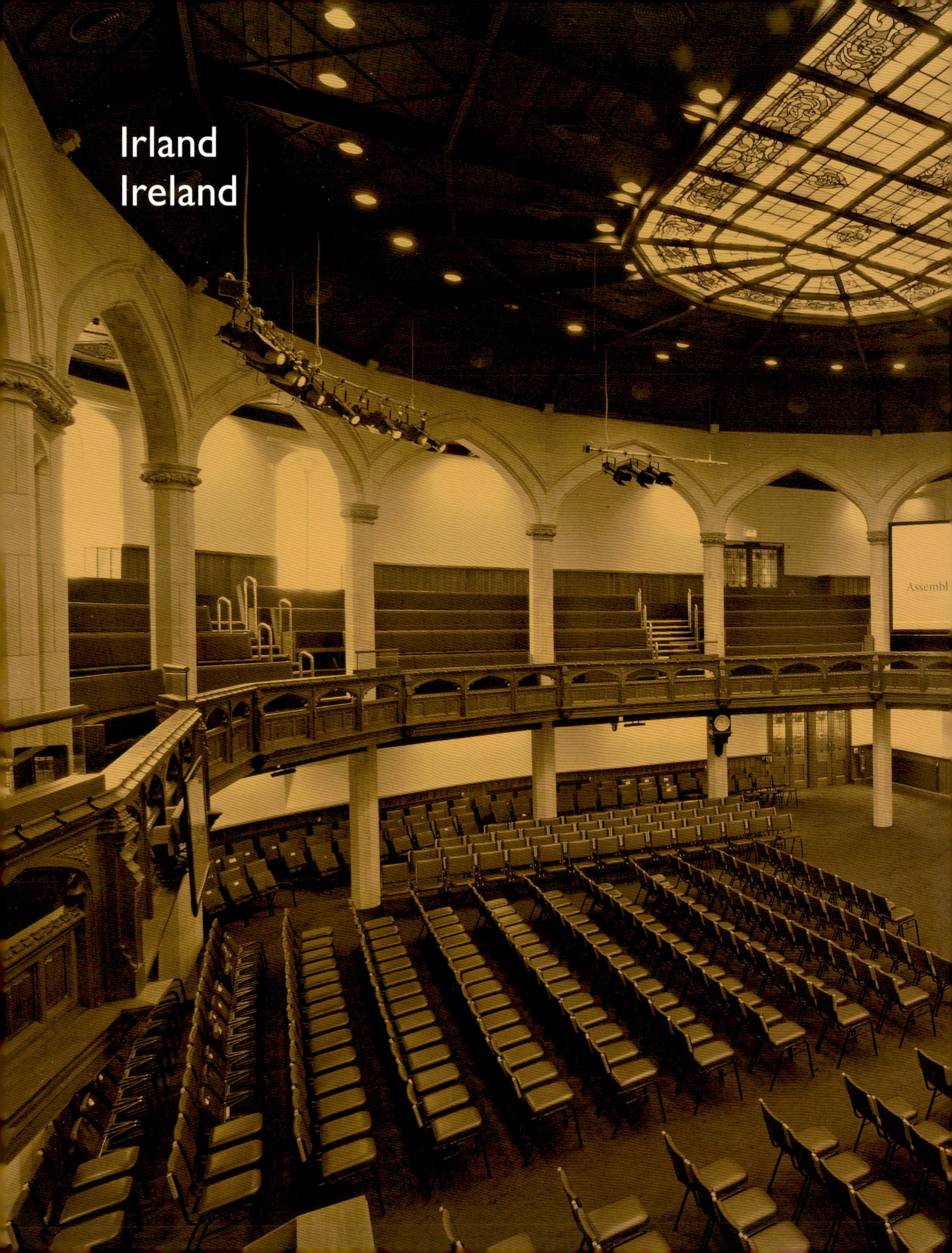

Assembly Buildings
CONFERENCE CENTRE

Steckbrief / General information

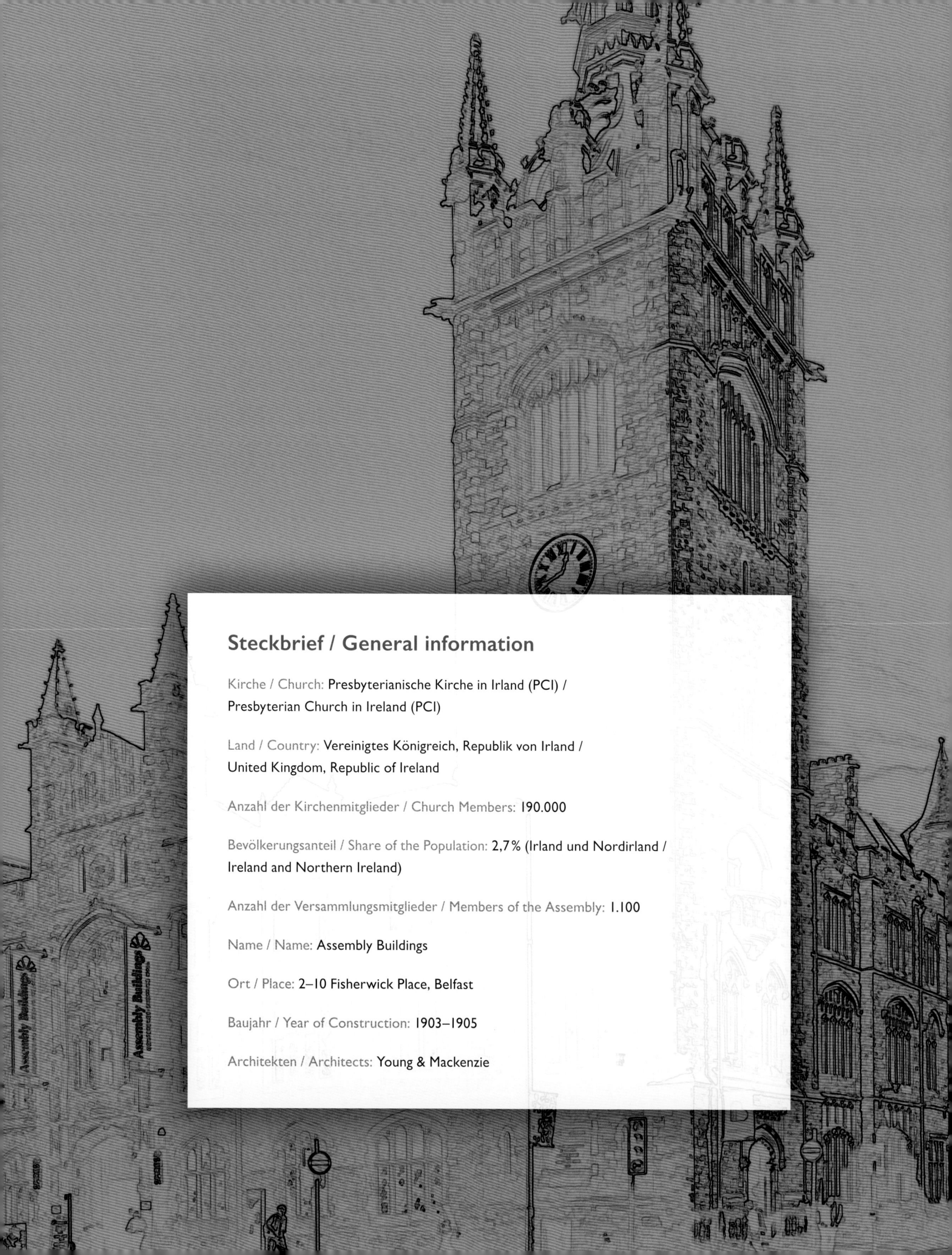

Kirche / Church: **Presbyterianische Kirche in Irland (PCI) / Presbyterian Church in Ireland (PCI)**

Land / Country: **Vereinigtes Königreich, Republik von Irland / United Kingdom, Republic of Ireland**

Anzahl der Kirchenmitglieder / Church Members: **190.000**

Bevölkerungsanteil / Share of the Population: **2,7 % (Irland und Nordirland / Ireland and Northern Ireland)**

Anzahl der Versammlungsmitglieder / Members of the Assembly: **1.100**

Name / Name: **Assembly Buildings**

Ort / Place: **2–10 Fisherwick Place, Belfast**

Baujahr / Year of Construction: **1903–1905**

Architekten / Architects: **Young & Mackenzie**

Raymond Robinson · Mark Smith

Die Assembly Buildings der Presbyterianischen Kirche in Irland

Die Presbyterianische Kirche in Irland und ihre Generalversammlung

Im frühen 17. Jahrhundert wanderten schottische Presbyterianer in die Provinz Ulster in Nordirland ein. Als Folge davon entstand in Irland eine presbyterianische Kirche. Heute ist die Presbyterianische Kirche in Irland (PCI) als gesamtirische Kirche die größte protestantische Konfession in Nordirland mit rund 200.000 Mitgliedern, die sich auf über 500 Gemeinden in ganz Irland verteilen.

Ihren Hauptsitz hat sie in Belfast in den *Assembly Buildings*, einem 1905 eröffneten Gebäudekomplex. Dieses historische Gebäude wurde im schottischen Baronialstil, einer lokalen Ausprägung der Neogotik, erbaut. Es hat einen hohen Glockenturm mit 12 Glocken, die als einziges in der Stadt noch funktionierende Glockenspiel zu jeder vollen Stunde über der Stadt Hymnen (und in der Adventszeit Weihnachtslieder) erklingen lassen. In diesem Gebäude wird die Generalversammlung der Kirche abgehalten (Abb. 1 und 2).

Die Generalversammlung ist die oberste Gesetzgebungs-, Verwaltungs- und Rechtsinstanz der Kirche und unterliegt, wie alle anderen ihr untergeordneten Gremien (Presbyterien und Gemeindeleitungen), der *Constitution and Government of The Presbyterian Church in Ireland*, der Verfassung, die als *The Code* bekannt ist. Bei der Generalversammlung kommen Presbyterianerinnen und Presbyterianer aus allen Gemeinden in Irland sowie Vertreterinnen und Vertreter der presbyterianischen Partnerkirchen und -organisationen aus aller Welt zusammen. Bei diesem Zusammentreffen von Menschen aus allen Teilen der Insel werden Entscheidungen getroffen, die das Leben und den Dienst der Kirche in den darauffolgenden Monaten und Jahren beeinflussen. Die Versammlung ist aber auch eine Zusammenkunft, um gemeinsam Gottesdienst zu feiern, zu beten und Christus die Ehre zu geben.

Der leitende Amtsträger der Generalversammlung und wichtigste öffentliche Repräsentant der PCI ist der Moderator, der ein jährliches Mandat innehat (Abb. 3). Die Generalversammlung besteht grundsätzlich aus allen aktiven sowie emeritierten Geistlichen, einem Ältesten aus jeder Gemeinde sowie weiteren Personen, denen die Vollversammlung die Teilnahme gestattet. Diakonissen sowie Frauen- und Jugendvertreterinnen und -vertreter sind zur Teilnahme und Beratung eingeladen, haben aber kein Stimmrecht. Ebenso sind Delegierte aus den weltweiten Partnerkirchen und den reformierten Kirchen aus Irland und dem Vereinigten Königreich eingeladen. Auch sie haben Rederecht, jedoch kein Stimmrecht.

Traditionell kommt die Generalversammlung in den *Assembly Buildings* in Belfast für drei oder vier Tage im Juni zusammen. Seit der ersten Generalversammlung, die 1840 in Belfast stattfand, hat sie aber auch zwanzigmal in den Städten Dublin, Armagh und Londonderry getagt. Im Jahr 2020 wurde die Generalversammlung zum ersten Mal in der Geschichte der PCI abgesagt – aufgrund der Covid-19-Pandemie. Stattdessen vereinbarte man andere Regelungen zur Durchführung der kirchenleitenden Aufgaben.

Während der Generalversammlungswoche werden den Mitgliedern Berichte zu den Ergebnissen der Arbeit der Räte, Kommissionen und Arbeitsgruppen im sogenannten »Blauen Buch« vorgelegt. In gesonderten Geschäftssitzungen diskutieren die Versammlungsmitglieder Finanz- und Missionsberichte und erörtern aktuelle ethische, theologische und politische Fragestellungen, bevor sie über die Annahme der einzelnen Berichte und über bestimmte darin enthaltene Resolutionen – ggf. in geänderter Form – abstimmen.

Viel Zeit widmet die Versammlung dem Gottesdienst und dem Hören auf das Wort Gottes. Es finden ein Abendmahlsgottesdienst und eine besondere Abendfeier statt, die – wie der größte Teil der Tagesordnung der Generalversammlung – für die Öffentlichkeit und die Medien zugänglich sind. Auch wird der Verlauf der Versammlung auf der PCI-Website per Livestream übertragen.

Der Moderator eröffnet die Versammlung mit einem Gottesdienst und sitzt der *General Assembly* vor, bis sein Nachfolger übernimmt. Der jeweilige Nachfolger, der üblicherweise im Februar in separat stattfindenden Versammlungen der neunzehn Kirchenbezirke (*Presbyteries*) designiert wurde, wird später im Verlauf der Verhandlungen in Anwesenheit von Gästen des öffentlichen Lebens von der Generalversammlung formell gewählt. Der neue Moderator leitet die Kirche bis zur nächsten Generalversammlung im Juni des Folgejahres.

Das 19. Jahrhundert war für den Presbyterianismus in Irland eine Zeit großer Expansion. In dieser Zeit schlossen sich zwei Körperschaften, die Synode von Ulster und die Sezessionssynode, zur Presbyterianischen Kirche in Irland zusammen. Sie kamen am 10. Juli 1840 zusammen, um die erste Generalversammlung zu konstituieren und den ersten Moderator der PCI zu wählen. Die Versammlung fand in der *Rosemary Street Presbyterian Church* in Belfast statt. Damals gehörten der Generalsynode von Ulster 292 Gemeinden und der Sezessionssynode 141 Gemeinden an. Schätzungsweise 400 Geistliche und Älteste waren im Rahmen der Versammlung anwesend, denen sich zwischen 3.000 und 4.000 weitere Bürgerinnen und Bürger zur Unterstützung anschlossen, nachdem eine Anzeige im *Belfast Newsletter* geschaltet worden war.

Die Geschichte der Assembly Buildings

Seit Mitte der 1860er Jahre wurde ernsthaft über die Notwendigkeit eines ständigen Sitzes für die Generalversammlung nachgedacht. Im Jahr 1865 sah sich der Missionsausschuss der PCI gezwungen, sich nach neuen Räumlichkeiten umzusehen. Schließlich wurde 1872 das Missionsgebäude in der May Street, einige Häuserblocks hinter dem heutigen Versammlungsgebäude, errichtet und diente fortan als Übergangslösung für die Generalversammlung. Der Bau existiert noch heute und wird derzeit von einem Unternehmen genutzt.

Es wurde erwogen, die *May Street Presbyterian Church*, welche eng mit Rev. Dr. Henry Cooke verbunden war, der

| Der Turm mit einem Glockenspiel ist das markanteste Merkmal der Assembly Buildings. | *The tower houses the city's only operational peal of 12 bells and is the most prominent feature of Assembly Buildings.*

2 Die Assembly Buildings wurden 1905 eröffnet. | *The Assembly Buildings were opened in 1905.*

1841 und 1862 zweimal das Amt des Moderators innehatte, umzugestalten oder neu zu errichten. Diese Pläne wurden jedoch nicht weiterverfolgt. Die *Central Presbyterian Association* unterbreitete der Generalversammlung im Jahr 1893 einen Vorschlag zur Errichtung eines eigenen Gebäudekomplexes – einschließlich einer großen Versammlungshalle – am Fisherwick Place in Belfast.

1897 hatte man sich auf diesen Standort in der Innenstadt geeinigt. Der Abriss der bestehenden *Fisherwick Presbyterian Church* (Abb. 4) und die Räumung des Geländes begannen im Jahr 1902. Die Gemeinde zog an ihren heutigen Standort an der Malone Road im Süden der Stadt und öffnete ihre Türen im Jahr 1904.

Mit der Planung des Gebäudes wurde das Architekturbüro Young & Mackenzie aus Belfast beauftragt, das von 1850 an mehr als ein Jahrhundert lang tätig war und für die Gestaltung vieler bekannter Bauwerke in Nordirland und darüber hinaus verantwortlich zeichnete. Ihre Gebäudeentwürfe aus der Hoch-Viktorianischen und Edwardianischen Ära sind besonders bemerkenswert. Ein Beispiel ihres Wirkens in Belfast sind die *Scottish Provident Buildings*. In ganz Ulster waren sie für die Gestaltung zahlreicher presbyterianischer Kirchen, Kaufhäuser, Schulen, Privathäuser und Villen verantwortlich – eine der bekanntesten ist das *Culloden Hotel* in Cultra, County Down, das zunächst ein Privathaus und später ein Bischofspalast der *Church of Ireland* war.

Das von Robert Young (1822–1917) gegründete Architekturbüro wurde überaus erfolgreich und spielte im späteren 19. Jahrhundert die bedeutendste Rolle im presbyterianischen Kirchenbau in Ulster.[1] Die Architekten zeichneten sich durch herausragende Fachkenntnisse aus und brachten Einflüsse aus den im auswärtigen Kirchenbau verbreiteten Baustilen – vor allem der Neogotik – in ihre Entwürfe ein. Das Architekturbüro trug damit maßgeblich zur Verbreitung dieser Stilrichtung bei und leitete damit in Ulster eine Stilwende ein.

Die Bauarbeiten an den *Assembly Buildings* begannen 1903. Am 5. Juni 1905 wurden die *Assembly Buildings* – oder *Church House*, wie sie damals hießen – zu Beginn der *General Assembly Week* durch den Herzog von Argyll, den Schwager König Edwards VII., offiziell eröffnet.

Young beschrieb seinen Entwurf für die *Assembly Buildings* in der Publikation *Belfast and the Province of Ulster* von 1909 folgendermaßen: »Es ist ein prächtiger Gebäudekomplex im schottischen Baronialstil mit einem Hauch von Gotik in seinen Ausschmückungen […] überragt von einem Turm mit offenen Bögen« (Abb. 5, 6, 7).

Das auffälligste Merkmal der *Assembly Buildings* ist eben dieser 52 Meter hohe Glockenturm, der von einer kupfernen Turmspitze gekrönt wird. Anlässlich der Generalversammlung von 1900 kommentierte das *Committee on Proposals* der *Central Presbyterian Association Belfast* die Entwurfspläne für das Gebäude wie folgt: »Das auffälligste äußere Merkmal des Gebäudes wird ein massiver Turm sein, dessen anmutige Spitze an viele historische Türme in Schottland erinnert und damit die Tatsache andeutet, dass unsere Kirche auf eine Geschichte zurückblicken kann, die von der fernen Vergangenheit des Landes unter Wallace und Bruce in die Zeit der Reformation durch Melville und Knox reicht.«

Das Projekt des Versammlungsgebäudes wurde durch den *Presbyterian Church Twentieth Century Fund*, Spenden von Kirchenmitgliedern und ein Darlehen der *Scottish Provident Institution* finanziert, das in den folgenden Jahren zurückgezahlt wurde. Die Gesamtkosten für das Grundstück und das Gebäude beliefen sich auf 74.000 Pfund Sterling (was heute 9,2 Millionen Britischen Pfund entspricht).[2]

Die Architektur der Assembly Hall

Der halbkreisförmige (oder D-förmige) Versammlungssaal ist um ein Podium, das sich im Zentrum der geraden Längsseite befindet, angeordnet. Die anderen Seiten werden durch eine Galerie gerahmt, die sich hinter Arkaden aus Tudor-Bögen befindet. Die Bögen stehen auf schlanken achteckigen Steinsäulen (zwei davon paarweise

3 »Brennend, aber blühend« ist ein Leitspruch der Presbyterianischen Kirche, hier als Relief am Platz des Moderators. | *»Burning but flourishing« is a motto of the Presbyterian Church, here on the seat of the Moderator.*

gegenüber dem Podium), deren Kapitelle mit naturalistischen Blattornamenten verziert sind. Diese funktionale Gestaltung gewährleistet von jedem Sitzplatz aus einen freien Blick auf das Podium. Im Jahr 1905 verfügte der ursprüngliche Saal über zwei Emporen; die akustische Gestaltung des Saals sorgte dafür, dass eine Person, die vom Podium aus ohne Verstärkung sprach, deutlich gehört werden konnte (Abb. 8). Heute ist die *Assembly Hall* mit den neuesten audiovisuellen Systemen ausgestattet. Nach der ersten umfassenden Renovierung des Gebäudes wurde es im Jahr 1992 um eine gewerbliche Nutzung ergänzt und das Erdgeschoss für den Einzelhandel umgestaltet. Dies hatte zur Folge, dass die *Assembly Hall* in den ersten Stock zog (Abb 9).

Die Bestuhlung im Parkett des Saals ist beweglich, sodass die Sitzordnung für die Wahl und Einsetzung des neuen Moderators, die Arbeitssitzungen, Gottesdienste, Abendmahlsfeiern und Abendveranstaltungen angepasst werden kann. Während der Generalversammlung werden sämtliche Räumlichkeiten des Gebäudes für verschiedene Zwecke genutzt. Vierzehn Besprechungsräume mit unterschiedlichen Kapazitäten, darunter auch die *Assembly Hall* selbst, stehen zur Verfügung (Abb. 10).

Der Moderator, der Schriftführer und der stellvertretende Schriftführer der Generalversammlung sitzen auf dem Podium. Abgesehen von einer kleinen Anzahl an Sitzplätzen, die denjenigen vorbehalten sind, die während der Sitzungen sprechen oder Fragen stellen, können die Mitglieder ihre Plätze frei wählen. Abstimmungen und Wortmeldungen sind nur vom Parterre des Saals aus möglich, nicht von der Besuchertribüne.

Ornamente und Glasfenster im neogothischen und Art nouveau Stil

An der Außenseite des Gebäudes befinden sich zahlreiche skulpturale Elemente wie Drachen, Eidechsen und Laubwerk, die für den spätgotischen Stil kennzeichnend sind. Der Haupteingang des Gebäudes wird von keltischen Spiralen, Weinblättern und 14 Engelsköpfen geziert (Abb. 11). Darüber befinden sich steinerne geflügelte Cherubim. Diese tragen Tafeln mit heraldischen Motiven des brennenden Dornbuschs, der Jahreszahl 1905 und den Wappen der wichtigsten Städte Irlands. Die irische Harfe von Leinster befindet sich in der Mitte und wird vom Wappen von Belfast überragt. Die der Howard Street zugewandte Fassade ist mit in Stein gemeißelten Wappen der irischen Städte auf einem halbrunden, vorspringenden Balkon versehen.

Im Gebäudeinneren, in der *Minor Hall*, befindet sich das Gedenkfenster für den Wohltäter David Graham Barkley (1835–1903). Es stellt die Tugenden Mäßigung, Glaube, Hoffnung, Nächstenliebe und Gerechtigkeit dar. In der *Assembly Hall* befindet sich je ein Buntglasfenster auf jeder Seite der zentralen Orgelpfeifen. Diese und weitere wertvolle Fenster wurden auf dem Höhepunkt der Unruhen in Nordirland, die als *The Troubles* bekannt wurden, zur sicheren Aufbewahrung entfernt. Sie wurden erst im Zuge der Renovierung im Jahr 1992 wieder eingesetzt. Eine weitere beachtenswerte Besonderheit ist das Carrickfergus-Fenster (Abb. 12), das sich im ersten Stock am Haupteingang zur *Assembly Hall* befindet. Dieses beeindruckende Fenster ist ein Geschenk des Presbyteriums

4 Die frühere Fischerwick Presbyterian Church, die 1899 abgerissen wurde, um Platz für die heutige Assembly Buildings zu schaffen. | *The Fisherwick Presbyterian Church was demolished in 1899 to make way for the current Assembly Buildings.*

5 Der Entwurf der Assembly Buildings. | *The sketch of the Assembly Buildings.*

6 Die *Assembly Buildings* dominieren noch immer den Fisherwick Place. | *The Assembly Buildings still dominate Fisherwick Place.*

von Carrickfergus, Irlands ältestem Presbyterium, und wurde 1992 zum Gedenken an den 350. Jahrestag der Geburtsstunde des Presbyterianismus in Irland im Jahr 1642 eingebaut.

Weitere Einblicke in die Kirchengeschichte bietet die ständige Besucherausstellung im Hauptfoyer des Gebäudes. Sie wurde 2019 eröffnet und zeigt die reiche Geschichte der Konfession und ihren Ort innerhalb des weltweiten Presbyterianismus sowie ihren Beitrag und ihre Bedeutung für die irische Gesellschaft.

Die Nutzung der Assembly Hall in der Vergangenheit und heute

Die *Assembly Buildings*, einschließlich der *Assembly Hall* selbst, sind heute ein etablierter, hochmoderner Konferenz- und Ausstellungsort. Jedes Jahr finden dort zahlreiche Veranstaltungen statt – von Aktivitäten unterschiedlichster Konfessionen, ökumenischen Dankgottesdiensten und internationalen christlichen Tagungen bis hin zu BBC-Aufnahmen, Business-Konferenzen sowie Veranstaltungen der öffentlichen Hand und der Regierung auf lokaler, nationaler und internationaler Ebene. Aufgrund der vielseitigen Nutzungsmöglichkeiten sind die Räumlichkeiten auch Schauplatz von Konzerten, Ausstellungen oder Unterhaltungsveranstaltungen.

Seit 1905 fanden in diesem Gebäude zahlreiche historische Ereignisse statt. Politische Versammlungen sind mittlerweile zwar nicht mehr erlaubt, vor über 100 Jahren aber war das noch anders: Am 1. Februar 1912 wurde in den *Assembly Buildings* die *Irish Presbyterian Anti Home Rule Convention* abgehalten, Damit wollten die Presbyterianer ihre Absage zum irischen Nationalismus erklären, ohne sich mit der anglikanischen *Church of Ireland* und dem unionistischen Oranier-Orden zu verbünden. Im selben Jahr, am 21. April, wurde ein Gedenkgottesdienst anlässlich des Untergangs der RMS Titanic abgehalten (Abb. 13). Das Schiff der White-Star-Line hatte die Belfaster Werft, in der es gebaut worden war, nur neunzehn Tage zuvor verlassen.

Im Juli 1937 wurde mit einem gemeinsamen Gottesdienst die Woche des Staatsbesuchs von König Georg VI. und Königin Elisabeth in Nordirland eingeleitet. Vierzig Jahre später, im Juni 1977, wurde in der *Assembly Hall* ein Dankgottesdienst für ihre Tochter, Königin Elisabeth II., anlässlich ihres silbernen Thronjubiläums abgehalten.[3]

Im Laufe ihrer Geschichte haben auch viele hochrangige Personen die *Assembly Buildings* und insbesondere die *Assembly Hall* besucht und dort gesprochen. Darunter befanden sich lokale, nationale und internationale Führungspersönlichkeiten, einschließlich des irischen Staatspräsidenten und von Mitgliedern der königlichen Familie. Prinzessin Anne, *The Princess Royal*, nahm hier im November 2022 an einer Veranstaltung teil, während ihre Schwägerin Diana, *The Princess of Wales*, im Juni 1992 zu Besuch war und zu diesem Anlass eine Steintafel in der *Assembly Hall* enthüllte.

Die *Assembly Buildings* hatten schon immer eine öffentliche Bedeutung. Sie sind nach wie vor das Verwaltungszentrum der Presbyterianischen Kirche in Irland und in der *Assembly Hall* trifft sich weiterhin die Kirche zur Generalversammlung.

Am besten wird der Zweck des Saals wahrscheinlich durch den Vers verdeutlicht, der unter den Überresten von zwei gewölbten ehemaligen Balkonen eingemeißelt ist, die sich ursprünglich an den Galerien auf beiden Seiten des Podiums befanden. Auf einem Spruchband, das von zwei Engeln gehalten wird, ist auf der linken Seite ein Auszug aus Psalm 107,32 zu lesen: »Praise Him in the Seat of the Elders (Rühmt ihn im Rat der Ältesten).« Auf der rechten Seite, wieder von zwei Engeln getragen, ist der Anfang des Psalmverses angeführt: »Exalt Him in the Assembly of the People (Erhöht Ihn in der Versammlung des Volkes).«

---

1 Paul Harron, Architects of Ulster: Young and Mackenzie, A Transformational Provincial Practice 1850–1960, Belfast 2016, 165–183.

2 General Assembly Minutes 1897–1906.

3 Records from the Presbyterian Historical Society of Ireland.

Raymond Robinson · Mark Smith

The Assembly Buildings of the Presbyterian Church in Ireland

The Presbyterian Church in Ireland and their General Assembly

Irish Presbyterianism has its origins in Scottish migrations to the northeast part of Ireland, in the historic province of Ulster, in the early 17th century. Today, while an all-Ireland Church, the Presbyterian Church in Ireland (PCI) is the largest Protestant denomination in Northern Ireland, having around 200,000 members belonging to 500-plus congregations throughout the island of Ireland.

Its headquarters is Assembly Buildings in Belfast and has been part of the cityscape since 1905. This historic landmark building was built in the gothic ›Scottish baronial‹ style, with a high clock tower that houses the city's only operational peal of 12 bells, which chimes hymns (and Christmas carols during Advent) across the city on the hour. It is in this building that the Church meets in General Assembly (Fig. 1 and 2).

The General Assembly is the Church's supreme legislative, administrative and judicial authority. It is the highest ›court‹ of the Church and, like all other subordinate courts (Presbyteries and congregational Kirk Sessions) it is governed by The Constitution and Government of The Presbyterian Church in Ireland, which is known as ›The Code‹.

It brings together Presbyterians from all PCI's congregations from across Ireland, along with overseas representatives of the denomination's partner churches and organisations from around the world. It is a coming together of people the length and breadth of the island, ›meeting in General Assembly‹, taking decisions that will affect the life and ministry of the Church in the coming months and years. It is also a coming together for fellowship, worship, prayer, and to bring glory to Christ.

The senior office bearer of the General Assembly, and PCI's principal public representative, is the Moderator of the General Assembly, which is an annual elected post (Fig. 3).

The Assembly consists principally of all active ministers, ministers emeritus and emerita, a representative elder from each congregation, along with others who the General Assembly permits to attend. Deaconesses, as well as women's and young people's representatives are invited to attend and deliberate, but they do not have a vote. Similarly, delegates from PCI's global partner churches, and reformed churches from Ireland and the UK, are also invited and may speak, but do not have a vote.

Traditionally, the General Assembly normally meets in Assembly Buildings in Belfast, for three or four days in June. Since the first General Assembly, held in Belfast in 1840, it has met on 20 occasions in the cities of Dublin, Armagh and Londonderry. In 2020, for the first time in PCI's history, the General Assembly was cancelled as a result of the Covid-19 pandemic. Other arrangements to conduct the church's business were agreed and put in place.

During ›General Assembly Week‹ the work of the General Assembly's Councils, Commissions, and Task Groups, contained in numerous reports, come before members in what is known as ›The Blue Book‹. During separate business sessions, from financial reports, to reports on mission at home and overseas, moral and theological matters, to political and government issues of the day, Members of Assembly debate and discuss them, before voting to receive each report, and on specific resolutions contained in them, which can also be amended.

As a time of fellowship, much time is given to worship and hearing the Word of God, with a Communion Service taking place and a special Evening Celebration, which, like the vast majority of the General Assembly's business, is open to the public and media outlets. Proceedings are livestreamed via PCI's website.

The Moderator opens business in a service of worship and chairs the General Assembly until his successor takes the chair. Their successor, who by convention is selected as Moderator-Designate when PCI's 19 Presbyteries meet separately across Ireland in February, is formally elected by the General Assembly, later on during the proceedings in front of invited civic guests. The new Moderator will lead the Church until its next meeting the following June.

The 19th century was a period of great expansion for Presbyterianism across Ireland. In that time two bodies, the Synod of Ulster and the Secession Synod, united to form the Presbyterian Church in Ireland. They met on 10 July 1840 to constitute the first General Assembly and elect PCI's first Moderator. It met in Rosemary Street Presbyterian Church in Belfast. At that time, there were 292 congregations in the General Synod of Ulster and 141 in the Secession Synod. It is estimated that some 400 ministers and elders made up the Assembly that day and between 3,000 and 4,000 members of the public joined them in support, after an advertisement had been placed in the Belfast Newsletter.

History of the Assembly Buildings

The need for a permanent home for the General Assembly had been seriously considered since the mid-1860s. In 1865 PCI's Mission Board was compelled to look for new premises. In 1872 the Mission Buildings were erected on May Street, a few blocks behind Assembly Buildings, and served the purposes of the General Assembly from that date as an interim measure. The building still exists today and is currently occupied by a business.

Consideration was given to remodelling, or reconstructing, May Street Presbyterian Church, which had been closely associated with Rev. Dr Henry Cooke, who served twice as Moderator in 1841 and 1862, but these were not pursued. In 1893 the Central Presbyterian Association brought a proposal to the General Assembly for a dedicated suite of buildings, including a major Assembly Hall at Fisherwick Place in Belfast.

By 1897 this city centre location was settled upon. The demolition of the existing Fisherwick Presbyterian Church (Fig. 4), and clearance of the site, began in 1902. The congregation moved to its existing location on the Malone Road, in the south of the city, opening its doors in 1904.

The architects who were chosen to design the building were Young & Mackenzie of Belfast, who thrived for over a century from 1850 onwards, and were also responsible for the design of many well-known structures across Northern Ireland and beyond.

Its building designs from the High Victorian and Edwardian eras are particularly notable. In Belfast, for example, they designed the Scottish Provident Buildings. Across Ulster, they were responsible for the design of many Presbyterian churches, warehouses, schools, private houses and villas – one of the most well-known being the Culloden Hotel at Cultra, County Down, initially a private residence and then a Church of Ireland bishop's palace.

Founded by Robert Young (1822–1917) it became an extraordinarily prolific in designing commercial, institutional, residential and ecclesiastical buildings. Their buildings followed programmatic ideas.

As for churches, Young & Mackenzie were the leading architects of new Presbyterian churches in Ulster during the later 19th century.[1] Its ecclesiastical work is

7 »Das auffälligste äußere Merkmal des Gebäudes wird ein massiver Turm sein«. | *»The most striking external feature of the building will be a massive Tower«.*

also significant because of the high level of technical skill demonstrated, and because of the influence of ecclesiastical designs from elsewhere – like the Gothic Revivalism, the firm's contribution to the popularisation of the various manifestations of this style in Ulster was immense, achieving a stylistic revolution.

Construction work on Assembly Buildings (or Church House as it was officially called then) commenced in 1903. On 5 June 1905 it was officially opened by the Duke of Argyll, the brother-in-law of King Edward VII.

Young's description of his own firm's design for Assembly Buildings in the 1909 publication ›Belfast and the Province of Ulster‹ reads »A magnificent pile of buildings in Scottish Baronial style with something of the Gothic in its enrichments […] covered with open arch spire« (Fig. 5, 6, 7).

The most prominent feature of Assembly Buildings is the 52-metre-high clock tower, which is topped by a crown spire in copper. At the General Assembly of 1900, the Committee on Proposals of Central Presbyterian Association Belfast commenting on the design plans for the building said, »The most striking external feature of the building will be a massive Tower, which culminates gracefully in a fashion that reminds one of many historic towers in Scotland, and is suggestive of the fact that our Church has a history behind her stretching back to Reformation times, and beyond them, to the far-off antiquity of the land of Wallace and Bruce, as well as Melville and Knox«.

The Assembly Building project was funded through the Presbyterian Church Twentieth Century Fund, Church member donations and a loan from The Scottish Provident Institution, which was repaid in subsequent years. The total cost of the site and buildings was £ 74,000 (equivalent to £ 9.2 million today).[2]

8 Die ursprüngliche Assembly Hall im Jahr 1905. | *The original Assembly Hall in 1905.*

9 Der renovierte Saal nach der Verlegung in den ersten Stock – mit nunmehr einer statt zwei Galerien. Im unteren Teil des Gebäudes wurden Geschäftslokale errichtet, die als zusätzliche Tagungsräumlichkeiten in den Assembly Buildings genutzt werden. | *The refurbished Hall after relocation to the first floor – with only one remaining gallery. A retail facility was built in the lower part of the building, which has since been reincorporated into the main Assembly Buildings as an additional conferencing facility.*

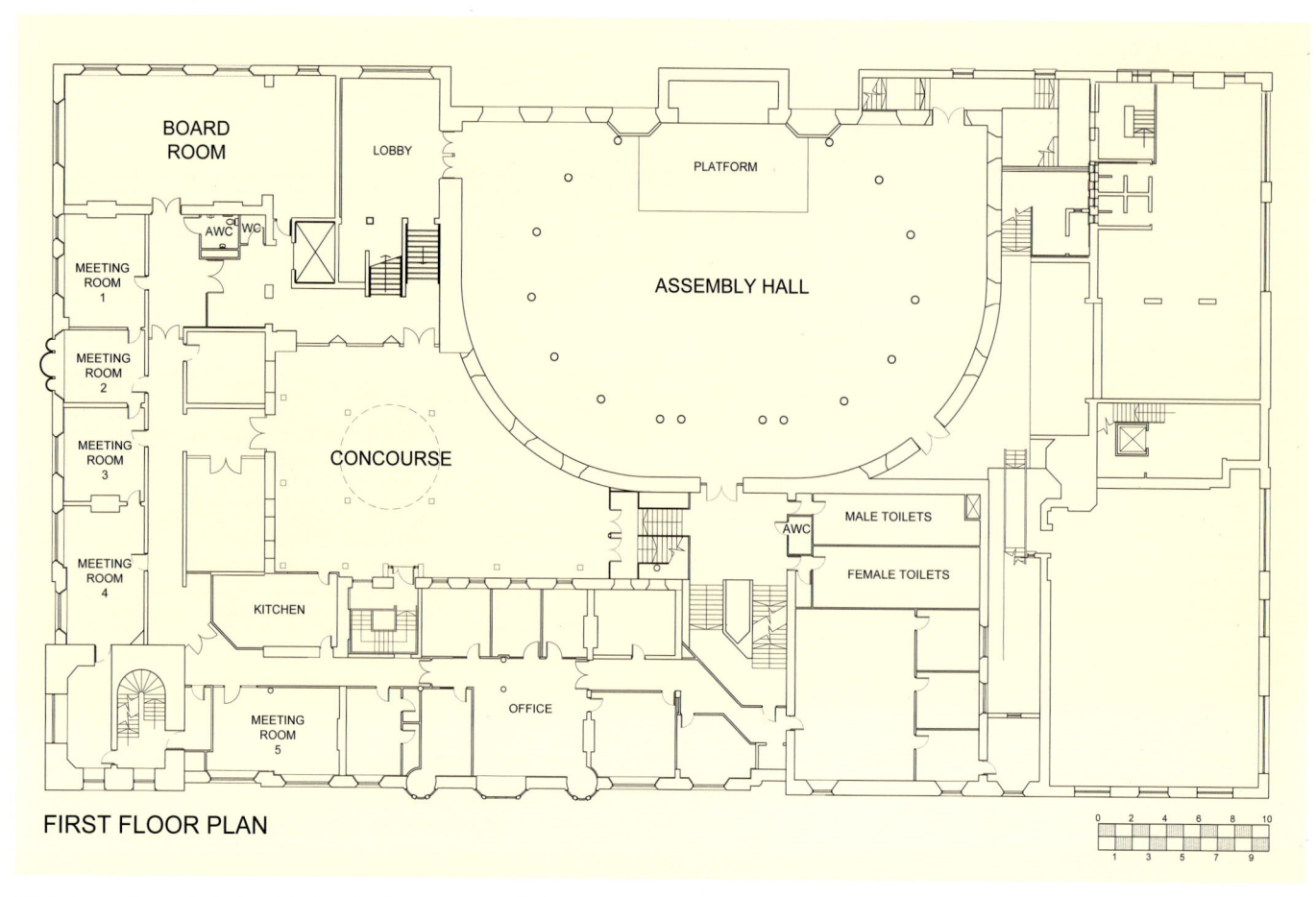

10 Auf zwei Etagen befinden sich vierzehn Tagungsräume. | *On two floors there are 14 meeting rooms.*

The chamber's architecture

The semi-circular (or D shaped) Assembly Hall is arranged around a platform on one of the longitudinal walls with a gallery suspended behind a running arcade of Tudor arches on thin octagonal stone columns (two of them paired facing the platform) with capitals carved with naturalistic foliage. This functional design ensures that everyone seated has a clear view of the platform. In 1905 the original room had two galleries and the acoustical design of the room ensured that a person speaking from the platform with no audio enhancement could be heard clearly (Fig. 8). The Assembly Hall today contains the latest in Audio-Visual systems. In 1992, after its first significant refurbishment, the building took on a commercial persona, providing a retail facility on the ground floor which resulted in the removal from the ground floor of the Assembly Hall and its reconstruction at first floor level.

The seating on the parquet floor of the Assembly Hall is not fixed, so the seating arrangement for each General Assembly is arranged and allocated as appropriate to facilitate the election and installation of the new Moderator, business sessions, worship and communion services, and Evening Celebration (Fig. 9). During the General Assembly, all the facilities in the building are used for various purposes. Assembly Buildings has 14 meeting rooms of various capacities, including the Assembly Hall itself (Fig. 10).

The Moderator, Clerk and Deputy Clerk of the General Assembly sit on the platform. Apart from a small number of allocated seats reserved for those speaking, or asking questions during business sessions, members can sit anywhere in the Hall. Voting and speaking is only permitted from the floor of the Assembly Hall, and not from the public gallery.

Ornamentation and glass windows in Neogothic and Art Nouveau Style

There is a significant amount of architectural sculpture on the outside of the building. Subjects include dragons, lizards, and foliage in keeping with the late Gothic style. At the main entrance of the building there is a Celtic spiral motif, vine leaves and 14 angel heads (Fig. 11). Above these is a carving of the Burning Bush and winged cherubs. These hold panels bearing heraldic burning bush motifs, the date 1905 and coats of arms of the main cities of Ireland. The Irish Harp of Leinster is centrally placed but with the Belfast coat of arms taking pre-eminence above it. On the Howard Street side of the building, carved coats of arms of Irish towns are contained on a semi-circular projecting balcony.

11 Tafeln mit den heraldischen Motiven des brennenden Dornbuschs befinden sich links und rechts oberhalb des Eingangs. | *Panels bearing the heraldic Burning Bush motifs are at the left and the right above the entrance.*

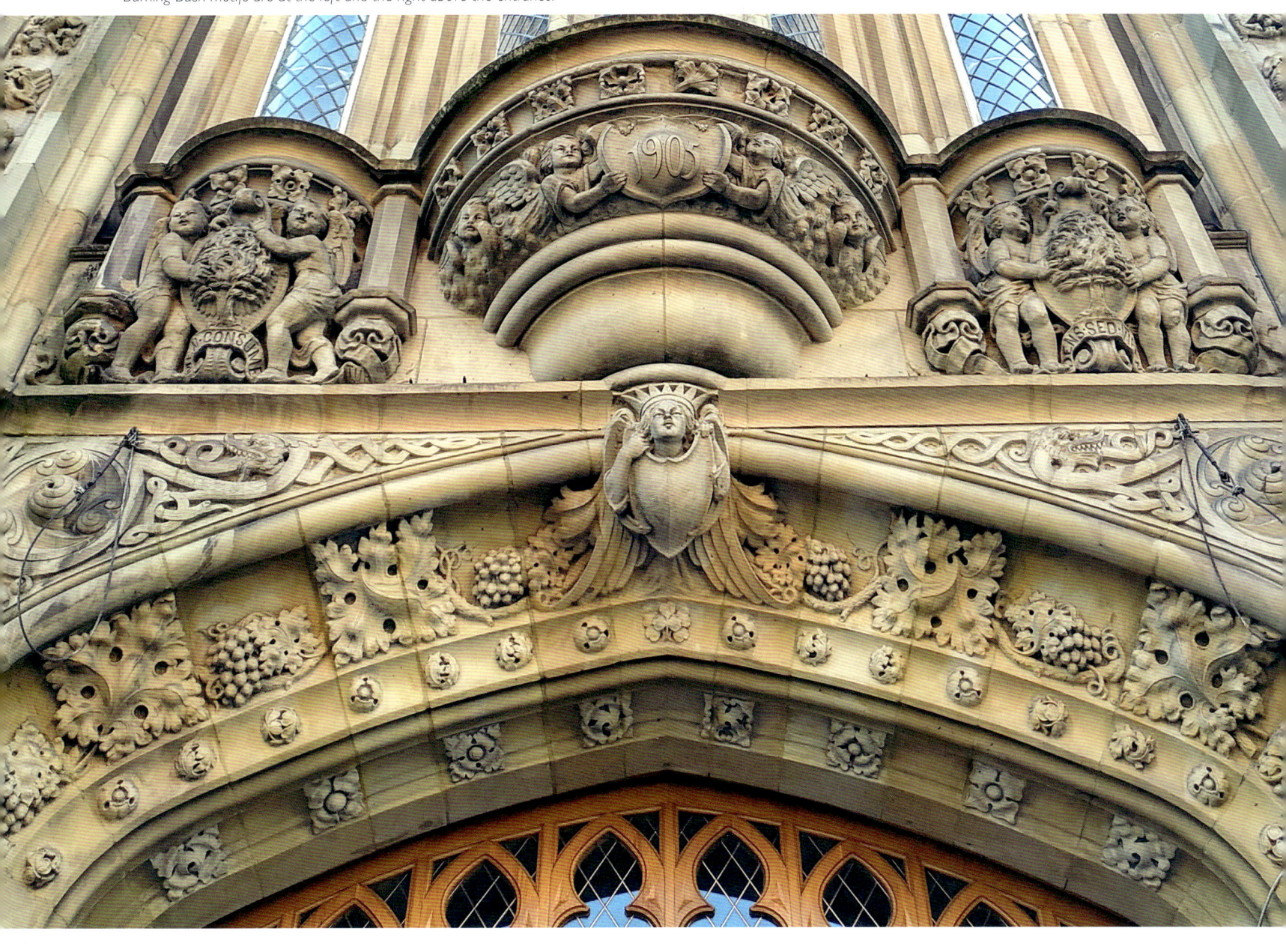

12 Das Carrickfergus-Fenster zur Erinnerung an das 350-jährige Bestehen des ältesten presbyterianischen Kirchenbezirks in Irland. | *The Carrickfergus Window to commemorate the 350th anniversary of the oldest presbytery in Ireland.*

Internally, in the Minor Hall, is the Barkley memorial window dedicated to David Graham Barkley (1835–1903), which depicts Temperance, Faith, Hope, Charity and Justice. The Assembly Hall contains two stained glass windows either side of the central organ pipes. These special windows, and others, were removed for safe keeping at the height of the civil disturbances that became known as ›The Troubles‹. They were only replaced during the 1992 refurbishment. Another notable feature, the Carrickfergus Window, is located on the first floor at the main entrance to the Assembly Hall (Fig. 12). Installed in 1992, this impressive window was a gift donated by the Presbytery of Carrickfergus, Ireland's oldest presbytery to commemorate the 350th anniversary that year of the ›birth‹ of Presbyterianism in Ireland in 1642.

Other aspects of the church's history can be found in the permanent visitor exhibition in the building's main foyer. Opened in 2019 it sets out the rich history of the denomination, its place within Presbyterianism and its contribution to, and place in, Irish society.

The chamber's usage in the past and today

Assembly Buildings, including the Assembly Hall itself, is also an established state-of-the-art conference and exhibition venue. Numerous events are held in Assembly Buildings each year and have included events and conferences for other Christian denominations, United Services of Thanksgiving, BBC recordings, international Christian conferences, commercial conferences, public sector and government conferences at local, national and international level. Due to its versatility, a wide variety of other events also take place there, as it is a venue for music, exhibitions and appropriate entertainment events.

Since 1905, many historic events have taken place in the building. While political meetings are no longer permitted, on 1 February 1912 the Irish Presbyterian Anti Home Rule Convention was held in Assembly Buildings. That same year, on 21 April, a Memorial Service was held for the loss of the White Star liner, RMS Titanic (Fig. 13). It had left the Belfast shipyard, where it had been built, just 19 days earlier.

In July 1937 a united service inaugurating the week of the state visit to Northern Ireland of King George VI and Queen Elizabeth was held. Forty years later, in June 1977, a United Service of Thanksgiving was held in the Assembly Hall for their daughter, Queen Elizabeth II, to mark the occasion her Silver Jubilee.[3]

Throughout its history many distinguished visitors, have also been to, and spoken in, Assembly Buildings and the Assembly Hall in particular. These have included, local, national and international leaders, including the President of Ireland, and members of the Royal Family. Princess Anne, The Princess Royal, attended an event in November 2022, while her late sister-in-law, Diana, The Princess of Wales, visited in June 1992, unveiling a stone plaque in the Assembly Hall to mark the occasion.

While Assembly Buildings has always had a ›public dimension‹ to it, it remains the administrative heart of the Presbyterian Church in Ireland, and the Assembly Hall, the place where the Church meets in General Assembly.

13 Die Ankündigung des Gedenkgottesdienstes anlässlich des Untergangs der »Titanic«. | *The Announcement of the Memorial Service for the Loss of »Titanic«.*

The purpose of the Hall is probably best encapsulated by the verse chosen to be carved beneath what remains of two arched former minstrel balconies, originally located at the end of the first-floor gallery, either side of the platform. Written on a banner held by two angels, from Psalm 107:32, to the left it reads, »PRAISE HIM IN THE SEAT OF THE ELDERS«. To the right, two more angels hold the beginning of the verse on another banner, »EXALT HIM IN THE ASSEMBLY OF THE PEOPLE«.

---

1 Paul Harron, Architects of Ulster: Young and Mackenzie – A Tranformational Provincial Practice 1850–1960, Belfast 2016, 165–183.
2 General Assembly Minutes 1897–1906.
3 Records from the Presbyterian Historical Society of Ireland.

Sachsen
Saxony

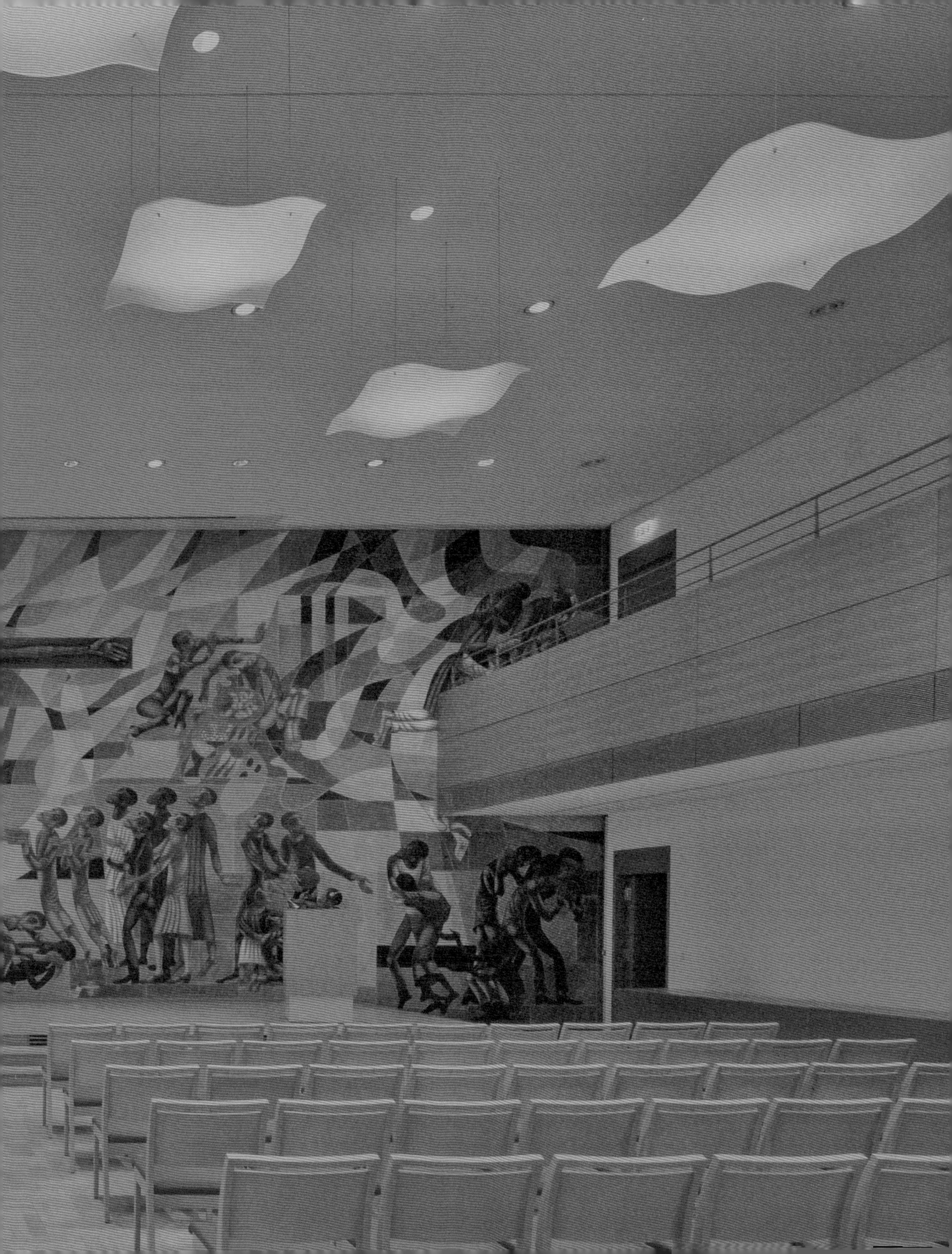

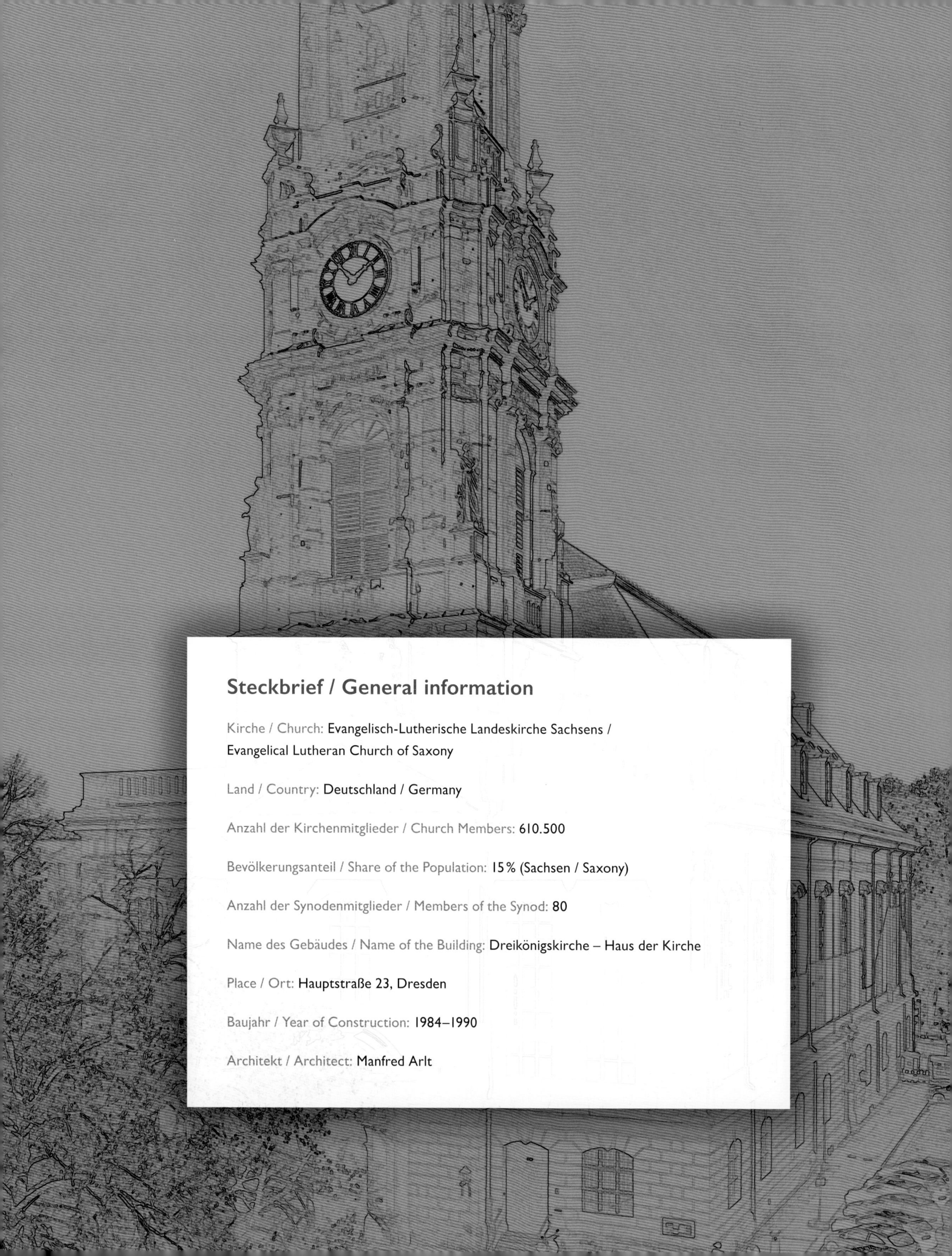

Steckbrief / General information

Kirche / Church: Evangelisch-Lutherische Landeskirche Sachsens / Evangelical Lutheran Church of Saxony

Land / Country: Deutschland / Germany

Anzahl der Kirchenmitglieder / Church Members: 610.500

Bevölkerungsanteil / Share of the Population: 15 % (Sachsen / Saxony)

Anzahl der Synodenmitglieder / Members of the Synod: 80

Name des Gebäudes / Name of the Building: Dreikönigskirche – Haus der Kirche

Place / Ort: Hauptstraße 23, Dresden

Baujahr / Year of Construction: 1984–1990

Architekt / Architect: Manfred Arlt

Bettina Westfeld

Von der Ständekammer in die Dreikönigskirche

Zweimal im Jahr versammeln sich die 80 Landessynodalen der Evangelisch-Lutherischen Landeskirche Sachsens zu ihren Tagungen im sakralen Mehrzweckbau *Dreikönigskirche – Haus der Kirche* in Dresden. Seit dem Herbst 1990 verfügt sie dort über einen eigenen Tagungsort, zeitweise gemeinsam mit dem Sächsischen Landtag. Diese Verbindung von staatlicher und kirchlicher Repräsentation zieht sich durch die gesamte über 150-jährige synodale Geschichte. Der Weg in die Dreikönigskirche war historisch weit, geographisch nicht. Die wechselvolle deutsche Geschichte und auch die Geschichte der sächsischen Landeskirche ist bis heute auf besondere Weise im synodalen Tagungsort präsent.

Beginn der Landessynode in der Ständekammer des Sächsischen Landtages

Die Plenarsitzungen der ersten Landessynode fanden ab dem 9. Mai 1871 – einen Tag vor dem Ende des Deutsch-Französischen Krieges – im Sitzungssaal der ersten Ständekammer des Sächsischen Landtages statt. Diese befand sich im Landhaus in Dresden, im heutigen Stadtmuseum (Abb. 1). Erst 1907 wurde das Ständehaus an der Brühlschen Terrasse zum Versammlungsort des Sächsischen Landtages und damit auch der Landessynode (Abb. 2). Das zwischen 1901 bis 1906 gebaute Ständehaus wurde von Paul Wallot (1841–1912) entworfen. Er ist auch der Architekt des Reichstags in Berlin. Der massive Trapezbau im Renaissancestil wurde mit Sandstein aus der Sächsischen Schweiz verkleidet. Mit seinem seitlich angefügten Turm und einer zum Platz zeigenden prächtigen Fassade diente er als eindrücklicher Repräsentationsbau des Sächsischen Landtages. Beim Luftangriff auf Dresden am 13./14. Februar 1945 wurde das Ständehaus fast vollständig zerstört.

Die Tagungsorte der ersten Landessynode zeigen die enge Verflechtung von Staat und Kirche im Königreich Sachsen. So wurde die erste synodale Sitzung vom sächsischen Minister für Kultus und öffentlichen Unterricht, Johann Paul Freiherr von Falkenstein, eröffnet. Die Aufsicht über Schule und Kirche in Sachsen unterstand dem Kultusministerium, weil der sächsische König sich zum katholischen Glauben bekannte. Mit dem Kultusminister waren insgesamt vier Minister in evangelischen Angelegenheiten beauftragt. Sie leiteten der Landessynode die zu beratenden Vorlagen zu und genehmigten die Beratungsergebnisse.

1868 wurden erstmals nach der Kirchen- und Synodalwahlverordnung Kirchenvorstände in den Kirchgemeinden gebildet. Unter dem Eindruck verschiedener revolutionärer Ereignisse in Sachsen und in ganz Europa seit dem Beginn des 19. Jahrhunderts stand die angemessene Partizipation auf der Tagesordnung. Mit der Einrichtung von Kirchenvorständen erhoffte sich die sächsische Regierung auch eine Stärkung der örtlichen Kirchgemeinden, um sie als Bollwerk gegen den wachsenden Einfluss der Sozialdemokratie zu ertüchtigen. Die Anfänge der Beteiligung in Kirchenvorständen und der Landessynode waren bescheiden. Das aktive Wahlrecht für den Kirchenvorstand übten ausschließlich Männer ab 25 Jahren aus, die männliche Kandidaten ab 30 Jahren wählen konnten. Die erste Frau wurde 1923 in einem Wahlkreis in Leipzig in die 12. Landessynode gewählt. Oberlehrerin Magdalene Focke, Mitglied der nationalkonservativen Deutschnationalen Volkspartei (DNVP), Leipziger Stadtverordnete

| Das Landhaus. Heute das Stadtmuseum in Dresden, früher Sitz des Sächsischen Landtags und Sitzungssaal der Landessynode. | *The Landhaus: today the Dresden City Museum, formerly the seat of the Saxon Parliament and the meeting hall of the first synod.*

und auch kurzzeitig im Jahre 1922 Abgeordnete des Sächsischen Landtags, bereicherte mit ihren schlagfertigen Redebeiträgen die bis dahin ausschließlich männlich dominierten Debatten.

Bis 1919 kam die Synode lediglich alle fünf Jahre zu einer ordentlichen Sitzung zusammen, dann allerdings für einen ganzen Monat. Bei einschneidenden Ereignissen wurden außerordentliche Synoden einberufen, wie beispielsweise während des Ersten Weltkrieges. Bis zu dessen Ende unterstand die Evangelisch-Lutherische Landeskirche Sachsens dem landesherrlichen Kirchenregiment. Die 1919 erfolgte Trennung von Staat und Kirche bedeutete große Veränderungen, auch für die synodale Arbeit. Die Freiheit und die Verantwortung synodalen Handelns erhöhten sich, da die Gültigkeit der Beschlüsse nicht mehr von der sächsischen Regierung in Frage gestellt werden konnte. Noch bis zum Ende der 1920er Jahre durften die Räume des Sächsischen Landtages für die Tagungen weiter genutzt werden, obwohl es heftige Auseinandersetzungen zwischen der evangelischen Kirche und den überwiegend sozialdemokratisch geführten Regierungen im Freistaat Sachsen gab. Bei den Streitigkeiten ging es vor allem um die Fragen der Erteilung von Religionsunterricht an staatlichen Schulen und um die Zahlung von Staatsleistungen.

In der Zeit des sogenannten Dritten Reichs (1933–1945) arbeitete die von der nationalsozialistischen Kirchenfraktion der »Deutschen Christen« dominierte Landessynode nur ein Jahr. Die Synodalen bezeichneten sich in Anlehnung an die von ihnen getragenen braunen Hemden der nationalsozialistischen SA als »braune Synode«. Am 4. Mai 1934 beschloss die Synode ihre Selbstauflösung. Eine für die sächsische Landeskirche zermürbende Zeit des Kirchenkampfes zwischen den »Deutschen Christen«, der »Mitte« und der »Bekennenden Kirche« begann.

Neubeginn in kirchlichen Räumen

Aber das synodale Leben in Sachsen endet nicht. Nur kurze Zeit nach der Selbstauflösung begannen Bekenntnissynoden der Bekennenden Kirche, die an unterschiedlichen Orten zusammenkamen, ihre Arbeit. Erst im April 1948 konnte eine neue Landessynode wieder ihre regulären Tagungen aufnehmen. Die »braune Synode« wurde für nichtig erklärt.

Nach dem Zweiten Weltkrieg waren ausschließlich kirchliche Räume Tagungsorte der sächsischen Landessynode. Zuerst nutzte man in Dresden das große Gemeindehaus der Auferstehungskirche und wechselte später in die Christuskirche in Dresden-Strehlen. Eine Tagung in staatlichen Räumen war bis zum Herbst 1989 undenkbar. Zu DDR-Zeiten lag ein großer äußerer Druck auf dem gesamten kirchlichen Leben. Das spannungsvolle Verhältnis zwischen Staat und Kirche bildete sich auch in der synodalen Arbeit ab. Die freiere Ausübung des Glaubens in der DDR sowie eine wachsende Anzahl von oppositionellen Gruppen, die in Kirchgemeinden einen Ort fanden, beschäftigte die Synoden.

Die Dreikönigskirche als Tagungsort der heutigen Synode

Die Herbsttagung der Landessynode im Jahr der Friedlichen Revolution 1989 endete mit einem gemeinsamen Gang vom Tagungsort im Gemeindehaus der Christuskirche zur Demonstration auf dem Dresdner Theaterplatz. Die Landessynode war zu DDR-Zeiten ein Lernort

2 Von 1907 bis 1933 tagte die Landessynode im Ständehaus. | *The synod met in the Ständehaus between 1907 and 1933.*

der Demokratie. Zahlreiche Christinnen und Christen trugen ihre Erfahrungen aus kirchlichen Gremien in die neugebildeten Parlamente oder Regierungen ein. Wie ein äußeres Zeichen für diese Verbundenheit war die Wahl des Tagungsortes des ersten nach 1989 frei gewählten Sächsischen Landtages. Vom 27. Oktober 1990 bis zum 17. September 1993 tagte er in der *Dreikönigskirche – Haus der Kirche*. Schon kurz vor der ersten Tagung des Landtages nutzte die 23. Landessynode vom 19. bis zum 23. Oktober 1990 das *Haus der Kirche* zum ersten Mal für ihre Herbsttagung (Abb. 3).

Die Dreikönigskirche (Abb. 4), deren spätmittelalterlicher Vorgängerbau bei einem Stadtbrand 1685 zerstört worden war, war nach Plänen des Baumeisters Daniel Pöppelmann (1662–1736), der auch den Dresdner Zwinger konzipiert hatte, bis 1739 im barocken Stil neu errichtet worden. Als Besonderheit galt der nach Westen und nicht nach Osten ausgerichtete Altar, auf dem die Geschichte von den klugen und törichten Jungfrauen dargestellt ist. Erst 1855 erhielt die Dreikönigskirche einen Turm (Abb. 5).

Bei der Bombardierung Dresdens am 13. Februar 1945 wurde die Dreikönigskirche mit Ausnahme des Turms und der Taufkapelle zerstört. Im Jahre 1977 genehmigte die DDR den Wiederaufbau der Kirchenruine. Im Frühjahr 1980 stimmte dem auch die Synode zu. Allerdings sollte der Kirchenbau nicht nur als Gottesdienststätte dienen, sondern mehreren kirchlichen Einrichtungen und vor allem für die Begegnung von Christen und Nichtchristen im Herzen der Stadt Dresden Raum geben.

In der Dresdner Innenstadt gab es bereits mehrere große Kirchengebäude und angesichts der fortschreitenden Säkularisierung nahm der Bedarf an Gottesdienststätten ab. Dem stand der erhöhte Bedarf an Räumen

3 Die Dreikönigskirche – seit 1990 Sitzungsort der Landessynode. 1990 bis 1993 tagte hier der erste demokratisch gewählte Landtag nach der Wende.
| *The Dreikönigskirche – venue of the synod since 1990. The first democratically elected parliament after the political change met here from 1990 to 1993.*

4 Die Dreikönigskirche ist ein barocker Bau von Daniel Pöppelmann, der auch den berühmten Dresdner Zwinger errichtet hat. | *The Dreikönigskirche is a baroque building by Daniel Pöppelmann, who also constructed the famous Dresden Zwinger.*

gegenüber, in denen diakonische Aufgaben, vor allem die Unterstützung von Menschen mit Behinderungen, ausgeführt werden konnten. Außerdem benötigte die Kirchentags- und Kongressarbeit einen Arbeitsort. In diesen Veranstaltungsformaten kamen seit der erzwungenen deutschen Teilung ab 1968 Christinnen und Christen zusammen, um aktuelle Themen und deren Relevanz für das Christsein in der DDR zu diskutieren und sprachfähig in der atheistischen Umwelt zu werden.

Dieses Anliegen spiegelt sich auch im konkreten Bauvorhaben wider. Es entstand ein sakrales Mehrzweckgebäude, das nach sechsjähriger Bauzeit am 9. September 1990 durch den sächsischen Landesbischof Johannes Hempel als *Haus der Kirche* eingeweiht wurde. Die Baukosten überstiegen die Möglichkeiten der Kirchgemeinde und der sächsischen Landeskirche jedoch bei weitem. Das Bauvorhaben konnte in ein Sonderbauprogramm für Kirchen in der DDR aufgenommen werden. Großzügige Spenden aus westdeutschen und westeuropäischen Kirchen ermöglichten so den Bau.[1]

Außen barocke Kirche – innen multifunktionaler Raum

Die ursprünglichen äußeren Formen des Kirchenbaus von 1739 wurden beim Wiederaufbau weitgehend wiederhergestellt. Im Inneren gibt es jedoch eine völlig neue Raumaufteilung. Nur noch ein Drittel der Fläche des Kirchenbaus steht jetzt für gottesdienstliche Zwecke zur Verfügung. Das gesamte Kircheninnere vom Fußboden bis zum Dachgeschoss wurde komplett neu gebaut. Der nun vorhandene Kirchenraum ist beim Betreten der Dreikönigskirche durch eine Glastür sichtbar. Dort hält die

5 Die Dreikönigskirche mit dem nachträglich errichteten Turm im barocken Stil. | *The Dreikönigskirche with the subsequently erected tower in baroque style.*

Landessynode ihre Gottesdienste und Andachten ab. Besonders hervorzuheben ist der von 1992 bis 1994 restaurierte 12 Meter hohe Altar, an dem die Kriegszerstörung sichtbar geblieben ist (Abb. 6).

Im Erdgeschoss hat eine Beratungsstelle der Diakonie für Menschen mit Behinderung ihren Platz. Außerdem bietet eine Mensa Begegnungsmöglichkeiten für alle Dresdnerinnen und Dresdner und Gäste der Stadt. Wechselnde Kunstausstellungen locken Menschen von der belebten Einkaufsmeile »Hauptstraße« in diesen besonderen Kirchenraum und stellen so auch die Arbeit der Landessynode in die Mitte der Gesellschaft.

Der Synodensaal

Die größte Neuerung beim Wiederaufbau der Dreikönigskirche ist der Festsaal im 2. Obergeschoss. Er bietet auf einer Fläche von 432 Quadratmetern 300 Menschen Platz. Dieser Saal ist seit 1990 Heimat der sächsischen Landessynode und ermöglicht eine zeitgemäße synodale Arbeit. Das siebenköpfige Präsidium sitzt den in Reihen hintereinander angeordneten Synodalen, den Vertreterinnen und Vertretern des Landeskirchenamtes sowie den Gästen gegenüber (Abb. 7).[2]

Die wuchtige und düstere Bestuhlung aus den 1990er Jahren wurde mittlerweile zu Gunsten einer freundlichen helleren ausgetauscht. Im kleinen Saal neben dem Festsaal hat während der Tagungen die Synodalkanzlei ihren Platz, die die Tagungen inhaltlich und organisatorisch begleitet.

Das Wandbild

Im Saal schauen alle Synodalen auf das monumentale Wandbild »Versöhnung« des Künstlers Werner Juza (1924–2022). Es weist – wie der nur teilrestaurierte Altar im Kirchenraum – auf besondere Weise auf die Geschichte des Hauses und auf Inhalte des christlichen Glaubens hin. Im Mittelpunkt des Bildes ist der gekreuzigte Christus zu sehen. Um ihn herum hat der Künstler die Gewaltorgien des 20. Jahrhunderts sichtbar gemacht. Eine Abendmahlsszene soll die Darstellung zu einem Bild der Hoffnung umwandeln (Abb. 8).

Der Saal wird nicht nur zwei Mal im Jahr als Sitzungssaal der Landessynode sowie für andere kirchliche Veranstaltungen genutzt, sondern auch von nichtkirchlichen Veranstaltern. Deshalb gibt es seit einigen Jahren die Möglichkeit, das eindrucksvolle Wandbild zu verhüllen (Abb. 9).

In Erinnerung daran, dass der Sächsische Landtag nach der Friedlichen Revolution 1989/90 über drei Jahre in der Dreikönigskirche tagte und das Wandbild in dieser Zeit ständiger Begleiter der Arbeit des Landtags war, wurde eine großformatige Fotoreproduktion des Gemäldes für das Bürgerfoyer des Parlaments angefertigt. Dort erinnert das Bild an den politischen Neuanfang in der Dreikönigskirche.

Resümee

Die verschiedenen Tagungsorte der sächsischen Landessynode im Verlauf ihrer Geschichte spiegeln ihr Verhältnis zur jeweiligen politischen Ordnung wider. In der Dreikönigskirche erhielt die Synode erstmals eine feste Bleibe in kirchlichen Räumen. Mit dem eindrücklichen Wandbild von Werner Juza vor Augen, waren die Synodalen nach dem Ende der deutschen Teilung in den 1990er Jahren aufgefordert, die kirchlichen Strukturen neu zu organisieren. Mit der Übernahme der volkskirchlichen Strukturen aus der alten Bundesrepublik in die Diasporasituation der sächsischen Landeskirche begann das bis heute andauernde Ringen um angemessene Strukturen und die beständige Suche nach der zeitgemäßen Verkündigung des Evangeliums in dieser Welt.

---

1 Seit 1973 existierte die Möglichkeit für die Kirchen in der DDR, über den DDR-Außenhandelskonzern Limex Baumaterialien zu beziehen. Während die großzügigen westlichen Unterstützerkirchen Geld in D-Mark bezahlten, erhielten die DDR-Kirchen den Wert in DDR-Mark. Dadurch kam die stets wirtschaftlich klamme DDR ausgerechnet über die ungeliebten Kirchen zur kompatiblen Währung, um dringend benötigte Rohstoffe wie Erdöl und weitere Bodenschätze einzukaufen. Aber nicht nur bei Baumaßnahmen, auch in der täglichen Arbeit wurden die Kirchen in der DDR intensiv aus dem Westen unterstützt.
2 Seit den 1960er Jahren werden bewusst Christinnen und Christen aus der weltweiten Ökumene eingeladen, um die Verbundenheit zu verdeutlichen und die Landessynode als Forum des Austauschs zu nutzen. Vor allem die Verbindungen nach Osteuropa werden gepflegt und erweisen sich besonders in Krisenzeiten als nötig.

Bettina Westfeld

From the Chamber of Estates to Three Kings Church

Twice a year the 80 members of synod of the Evangelical Lutheran Church of Saxony convene for their sittings in the multipurpose church building *Dreikönigskirche (Three Kings Church) – Church House* in Dresden. Since autumn 1990 the Lutheran Church has had its own Synod Hall, shared at one time with the Parliament of the Free State of Saxony. This connection runs through the whole 150 years (and more) of synodal history. While the road to *Dreikönigskirche* was historically long, geographically there was only a small distance to cover. To this day, the vicissitudes of German history and the history of the Evangelical Lutheran Church of Saxony are intertwined at the place where Synod meets.

The Saxon Synod starts life in the chamber of the Saxon Parliament

The plenary sessions of the first Saxon Synod took place from 9 May 1871 – one day before the end of the Franco-Prussian War – in the Plenary Hall of the first *Ständekammer* (Chamber of Estates) of the Saxon Parliament. This was located in the *Landhaus* in Dresden, now the city museum (Fig. 1). It took until 1907 for the *Ständehaus* (House of Estates) at Brühl's Terrace to become the venue for the Saxon Parliament and thus also of Synod (Fig. 2). The *Ständehaus*, built between 1901 and 1906, was designed by Paul Wallot (1841–1912), who was also the architect of the *Reichstag* in Berlin (now the seat of the *Bundestag* – Federal Parliament). The massive trapezium-shaped building in Renaissance style was faced in sandstone from the Saxon Switzerland region. With its laterally adjoining tower and a splendid exterior facing the square, it was an impressive ceremonial building for the Saxon Parliament. The *Ständehaus* was almost entirely destroyed during the air raid on Dresden of 13/14 February 1945.

The meeting hall of the first Saxon Synod shows how closely church and state were intertwined in the kingdom of Saxony. The first session of synod was opened by Johann Paul Freiherr von Falkenstein, the Saxon Minister of Education and Public Instruction. The education ministry had oversight over schools and the church in Saxony because the King of Saxony was a Catholic. The education ministry assigned a total of four ministers to deal with Protestant affairs. They forwarded the documents for discussion to Synod and approved the results of the deliberations.

1868 saw the first formation of parish councils according to the Church and Synodal Electoral Order. As a result of various revolutionary events in Saxony and the whole of Europe since the early 19th century, appropriate participation was on the agenda. In addition, through establishing parish councils the Saxon government hoped to strengthen local parishes to become a bulwark against the growing influence of social democracy. The beginnings of participation in parish councils and the Saxon Synod were modest. Only men over 25 years of age exercised the right to vote for the parish council and they could only elect male candidates aged over 30.

The first woman was elected to the 12th Saxon Synod in 1923, in an electoral district in Leipzig. A senior teacher, Magdalene Focke was a member of the national-conservative German National People's Party (DNVP), a member of the Leipzig City Council and briefly, in 1922, a member of the Saxon Parliament. She enlivened the hitherto exclusively male-dominated debates with her quick-witted interventions.

Until 1919 Synod only convened every five years in ordinary session, but then for a whole month. Extraordinary synods were called to deal with critical matters, for instance during the First World War. Up to this time the Evangelical Lutheran Church of Saxony was subject to the church regime of the respective government. The subsequent separation of church and state in 1919 entailed major changes, also for the work of Synod. It brought increased freedom and responsibility for synodal action as the government of Saxony could no longer call into question the validity of decisions. By the end of the 1920s, Synod was again permitted to use the premises of the Saxon Parliament although there were heated arguments between the Lutheran Church and the mainly social-democratic governments in the Free State of Saxony. These were mainly about questions concerning religious instruction at state schools and the state's payments to the church.

During the so called Third Reich (1933–1945) the National Socialist group of »German Christians« dominated the Synod in the first year of the Nazi Regime. The members of synod called themselves the »brown Synod« with reference to the brown shirts of the Nazi paramilitary group SA. On May 4 1934, Synod voted to dissolve itself. A period of church struggle between the »German Christians«, the »Moderates« and the »Confessing Church« began within the Evangelical Lutheran Church of Saxony.

A new start in church premises

This self-dissolution was not the end of synodal life in Saxony, however. Shortly afterwards, the Confessional Synods of the Confessing Church began, meeting at different places. The Synod of the Evangelical Lutheran Church of Saxony was only able to resume its regular sessions in April 1948. The »brown Synod« was declared to be abolished.

After the Second World War, the Saxon Synod met only in church premises. It first convened in the big parish centre of Dresden's Church of the Resurrection and later moved to Christ Church in Dresden-Strehlen. Until autumn 1989, the very idea of meeting in state premises was unthinkable. During the existence of the German Democratic Republic (GDR) the whole of church life underwent great external pressure. The tense relationship between church and state was also reflected in the work of Synod. Synods discussed ways of practising faith more freely in the GDR and also the issues involved in allowing a growing number of opposition groups to meet in parish premises.

6 Der beschädigte Altar wurde in den Neubau integriert.
The damaged altar was integrated into the new building.

Dreikönigskirche as the venue for synod today

The autumn session of the Saxon Synod in 1989, the year of the peaceful revolution, ended with everyone walking from the venue in the Christ Church parish hall to the demonstration at Dresden's Theatre Square. In GDR times, Synod was a place to learn democracy. Many Christians brought their experiences from church bodies into the newly formed parliaments or governments. The first freely elected Saxon Parliament's choice of assembly hall was an outward sign of these close ties: from 27 October 1990 until 17 September 1993 it met in *Dreikönigskirche – Church House*. Shortly before this inaugural session of the Saxon Parliament, the 23rd Synod also convened at Church House for the first time, from 19 to 23 October 1990, for its autumn session (Fig. 3).

The late medieval predecessor of *Dreikönigskirche* was destroyed in a town fire in 1685, whereupon the church was completely rebuilt by 1739 in Baroque style (Fig. 4), based on the plans of master builder Daniel Pöppelmann (1662–1736), who also designed the Dresden *Zwinger*. A special feature was the altarpiece facing westward, not eastward, which depicts the parable of the wise and foolish virgins. The tower was not added to the church building until 1855 (Fig. 5).

The bombing of Dresden on 13 February 1945 destroyed the church with the exception of the tower and the baptismal chapel. In 1977 the GDR approved the reconstruction of the severely damaged building. In spring 1980, Synod endorsed that decision. However, the church was no longer to be used solely for worship. Instead, it was to accommodate several church facilities and, above all, offer space for encounter between Christians and non-Christians in the heart of the city of Dresden.

7 Seit 1990 tagt die sächsische Landessynode in dem damals errichteten Festsaal. | *Since 1990, the Saxon synod has been meeting in the Festival Hall built at that time.*

8 Die Synode vor Werner Juzas Wandbild »Versöhnung«. | *The Synod in front of Werner Juza's mural »Reconciliation«.*

There were already several large church buildings in the inner city, in view of continuing secularisation, the demand for places of worship was declining. By contrast, there was a growing need for premises for diaconal activities, particularly to support people with disabilities. In addition, space was needed for big church gatherings and conferences. Since the forced division of Germany, Christians had started holding such encounters in 1968, in order to discuss current topics and their relevance for Christian life in the GDR and to find ways of articulating their faith in an atheistic environment.

This concern was reflected in the building plans. A multipurpose church complex was designed and, after six years of construction work, inaugurated as Church House on 9 September 1990 by Saxony's Lutheran Bishop Johannes Hempel. The building costs far exceeded the resources of the parish and the Evangelical Lutheran Church of Saxony. However, the project was eligible for inclusion in a special GDR church construction programme. Then it was possible to finance the building by means of generous donations from churches in western Germany and western Europe.[1]

Outside a baroque church – inside a multifunctional space

The exterior of the church building dating from 1739 was largely restored to its original shape. Inside, however, there was a completely new distribution of space. Only one third of the previous church area is now available for worship purposes. The whole interior was completely rebuilt, from the floor to under the roof. The church space now available is visible through a glass door right from the entrance to the *Dreikönigskirche* complex. That is where Synod also holds its worship services and devotions. Particularly noteworthy is the 12-metre-high altarpiece, which was restored from 1992 to 1994 but still shows signs of war damage (Fig. 6). A diaconal advisory service for people with disabilities continues its ministry on the ground floor. In addition, a cafeteria provides the desired opportunities for encounter between all the residents of Dresden and visitors to the city. Temporary art exhibitions invite people from the lively shopping precinct (*Hauptstraße*) to enter this special church space, and likewise bring the work of Synod to the centre of society.

The Synod Hall

The greatest innovation in the reconstruction of Church House is the Festival Hall (*Festsaal*) on the second floor. It can accommodate 300 people on an area of 432 square metres. Since 1990 this hall has been the home of the Saxon Synod and has provided modern working conditions. The group of seven presiding officers sit opposite the parallel rows of synod members, staff of the central church office and guests (Fig. 7).[2] The dark, heavy chairs from the 1990s have since been replaced by lighter, brighter seating. During the sessions of Synod, the small room next to the Festival Hall is occupied by the Synod office, which organizes its agenda and administrative business.

The monumental mural

Everyone sitting in the body of the hall look up at the monumental mural »Reconciliation« by the artist Werner Juza (1924–2022). Like the incompletely restored altarpiece in the church, it evokes the history of the building and the content of Christian faith in a special way. The picture focuses on the crucified Christ. The artist has portrayed the orgies of violence in the 20th century. And, at the same time, it is a picture of hope, also depicting the Lord's Supper (Fig. 8).

The hall is not just used twice a year as a Synod Hall and for other church events – it is also rented out for non-church events. Consequently, for some years now there has been an option to cover up the impressive mural (Fig. 9).

Since the Saxon Parliament assembled in Church House for three years after the Peaceful Revolution of 1989/90, the picture was a constant companion of the parliamentary work during that period. In memory of those years, a large-scale photographic reproduction of Werner Juza's mural hangs in the lobby of the House of Parliament, recalling the new political beginning in the *Dreikönigskirche* complex.

In short

The different venues of the Saxon Synod throughout its history reflect its relationship with the respective political order. Synod received its first fixed location in church premises at *Dreikönigskirche – Church House*. In the 1990s, and contemplating the impressive mural by Werner Juza, the members of synod were called upon to reorganise church structures now that the two Germanies were no longer divided. With the transfer of ›people's church‹ (*Volkskirche*) structures from the old Federal Republic onto the diaspora situation of the Evangelical Lutheran Church of Saxony the struggle for appropriate structures began and continues to this day as does the quest of proclaiming the Gospel in contemporary times.

---

1 From 1973 it was possible for churches in the GDR to procure building materials via the GDR foreign trade company Limex Baumaterialien. While the generous western supporter churches paid in deutschmarks, the GDR churches received the equivalent in DDR-marks. That way the GDR, which was perpetually hard up, gained access to the compatible currency through the unloved churches, of all things, which it used to buy urgently needed raw materials like crude oil and other minerals. But the churches in the GDR were intensively supported by the West not only with building projects but also in their daily work.

2 Since the 1960s, Christians from the international ecumenical movement have been invited to attend, specifically to highlight our unity and use the Saxon Synod as a forum for sharing. Above all, connections are maintained with eastern Europe and prove to be necessary particularly in times of crisis.

9 Der Sitzungssaal wird auch für Konzerte und andere Veranstaltungen genutzt. | *The meeting hall is also used for concerts and other events.*

Autorenverzeichnis

Gabriella Ballesio leitete das Archiv der *Tavola Valdese* in Torre Pellice.

Dr. Simone Baral arbeitet als Historiker für das Archiv der *Tavola Valdese* in Torre Pellice.

Sabine Blütchen ist Präsidentin der Synode der Evangelisch-Lutherischen Kirche in Oldenburg.

András Czanik ist Mitarbeiter im Synodenbüro der Reformierten Kirche in Ungarn.

Prof. Dr. Martin Friedrich war Studiensekretär der Gemeinschaft Europäischer Kirchen in Europa (GEKE).

Máté Millisits ist Kunsthistoriker und Museologe für Zeitgeschichte in Budapest.

Prof. Dr. Peter Opitz ist Professor emeritus für Kirchen- und Dogmengeschichte von der Reformationszeit bis zur Gegenwart am Institut für Schweizerische Reformationsgeschichte der Universität Zürich.

Raymond Robinson leitet die Konferenz- und Organisationsabteilung der *Presbyterian Church in Ireland*.

Mark Smith ist Pressereferent der *Presbyterian Church in Ireland*.

Rosalind Taylor ist Architektin für Denkmalpflege und war an der Modernisierung des *Assembly Buildings* in Edinburgh maßgeblich beteiligt.

Bettina Westfeld ist Präsidentin der Synode der Evangelisch-Lutherischen Landeskirche Sachsens.

Index of Authors

Gabriella Ballesio is the former director of the Archive of the *Tavola Valdese* in Torre Pellice.

Dr Simone Baral works as a historian for the Archive of the *Tavola Valdese* in Torre Pellice.

Sabine Blütchen is President of Synod of the Evangelical Lutheran Church in Oldenburg.

András Czanik is a staff member in the Synod Office of the Reformed Church in Hungary.

Prof. Dr Martin Friedrich is the former study secretary of the Communion of European Churches in Europe (CPCE).

Máté Millisits is an art historian and museologist for modern and recent history in Budapest.

Prof. Dr Peter Opitz is Professor Emeritus of church and dogma history from the Reformation to the present, at the Institute for Swiss Reformation History of the University of Zurich.

Raymond Robinson is Head of Conferencing & Operations at the Presbyterian Church in Ireland.

Mark Smith is press officer of the Presbyterian Church in Ireland.

Rosalind Taylor is a conservation architect and was closely involved in adapting and modernising the Assembly Buildings in Edinburgh.

Bettina Westfeld is President of Synod of the Evangelical Lutheran Church of Saxony.

Fotonachweise / Credits

Synoden im Protestantismus / Synods in Protestantism
1: Hervé Champollion / akg-images
2: akg-images
3: Uwe Dittmer
4: Franz Krüger, Reiterporträt Friedrich Wilhelms III. von Preußen (1770–1840), Eremitage, Sankt Petersburg, Russland
5: Kirchenordnung für die evangelischen Gemeinden der Provinz Westphalen und der Rheinprovinz, Koblenz 1835, Fotoaufnahme des Buches aus der Archivbibliothek der Evangelischen Kirche im Rheinland
6: Archiv der Evangelischen Kirche im Rheinland, 8SL 046 (Bildarchiv), 80019

Anfänge der evangelischen Synodalkultur in der »reformierten« Reformation / The Beginnings of Protestant Synodal Culture in the »Reformed« Reformation
1: Zentralbibliothek Zürich, Ms B 316, Bl. 75v.
2: © Heinrich Stürzl, Wikimedia Commons, CC BY-SA 4.0
3: Bibliothèque du Protestantisme français
4: Bildarchiv der Johannes a Lasco Bibliothek Emden, Nr. 0084: Sammlung Gisa Majert 03, Bild 12
5: Stadt- und Kreisarchiv Düren, Depositum Evangelische Gemeinde zu Düren (45) A 1-4, Seite 1
6: Stadt- und Kreisarchiv Düren, Depositum Evangelische Gemeinde zu Düren (45) A 1-4, Seite 14
7: Pouwels Weyts de Jonge (Dordrecht, 01-01-1585 - Delft, 26-05-1629), Public domain, via Wikimedia Commons
8: John Rogers Herbert, Public domain, via Wikimedia Commons

Gegenwärtige Herausforderungen evangelischer Synoden / Challenges to Protestant Synods
1: Evangelische Kirche in Hessen und Nassau (EKHN)
2: Gemeinschaft evangelischer Kirchen in Europa / Communion of Protestant Churches in Europe (GEKE/CPCE), Oliver Hochstrasser
3: Evangelisch-reformierte Kirche, Ulf Preuß
4: Evangelischer Pressedienst (EPD), Matthias Rietschel
5: Evangelisch-reformierte Kirche Schweiz (EKS), Nadja Rauscher
6: Českobratrská církev evangelická
7: Union des Églises protestantes d'Alsace et de Lorraine (UEPAL)
8–10: The United Reformed Church

Der Synodensaal der Evangelischen Waldenserkirche / The Synod Hall of the Waldensian Evangelical Church / L'aula sinodale della Chiesa evangelica valdese
1, 2, 4, 6, 8, 9: Archivio Valdese
10–18: Daniele Vola
3: PurpleImages (i-stock-1207574644)
5: Henry Peyrot

Das Assembly Building der Kirche von Schottland / The Assembly Building of the Church of Scotland
1: © Kim Traynor, Wikimedia Commons, CC BY-SA 3.0
2, 3, 7, 10: Church of Scotland
4: Free Church of Scotland
5: With permission of the University of Glasgow Archives & Special Collections, Hill and Adamson (HA 0749)
6: Artur Bogacki (shutterstock_2347019727)
8: Lee Pearson (i-stock-1392710148)
9: Will Knight
11, 12, 14: School of Divinity, Edinburgh
13: Public Information Scottish Parliament
15: Assembly Festival

Das Synodengebäude der Reformierten Kirche in Ungarn / The Synod Building of the Reformed Church in Hungary / A Magyarországi Református Egyház Zsinati Székháza
1: Csengő-Tschörner András gyűjteménye
2, 3, 6, 8, 10–15: Sebestyén László
4, 7, 9: Magyarországi Református Egyház
5: Aufnahme Hajós Alfréd, 1896, Public domain, via Wikimedia Commons

Die Assembly Buildings der Presbyterianischen Kirche in Irland / The Assembly Buildings of the Presbyterian Church in Ireland
1: Maria Albi (shutterstock_2370147639)
2: princeztl (shutterstock_804559251)
3, 5, 6, 8–13: Presbyterian Church in Ireland (PCI)
4, 7: © 2022 Future Belfast

Von der Ständekammer in die Dreikönigskirche / From the Chamber of Estates to Three Kings Church
1: Stadtmuseum Dresden, Franz Zadnicek
2: Institut für Denkmalpflege, Arbeitsstelle Dresden
3, 4–6, 9: Haus der Kirche, Jens Ahner
7, 8: Evangelisch-Lutherische Landeskirche Sachsens

Doppelseiten / Double pages
Essays: Gemeinschaft evangelischer Kirchen in Europa (GEKE) / Communion of Protestant Churches in Europe (CPCE), Oliver Hochstrasser
Italien/Italy/Italia: Daniele Vola
Schottland/Scotland: School of Divinity, Edinburgh
Ungarn/Hungary/Magyarország: Sebestyén László
Irland/Ireland: Presbyterian Church in Ireland
Sachsen/Saxony: Haus der Kirche, Jens Ahner

Steckbriefe / General information
Italien/Italy/Italia: Daniele Vola
Schottland/Scotland: shutterstock_548473033
Ungarn/Hungary/Magyarország: Sebestyén László
Irland/Ireland: Presbyterian Church in Ireland
Sachsen/Saxony: Haus der Kirche, Jens Ahner

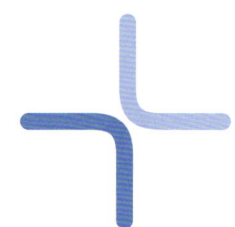

Umschlagabbildung: Assembly Hall der Kirche von Schottland, Rechte bei School of Divinity, Edinburgh

Bibliographische Informationen der Deutschen Nationalbibliothek:
Die Deutsche Nationalbibliothek verzeichnet diese Publikation
in der Deutschen Nationalbibliographie; detaillierte bibliographische Daten
sind im Internet über https://dnb.de abrufbar.

1. Auflage 2024
© 2024 Verlag Schnell & Steiner GmbH, Leibnizstraße 13, 93055 Regensburg
Umschlaggestaltung: Julie August
Satz: typegerecht berlin
Druck: Gutenberg Beuys Feindruckerei GmbH, Langenhagen

ISBN 978-3-7954-3642-1

Alle Rechte vorbehalten. Ohne ausdrückliche Genehmigung des Verlags ist es nicht gestattet,
dieses Buch oder Teile daraus auf fototechnischem oder elektronischem Weg zu vervielfältigen.

Weitere Informationen zum Verlagsprogramm erhalten Sie unter:
www.schnell-und-steiner.de